Henry Parry Liddon

**Easter in St. Paul's**

Sermons bearing chiefly on the resurrection of our Lord

Henry Parry Liddon

**Easter in St. Paul's**

*Sermons bearing chiefly on the resurrection of our Lord*

ISBN/EAN: 9783741182884

Manufactured in Europe, USA, Canada, Australia, Japa

Cover: Foto ©Andreas Hilbeck / pixelio.de

Manufactured and distributed by brebook publishing software (www.brebook.com)

Henry Parry Liddon

**Easter in St. Paul's**

# Easter in St. Paul's

SERMONS

BEARING CHIEFLY ON THE RESURRECTION OF

## OUR LORD

By H. P. LIDDON, D.D., D.C.L.

CANON RESIDENTIARY AND CHANCELLOR OF ST. PAUL'S

*IN TWO VOLUMES*
VOL. II.

*Surrexit Dominus verè. Alleluia*

SECOND EDITION

RIVINGTONS
WATERLOO PLACE, LONDON
MDCCCLXXXVII

# CONTENTS.

## SERMON XIX.
### THE PEACE OF CHRIST.

St. John xx. 19.

*The same day at evening, being the first day of the week, when the doors were shut where the disciples were assembled for fear of the Jews, came Jesus and stood in the midst, and saith unto them, Peace be unto you.* . . . . . 1

Preached at St. Paul's on Low Sunday, April 23, 1876.

## SERMON XX.
### THE MODEL OF OUR NEW LIFE.

Rom. vi. 4.

*That like as Christ was raised up from the dead by the glory of the Father, even so we also should walk in newness of life.* . 19

Preached at St. Paul's on Easter Day, April 17, 1870.

## SERMON XXI.
### SEEKING THINGS ABOVE.

Col. iii. 1.

*If ye then be risen with Christ, seek those things which are above, where Christ sitteth on the right hand of God.* . . . 37

Preached at St. Paul's on Low Sunday, April 4, 1880.

## Contents.

## SERMON XXII.
### FAITH'S CONQUEST OF THE WORLD.

1 St. John v. 4.

*This is the victory that overcometh the world, even our faith.* . 51

Preached at St. Paul's on Low Sunday, April 16, 1882.

## SERMON XXIII.
### THE RAISER OF THE DEAD.

Phil. iii. 20, 21.

*The Lord Jesus Christ: Who shall change our vile body, that it may be fashioned like unto His glorious body, according to the working whereby He is able even to subdue all things unto Himself.* . . . . . . . . 66

Preached at St. Paul's on the Third Sunday after Easter, April 26, 1874.

## SERMON XXIV.
### THE LORD'S DAY.

Rev. i. 10.

*I was in the Spirit on the Lord's Day.* . . . . 81

Preached at St. Paul's on the Second Sunday after Easter, April 8, 1883.

## SERMON XXV.
### THE LORD OF LIFE.

St. John xiv. 19.

*Because I live, ye shall live also.* . . . . . 100

Preached at St. Paul's on the Third Sunday after Easter, April 22, 1877.

*Contents.*

## SERMON XXVI.
### THE VICTORY OF EASTER.
1 St. John v. 4, 5.

*That which is born of God overcometh the world: and this is the victory that overcometh the world, even our faith. Who is he that overcometh the world, but he that believeth that Jesus is the Son of God?* . . . . . . . . 115

Preached at St. Paul's on the Second Sunday after Easter, April 23, 1871.

## SERMON XXVII.
### THE GOOD SHEPHERD.
St. John x. 11.

*Jesus said, I am the Good Shepherd.* . . . . 131

Preached at St. Paul's on the Second Sunday after Easter, April 14, 1872.

## SERMON XXVIII.
### REVERENCE.
Rev. i. 17, 18.

*And when I saw Him, I fell at His feet as dead. And He laid His Right Hand upon me, saying unto me, Fear not; I am the First and the Last: I am He that liveth, and was dead; and behold, I am alive for evermore, Amen; and have the keys of hell and of death.* . . . . . . . . 146

Preached at St. Paul's on the Second Sunday after Easter, April 27, 1873.

## SERMON XXIX.
### ENDURANCE OF WRONG.
1 St. Peter ii. 19.

*This is thankworthy, if a man for conscience toward God endure grief, suffering wrongfully.* . . . . . 162

Preached at St. Paul's on the Second Sunday after Easter, April 15, 1877.

## SERMON XXX.

### CHRIST OUR EXAMPLE.

1 St. Peter ii. 21.

*Leaving us an example, that ye should follow His steps.* . . 177

Preached at St. Paul's on the Second Sunday after Easter, April 27, 1879.

## SERMON XXXI.

### TRUTH THE BOND OF LOVE.

2 St. John 1, 2.

*The Elder unto the elect lady and her children, whom I love in the truth ; and not I only, but also all they that have known the Truth ; for the Truth's sake, Which dwelleth in us, and shall be with us for ever.* . . . . . . . 195

Preached at St. Paul's on the Third Sunday after Easter, April 30, 1871.

## SERMON XXXII.

### FREEDOM AND LAW.

1 St. Peter ii. 16.

*As free, and not using your liberty for a cloke of maliciousness, but as the servants of God.* . . . . . 211

Preached at St. Paul's on the Third Sunday after Easter, April 21, 1872.

## SERMON XXXIII.

### JESUS THE ONLY SAVIOUR OF MEN.

1 Cor. i. 13.

*Was Paul crucified for you?* . . . . . 224

Preached at St. Paul's on the Third Sunday after Easter, April 20, 1890.

## SERMON XXXIV.
### THE APOSTOLIC COMMISSION.
St. Matt. xxviii. 18-20.

*And Jesus came and spake unto them, saying, All power is given unto Me in heaven and in earth. Go ye therefore, and teach all nations, baptizing them in the Name of the Father, and of the Son, and of the Holy Ghost; teaching them to observe all things whatsoever I have commanded you: and lo, I am with you alway, even unto the end of the world. Amen.* . . . 240

Preached at St. Paul's on the Third Sunday after Easter, April 30, 1882.

## SERMON XXXV.
### WITNESSES FOR JESUS CHRIST.
Acts i. 8.

*Ye shall be witnesses unto Me.* . . . . . 259

Preached at St. Paul's on the Third Sunday after Easter, April 17, 1864.

## SERMON XXXVI.
### DIVINE TEACHING GRADUAL.
St. John xvi. 12, 13.

*I have many things to say unto you, but ye cannot bear them now. Howbeit when He, the Spirit of Truth, is come, He will guide you into all truth.* . . . . . . 279

Preached at St. Paul's on the Fourth Sunday after Easter, April 28, 1872.

## SERMON XXXVII.
### DIVINE TEACHING GRADUAL.
St. John xvi. 12.

*I have many things to say unto you, but ye cannot bear them now.* 294

Preached at St. Paul's on the Fourth Sunday after Easter, April 22, 1883.

# SERMON XIX.

## THE PEACE OF CHRIST.

St. John xx. 19.

*The same day at evening, being the first day of the week, when the doors were shut where the disciples were assembled for fear of the Jews, came Jesus and stood in the midst, and saith unto them, Peace be unto you.*

THIS was our Blessed Lord's fifth appearance on the day of His rising from the dead. First, He had met some devoted women, in the early morning, as they were on their way to tell the disciples that the sepulchre was empty. He met them, saying, "All hail;" and they in their joy held Him by the feet and worshipped Him.[a] Next, somewhat later, He appeared to Mary Magdalene in the garden, outside the sepulchre, which Peter and John had just left. She knew Him by His way of pronouncing her name, Mary; she would have seized Him in her ecstasy, but He said, "Touch Me not."[b] Thirdly, in the afternoon He joined two sad travellers, walking along the road to Emmaus,[c] and after they had poured out to Him their tale of disappointment and perplexity,—disappointment at the seeming failure of their hopes for the redemption of Israel, and perplexity at the strange

[a] St. Matt. xxviii. 9.  [b] St. John xx. 14-17.
[c] St. Luke xxiv. 13-31.

rumours which had reached them as to what had happened in the morning of the day,—He first interested them by showing how all that had occurred was in accordance with prophecy, and then He revealed Himself to them in the Sacrament of His love, and vanished from sight. On their return to Jerusalem they found that at some earlier hour He had appeared to St. Peter alone;[a] but of this fourth apparition no details are preserved. And now the evening had come. The story of the empty grave had made its way, no doubt before this, very widely in Jerusalem, and had produced its effect upon the passions of the great and upon the passions of the multitude. The official explanation was circulated without loss of time; what had happened was represented as a pious fraud on the part of the disciples. But there must have been many men who repeated this, and who tried to persuade themselves of its truth by a process of constant repetition while at heart they suspected something else. They felt that the antecedents of the Prophet of Nazareth made something else at least possible. They knew that His immediate followers were men with no resources at command, no skill or craft of purpose, no social influence. Still there was the empty grave; it had been emptied in some way, that was certain; it might after all have been emptied by some unearthly power. Who could say? This sort of suspicion would probably have haunted the brain of many a Jew; and any such suspicion would of course have made the religious system or creed which occasioned it an object of fear, of suppressed, unacknowledged fear, of fear which tried to evaporate in expressions of affected contempt, but which obstinately survived the experiment. And fear, we all know, is wont to be cruel. Especially fear of an unknown religious influence

[a] St. Luke xxiv. 33, 34.

is apt to be cruel beyond other varieties of fear; it has been guilty of some of the worst crimes that have disgraced human history. The disciples would have been well aware of the strength and character of this public feeling in Jerusalem; so they naturally kept themselves out of sight; they did not wish to provoke violence by showing themselves at nightfall in the public streets. Thus they were assembled in an upper room, mainly for fear of the Jews, when "Jesus came and stood in the midst, and saith unto them, Peace be unto you."

He came; they knew not how; they knew only that the chamber was strongly secured against intrusion or surprise. No bolt was withdrawn; no door was opened; no breach was made in the wall of their place of assembly; there was no visible movement as from without to within, or from point to point. One moment they were, as they thought, alone; and the next, they looked, and lo! an outline, a Form, a visible Body and Face, a solid human frame was before them, as if created out of the atmosphere which they breathed. "Jesus came, and stood in the midst, and saith unto them, Peace be unto you." They gazed at Him; they gazed at each other in bewilderment and terror. They supposed that they had seen a "spirit;"[a] they were with difficulty reassured—so St. Luke's report seems to imply—by the means which our Lord took to convince them that a body of flesh and bones was before them. At last they were glad when they saw the Lord.[b]

Brethren, it would be interesting to dwell at length on the character of our Lord's Easter appearances, as illustrating the nature of His presence in the Christian Church; but this would not leave us time for considering the words which He uttered; words which are always

[a] St. Luke xxiv. 37.   [b] St. John xx. 20.

full of comfort and invigoration for Christians, but especially so in connection with the yearly festival of the Resurrection. Jesus said, "Peace be unto you."

I.

Peace be unto you! Remark that this greeting was customary among the Jews and other Eastern nations in that age. It was, with slight variations, of high antiquity. With a like expression the steward of Joseph's house calmed the anxiety of his master's brethren,[a] and Jethro gave his permission to his great son-in-law to revisit Egypt,[b] and Eli soothed the troubles of the sorrowing Hannah,[c] and Jonathan concluded his pathetic compact with David.[d] With a like greeting David's young men were instructed to preface their demand on the churlish sheep-farmer, Nabal, on Mount Carmel,[e] and David himself was recognised as king in the review of the forces at Ziklag,[f] and Absalom was empowered to pay the vow in Hebron, the pretext that veiled his plans for rebellion,[g] and the Syrian Naaman, who after his cure in the waters of the Jordan had returned to make his acknowledgments to the prophet of Israel, was dismissed by Elisha.[h] "Peace be unto thee,"—"Go in peace,"—the expression is varied according to the circumstances of the person addressed. If a psalmist is blessing the holy city he exclaims,

> "Peace be within thy walls,
> Prosperity within thy palaces.
> For my brethren and companions' sakes
> I will now say, Peace be within thee."[i]

---

[a] Gen. xliii. 23.   [b] Exod. iv. 18.   [c] 1 Sam. i. 17.
[d] 1 Sam. xx. 42.   [e] 1 Sam. xxv. 6.   [f] 1 Chron. xii. 18.
[g] 2 Sam. xv. 9.   [h] 2 Kings v. 19.   [i] Ps. cxxii. 7, 8.

Even the heathen kings of the East had learnt this language. Achish dismisses David from Gath, where the jealousy of the Philistine lords made his presence unsafe, with "Go in peace;"[a] Nebuchadnezzar prefaces his proclamation to his subject states by the words, "Peace be multiplied unto you."[b] When the jailer at Philippi tells Paul and Silas that the magistrates had ordered their release, he desires them to depart, and go in peace.[c] When St. James is describing, not without irony, the conduct of rich Christians, who are full of sympathy for the poor and do nothing to help them, he makes them say to the objects of their sterile compassion, "Depart in peace, be ye warmed and filled."[d]

Thus observe, first, that this invocation of peace, at beginning or ending of intercourse, was already ancient. Next, that in our Lord's day it had become just as much part of the social habits of the people as the custom of saying "Good-morning" is among ourselves. All the Semitic peoples, the Syrians, the Arabians, and, as we know from the Talmud, the Jews of the Dispersion, used it as a matter of course. In earlier days, no doubt, men had invoked peace from Heaven with the utmost deliberation and seriousness. In the age of the kings and prophets the phrase had still a living meaning: the speaker had actually prayed for the blessing of peace on the person whom he addressed. It is a gradual process by which the real fresh language of primitive times is stiffened into the unmeaning forms of the society of a later age; but as far as this expression is concerned, the process was already complete in our Lord's day. And yet He did not scruple to avail Himself of the conventional phrase. When He dismissed the woman with the issue of blood, who had cured herself by touching Him in the crowd,

[a] 1 Sam. xxix. 7. [b] Dan. iv. 1. [c] Acts xvi. 36. [d] St. James ii. 16.

He bade her "go in peace."[a] When He blessed the Magdalene, who had washed His feet in the house of Simon the Pharisee, "Thy faith hath saved thee," He said; "go in peace."[b] He instructed His disciples on entering a house to say, "Peace be to this house."[c] And His Apostles continue the language of their Master. St. Peter closes his First Epistle with "Peace be with all that are in Christ Jesus;"[d] St. John writes to Gaius, "Peace be to thee;"[e] St. Paul wishes peace to the brethren at Ephesus,[f] peace to those who walk according to the rule of the Cross, in Galatia.[g]

But it would be a great mistake to infer that because our Lord and His Apostles used conventional language, they used it conventionally. A conscientious man in all ages will do what he can to mean all that he says, even when he uses words which are prescribed by custom or etiquette. And among the great men who have appeared in different ages as teachers of mankind, the majority have been less forward to employ new language than to breathe a new meaning into old words. In Him Who was no mere man, our Lord Jesus Christ, this latter method is especially observable. He picks up, as it were from the road-side, the common words and phrases which fall from men as they saunter unthinkingly through life; and He restores to this language its original power, I might say its original sanctity, as the native product of an immortal soul. He invigorates the form, from which during the lapse of ages its meaning has evaporated, with a new spirit. "Peace be unto you." No doubt many a Rabbi used that phrase, before and after, in the schools of Jerusalem, as the mere symbol of a self-respect which

[a] St. Mark v. 34.   [b] St. Luke vii. 50.   [c] St. Luke x. 5.
[d] 1 St. Pet. v. 14.   [e] 3 St. John 14.   [f] Eph. vi. 23.
[g] Gal. vi. 16.

prudently respects others in daily intercourse. But, be sure, no one word of Jesus Christ was merely conventional, from His first lispings in infancy until His last charge on the Mount of the Ascension. His work was to bring reality in all its shapes into human life; reality in dealing with God, with other men, with self; reality in thought, in conscience, in the exercise of the affections, and, as Isaiah had especially foretold, in the use of language.[a] Once before, in the supper-room, He had used words which rescued the blessing of peace, as uttered by Himself, from the unmeaning formalism of the society of the day. "Peace I leave with you, My peace I give unto you: not as the world giveth, give I unto you."[b] And when He stood among His Apostles, on the evening of the day of His return from the habitations of the dead, it was with a fulness of meaning—such as the phrase had never had before—that He uttered His "Peace be unto you."

The word which is translated "peace" does not, in the original, mean only or chiefly rest, or the absence of disturbance. The Hebrew root-word means *whole, entire;* it is applied to a person or thing which is as it should be according to its origin or capacity. Of this state of well-being, freedom from disturbance is either a condition or a result. Yet here, as so often else in the history of language, the incidental meaning of the word has permanently displaced the original; and we translate it by an expression which never suggests to us English the idea of completeness, but only that of tranquillity or rest. But when our Lord, speaking as He did in Syro-Chaldee, used the word, He had His eye no doubt, at least partially, on its original sense. He meant not merely tranquillity, but that which leads to it. He meant wellbeing; and wellbeing not in any of the contracted and earthly senses which limit

[a] Isa. xxxii. 5.     [b] St. John xiv. 27.

it to the things of this life, but wellbeing in its largest sense, as affecting the highest interests of a being like man.

## II.

Peace be unto you! What would have been the sense suggested by the blessing to those who heard it in the upper chamber?

Not, Peace with the Jews without! That could not be. Of the relations between His followers and the world which rejected Him our Lord had said, "Think ye that I am come to send peace on earth? I tell you, Nay; but rather division."[a] His followers indeed were, in Apostolic words, so much as lieth in them, to live peaceably[b] with all men. But this region of possible intercourse could only extend where the truths of faith were not imperilled; no loyal soldier of Christ might for a moment affect indifference to the claims of the Faith. Peace with the Jews at that time, like peace with the non-Christian world in later ages, was only to be had by an unqualified surrender of the honour and cause of Christ. And therefore it was impossible.

Nor, secondly, as it seems, did He then mean, Peace among yourselves! Doubtless the blessing of peace among Christians is of priceless value; for its own sake, as involving the best spiritual blessings to those concerned, and as an evidence to the world of the truth of our Lord's Religion. "By this shall all men know that ye are My disciples, if ye have love one towards another."[c] But this peace was not then especially needed! The instinct of self-preservation drew and kept together the hearts of the

[a] St. Luke xii. 51.     [b] Rom. xii. 18.     [c] St. John xiii. 35.

servants of the Crucified. The sad day of divisions among Christians was yet to come: for a while the first believers were of one heart and of one soul, and had all things common.[a] It was otherwise, even before the Apostles had left the earth. "I hear," writes St. Paul to the Corinthians, "that there are divisions among you, and I partly believe it."[b] The endeavour to keep the unity of the Spirit in the bond of peace[c] was scarcely less difficult in the later Apostolic age than it is now. But on the day of the Resurrection the disciples had met as do members of a family under the pressure of a great anxiety. There is no thought of division, when hearts are simultaneously open to those fears, hopes, sympathies, which really take possession of the soul.

The gift which our Lord breathed on the assembled disciples was peace in their individual souls. It was a sense of protection which conquers or ignores fear. There they were, when He appeared, huddled together for fear of the Jews. The Jews, they knew, were outside, seeking an opportunity for arresting, insulting, prosecuting, murdering them. They could hear, perhaps, the discordant cries of the fierce and cruel fanaticism which is always ready to urge forward a religious persecution; and which is ostentatiously brutal, or ostentatiously decorous, according to circumstances. They knew what measure had been dealt to their Master. What could they, His disciples, expect? Had not He forewarned them in His Agony: "If they do these things in the green tree, what shall be done in the dry?"[d] and did not that saying apply in its degree to themselves, as more directly and overwhelmingly to the people at large? They were agitated, convulsed,

[a] Acts iv. 32.  
[b] 1 Cor. xi. 18.  
[c] Eph. iv. 3.  
[d] St. Luke xxiii. 31.

almost paralysed with fear. Any new tragedy was possible at any moment. And in view of this possibility, all was disquiet and confusion.

Then He came, they knew not how, the doors being shut, and said, "Peace be unto you." They had heard rumours of His Resurrection; but they had not realised what it meant. They did not think of Him as One Whom they would see again with their bodily eyes. They supposed, St. Luke reports, that they had seen a spirit. Our Lord told them to touch Him freely, and convince themselves that He was really a form of flesh and blood. He asked for some food, and ate it before them, with the same object. Then, as St. John tells us, He repeated the words a second time, "Peace be unto you." They knew now that He was there. And from His lips the blessing of peace meant safety, in some way or other, from every adversary. They knew His love and His power. The Jewish persecutor might rage on; the disciples heeded not. They were no longer alone. It was not that the old dangers had ceased; but danger had lost its sway over their imaginations and their wills. He had lifted them into a new atmosphere of thought and feeling and resolve. He had given them His peace.

This is a primary effect of Christ's blessing of peace, whispered from age to age in the upper chambers of Christian souls. It distracts attention from things without. It does not destroy them. Sickness, death, the loss of friends, the opposition of those who have no true faith in and love for Jesus Christ, the bad tempers, the prejudices, the follies of those around us, the troubles and heartaches of the natural life, remain as before. But they no longer absorb attention. The eye of the soul is turned upward; it is fixed on the Divine and the Eternal. These outward troubles still have their importance. But they

XIX] *The Peace of Christ.* 11

are seen in their true proportions; they do not obscure the higher realities. They are not feared. Jesus has said, Peace be unto you!

### III.

Peace be unto you! Did this only confer freedom from anxiety on the waiting disciples? "That we being defended from the fear of our enemies" should "pass our time in rest and quietness,"[a] is doubtless an integral part of the gift of peace. But it is not the only or the chief part of it. The root of peace is deeper. The soul must be resting on its True Object; or the tumult within will continue in thought, in affection, in will, in conscience.

The Crucifixion of our Lord had thrown His disciples into the greatest mental perplexity. They had trusted that it had been He that should have redeemed Israel.[b] They had believed that God, remembering His mercy, had holpen His servant Israel, as He had promised to their forefathers,[c] by sending His Son. They had followed our Lord, with their eye upon the prophecies to which He constantly appealed. And although they had been often inappreciative, or even self-willed; although they had mistaken earthly images for heavenly realities, and a kingdom of sense for the kingdom which stretches away beyond the senses, but is not therefore the less real; yet on the whole, they had gone on, putting their thoughts about Him into order, and preparing for a future which seemed glorious and imminent. Upon this state of mind the Arrest, the Crucifixion, the Burial, burst like a thunderbolt. True, prophecy had foretold it; He Him-

[a] Second Collect at Evening Prayer.
[b] St. Luke xxiv. 21. [c] St. Luke i. 54, 55.

self had foretold it. But the human mind has a strange power of closing its ear to the unwelcome when it is half-comprehended. To the disciples it seemed as if a dense impenetrable gloom had settled down upon all their hopes, or rather, as if their thoughts about their Master had been thrown into irremediable confusion.

This was their mental condition when, passing through the closed doors, He said, "Peace be unto you." His words describe the intellectual effect of His mere appearance. The sight of Jesus, risen from His grave, restored order to the thoughts of the disciples. The Crucifixion was no longer the ruin of their faith, if it was followed by the Resurrection. And here was the Risen One Himself! The prophecies were consistent after all; there was no longer a seeming contradiction between the Word of God and the verdict of experience.

This is still the work of Jesus in the world; when He is recognised by souls, He blesses them with intellectual peace. Without Him the belief in a Holy God is embarrassed by the gravest perplexities. There is the world, said to be presided over by an all-good, all-powerful Being, yet full of suffering, and without any certain prospect of alleviation; nay, worse still, full of sin, but without any appearance of remedy. Why are we here? whither are we going? what is the destiny of the beings about us? are inquiries which a moral theism suggests, but which it cannot answer. All the great haunting questions about life and destiny are unanswered, to any real purpose, until Jesus appears. And He brings with Him, for those who will have it, intellectual peace.

It is indeed sometimes mistakenly supposed that a Christian knows no mental peace, but the peace of mental stagnation; and that in order to be what is oddly called a thinker, a man must needs be a sceptic. It is of course true that a Christian is not for ever re-opening questions which he believes to have been settled on the authority of God Himself. And it may therefore be conceded that a sceptic considers a larger number of questions to be really debatable than does a Christian. But this is the only admission that need be made. To believe is not to condemn thought to inertness and stagnation; a man does not do less work at mathematics because he starts with holding the axioms to be beyond discussion. On the contrary, a fixed creed, like that of the Christian, imparts to life and nature such varied interest, that, as experience shows, it fertilises thought; the human intelligence has on the whole been cultivated most largely among the Christian nations. Look at a mind like that of Pascal. His thought is not less active in all directions, because he believes that God has spoken, and that God's word is sure. His serenity of soul is not less assured, because he is constantly inquiring, learning, comparing, analysing, inferring, objecting, concluding; for him the great certainties do not change.

Reflect, again, that the disciples had, for the moment, by the death of Jesus Christ, lost the Object of their affections. How much they already loved our Lord they did not know until He was removed. Now that He was, as they thought, in His grave, they felt what He had been to them: they felt the void, the weary, restless void, of an aching heart. When then Jesus appeared He brought peace to their hearts. The wasting fever of unsatisfied affection no longer kept them in continuous restlessness. He appeared; and "I have found Him Whom my soul loveth, and will not let Him go,"[a] was the feeling of each disciple. That feeling meant peace.

[a] Song of Solomon iii. 4.

Who does not know how largely the peace of the soul depends on the due employment of the affections? Mental satisfaction does not alone bring peace, if the heart remains unsatisfied. And that which satisfies the heart is beauty; that Uncreated and Eternal Beauty of Which all earthly beauty is but the shadow. It is an instinctive perception of this which makes people marry early: they hope to find, in family life, the satisfaction of their affections, and the peace which that satisfaction brings. And, so far as anything earthly can satisfy a longing which is made for eternity, family life, under moderately favourable circumstances, gives them what they want; gives it them in its measure, and for a time. Sooner or later trouble and death make havoc of this peace. Only one Being satisfies the affections in such sort, that the soul's peace is insured beyond risk of forfeiture. In Him we find that which we can love perfectly, perseveringly, without risk of disappointment. "Thou wilt keep him in perfect peace whose mind is stayed on Thee, because he trusteth in Thee."[a]

Another effect of our Lord's Crucifixion had been that it had disturbed all the plans for action and life which had been formed by the Apostles. They had gradually been learning to look forward to the establishment of a new kingdom upon earth, and to their own places in it, and their work for it. These visions of a bright future now seemed to have vanished beyond recall. The Apostles were like men who had just failed in business. For the moment, the sky is overcast; there is nothing to be done, nothing to be hoped for; all is despair. And the will, the energetic and sovereign faculty of the soul, suddenly set free from the tension of continuous

[a] Isa. xxvi. 3.

XIX]      *The Peace of Christ.*      15

effort, falls back upon itself, and becomes within the soul a principle of disturbance. No men know less of inward peace than the unoccupied. A leading secret of peace is work. When then our Lord appeared, with the words "Peace be unto you," He uttered them because He restored to the disciples that sort of peace which comes with occupation pursued under a sense of duty. They had been a prey to all the miseries of hopeless inaction; in seeing Him they saw a career again open itself before them. They knew now that He was alive; that His Kingdom was still a reality, or rather, more a reality than ever before; and that in it they had each an assigned task, in the performance of which their peace of soul would be insured.

There are hundreds of persons in London who do not know what peace is, mainly because they have not enough, or rather anything, to do. They do not know how to get through the day, much less the week. They may have at command money, friends, amusements. But these things do not really secure peace of soul. And many a working man, who does not know how to get into the day what he has to do, supposes that the condition of these idle people is a thing to be envied. No mistake can well be greater. Depend on it, work guarantees the peace of the soul; because the soul must be active in some way, and work secures healthy action. The man who has no regular occupation has his mind and heart full of restless, impracticable, morbid thoughts and feelings, which are fatal to peace. "The happiest days of my life"—they were the words of one of the wisest of men—"have been those in which I have had the most work to do, with fair health and strength to do it."

But the peace which man needs most especially, and which our Lord gives most abundantly, is that of the conscience. Did the Apostles as yet understand in detail how their Master would reconcile them to God? It is difficult to say. They knew that this reconciliation was, in some way, to result from His Mission and Life. They knew from the Law, under which they had been educated, that they were sinful; and that God was of purer eyes than to behold iniquity.[a] In His last discourse our Lord had encouraged them to come to the Father by Him.[b] He had before spoken of giving His life a ransom for many.[c] At the Institution of the Eucharist He had said, "This is My Blood, Which is shed for many for the remission of sins."[d] But if the violence of His enemies had indeed prevailed, this Redemption was a mere matter of phrase and conjecture; His Life was essential to the completion of His work. As for the disciples, they had for a while lost sight of Him. They knew not whether they were saved, after all. They had lost that peace which comes from a sense of union with God.

When then our Lord appeared with His "Peace be unto you," He restored peace, because He restored the sense, however indefinite as yet, of pardon for past sin, and of reconciliation with God. Without this there can be no true peace for the soul of man. "The heart," left to itself, "knoweth its own bitterness."[e] All have sinned;[f] and "the wicked are like a troubled sea."[g] Only in union with Jesus, the Perfect Moral Being Who reconciles to God, can the soul find that peace which a sense of being pardoned brings.

Perhaps no Christian, since the days of the Apostles,

---

[a] Hab. i. 13.  [b] St. John xiv. 6.  [c] St. Matt. xx. 28.
[d] St. Matt. xxvi. 28.  [e] Prov. xiv. 10.
[f] Rom. iii. 23.  [g] Isa. lvii. 20.

XIX] *The Peace of Christ.* 17

has illustrated the true peace of soul which Jesus Christ gives at Easter so fully as the great Augustine. Read that pathetic story of his early life which he gives in his Confessions. What a restless life was his before his conversion! The intellect tossed about on the waves of speculation, without solid hold on any one reassuring truth. The heart distracted between the ideals presented by false philosophies, and the ideals suggested by sensuality. The will unable to fasten on any serious duty; the victim of a feverish unsettlement, or of a capricious languor. The conscience profoundly stirred by the terrible conviction that the Son of Peace was not there, and alternating between the phase of insensibility and the phase of agony. Then came his conversion, and with it what a change! Peace in his understanding, which now surveys, with a majestic tranquillity, the vast realms of revealed truth; more penetratingly, more comprehensively, than any Christian since St. Paul. Peace in his heart, which now turns its undistracted and enraptured gaze upon the Eternal Beauty Who, as he says, is always ancient yet always young. Peace in his will, for which the problem of duty has been simplified: he knows what he has to do, and he does it with all his might. Peace in his conscience. There is no longer any sense of an inward feud with the Law of Absolute Holiness. All has been pardoned through the Blood of Jesus; all is possible through His grace.

Brethren, what do we know of this Easter peace; this peace of mind, of heart, of will, of conscience? Let us not mistake for it some false peace; mere brute insensibility of soul, which will only last so long as health lasts, and will desert us in the closing scene. We need a peace which the world cannot give. We need this prerogative gift of Christ; His great Easter blessing. We have seen it in others; but we cannot analyse it. It pervades their life it plainly keeps their hearts and minds in the knowledge and love of God. But in itself it passes understanding. Its presence is traceable in the quiet resolve which is never disturbed by the ever-varying circumstances of the passing years; in the well-compacted harmony of the faculties; in the undertone of thankfulness and praise which is proof against the tragical possibilities of the days to come. This peace is no more touched by the troubles of life than the depths of the ocean are stirred by the storm which sweeps its surface. This peace is an inalienable possession; inalienable, except by the act of him who possesses, and who may, of course, forfeit it. Let us pray God, if in His mercy He has given it us, that we may keep it to the end. Let us pray Him, if as yet He has for our sins withheld it, that He will, for His Blessed Son's sake, crown our festival with this priceless blessing.

# SERMON XX.

### THE MODEL OF OUR NEW LIFE.

ROM. VI. 4.

*That like as Christ was raised from the dead by the glory of the Father, even so we also should walk in newness of life.*

EASTER DAY is like the wedding-day of an intimate friend: our impulse as Christians is to forget ourselves, and to think only of the great Object of our sympathies. On Good Friday we were occupied with ourselves; with our sins, our sorrows, our resolutions. If we entered into the spirit of that day at all, we spread these out, as well as we could, before the dying eyes of the Redeemer of the world; we asked Him, of His boundless pity, to pardon and to bless us. To-day is His day, as it seems, not ours. It is His day of triumph; His day of re-asserted rights and recovered glory; and our business is simply to forget ourselves; to intrude with nothing of our own upon hours which are of right consecrated to Him; to think of Him alone; to enter with simple, hearty, disinterested joy upon the duties of congratulation and worship which befit the yearly anniversary of His great victory. "This is the day which the Lord hath made: let us rejoice and be glad in it."[a]

Such are the first thoughts of loyal and loving Chris-

[a] Ps. cxviii. 24.

tians: but they are not exclusively encouraged by the Apostles of Christ. Our Lord does not really end His work for us on Calvary; He does not suffer for us, and triumph only for Himself. We have a share in His triumph not less truly than in His sufferings:—

"Thou knowest He died not for Himself, nor for Himself arose,
  Millions of souls were in His heart, and thee for one He chose:
  Upon the palms of His pierced hands engraven was thy name.
  He for thy cleansing had prepared His water and His flame.
  Sure thou with Him art risen; and now with Him thou must go
    forth,
  And He will lend thy sick soul health, thy strivings might and
    worth.
  Early with Him thou forth must fare, and ready make the way
  For the descending Paraclete, the third hour of the day."[a]

Not other than this is the language of St. Paul. If Christ died for us, He rose for us too. If He died for our sins, He rose again for our justification.[b] If He is our model in His death, He is also our model in His resurrection from the dead. "We have been buried with Him," says the Apostle, "by baptism into death, that like as Christ was raised up from the dead by the glory of the Father, even so we also should walk in newness of life."

## I.

"Like as—even so." St. Paul's words will suggest to a great many minds a question which must here be answered. What is the connection, they will say, between the raising Christ's Body from the dead, on the one hand, and our "walking in newness of life" on the other? Material things may be compared to material; spiritual things to spiritual; the resurrection of one body to the resurrection

[a] *Lyra Innocentium.*  [b] Rom. iv. 25.

of another; the conversion of one soul to the conversion of another. But if you pass these limits; if you compare a transaction in the world of spirits, as is a moral renovation, to a transaction in the world of sense, as is the resurrection of a corpse, do you not get forthwith into the region of the arbitrary and the fanciful? May you not, upon such vague principles of comparison as this, compare anything you like to almost anything else? and is not your comparison at best rather an ingenious exercise of the inventive fancy than a serious assertion of any real connection between two very dissimilar facts? This is probably the kind of question that is raised in the prosaic and realistic, or, as it would term itself, the practical mind of our day: and we do well therefore at once to ask, What is that common point between Christ's resurrection on the one hand, and the "newness of a Christian life" on the other, which St. Paul probably has in his thoughts, and which serves to explain his language?

The answer is, that the source, the motive power of the two things,—of Christ's resurrection, and of the Christian's new life,—is one and the same. They are equally effects of one Divine agency. They belong indeed, themselves, to two different spheres of being. But that does not interfere with the fact of one common cause lying at the root both of one and the other. St. Paul glances at this truth when he prays that the Ephesians may know " what is the exceeding greatness of God's power to us-ward who believe, according to the greatness of His mighty power, which He wrought in Christ, when He raised Him from the dead."[a] Why should God's power, as shown to us Christians, be thus in correspondence with the power which He wrought at the Resurrection of Christ? Why? Because the same Divine Artist shows His hand in either

[a] Eph. i. 19, 20.

work: because the Resurrection of Christ is in one sphere what the Baptismal New Birth or the Conversion of a Soul is in another; because the manner and proportion of the Divine action here at the tomb of Christ, where it is addressed to sight and sense, enables us to trace and measure it there in the mystery of the soul's life, where it is for the most part addressed to spirit.

May not something of the same kind be observed in the case of the human mind? Our faculties, indeed, are very limited; and a mind capable of writing a great poem, or history, or work of fiction, and also of governing a great country, is not often to be met with in the page of history. Business capacity is often fatal to literary skill; men who write books are as a rule unpractical. But when we do find the two things combined in a royal author, or in a literary statesman, it is reasonable to compare the book with the policy of the king or the minister, on the ground that both are products of one mind. And it is further reasonable to expect that, allowing for the great difference of circumstances under which books are written and government is carried on, there will be certain qualities, evidently common to the two forms of work; that the book will sometimes recall the statesman, and the public policy of the country will be now and then more intelligible when placed in the light of some marked peculiarities of the author.

Such as this is St. Paul's position when he makes a comparison between Jesus Christ Risen from the grave, and a soul walking in the newness of its life. Both are the works of a single Agent; of one Powerful, Wise, and Loving Will. "The glory of the Father," which is said to have raised Christ from the dead, means the collective perfections of the Godhead; the Love, Justice, and Wisdom, as well as the Power of God. St. Paul, indeed,

# XX]  *The Model of our New Life.*  23

in several places speaks of Christ's Resurrection as the work of the Father;[a] St. Peter, as the work of God, at least in two.[b] But this does not exclude the agency of Christ's Own Divine Power in His Resurrection. Had He not said of His Body, that if this temple were destroyed, in three days He would raise it up?[c] Had He not proclaimed, that as the Father raiseth up the dead and quickeneth them, even so the Son quickeneth whom He will?[d] Was He not announcing Himself, on the very eve of His sufferings, to be majestically free whether in life or death? "No man taketh My Life from Me, but I lay it down of Myself; I have power to lay it down, and I have power to take it again."[e] Do not Scripture and the Creeds alike state that Christ *rose* from the dead the third day; meaning that He was not simply passive, that in some sense the act of resurrection was His Own? The great Apostles, then, cannot be understood to ascribe Christ's Resurrection to the Father in such sense as to exclude the agency of the Son or of the Spirit. St. Paul's point is, that the Resurrection is a Divine work, and as such it occupies common ground with the new birth or conversion of a soul.

For, indeed, no truth is more clearly revealed to us than this, that spiritual life, whether given us at our first new birth into Christ, or renewed, after penitence, in later years, is the free gift of the Father of all spirits, uniting us by His Spirit to His Blessed Son. Nature can no more give us newness of life, than a corpse can rise from the dead by its unassisted powers. "That which is born of the flesh is flesh."[f] A sense of prudence, advancing years, the tone of society around us, family influences,

[a] Rom. vi. 4; viii. 11; Gal. i. 1.    [b] Acts ii. 24, 32.
[c] St. John ii. 19, 21.    [d] St. John v. 21.
[e] St. John x. 18.    [f] St. John iii. 6.

may remodel the surface form of our daily habits. But Divine grace alone can turn the inmost being to God; can "raise it from the death of sin to the life of righteousness;" can clothe it in that new man "which after God is created in righteousness and true holiness."[a]

Reflect, brethren, on the reality of spiritual death, linked as it often is in one and the same man, as if by a ghastly ligament, to the highest animal and mental life. The body is in the full flush of its powers; the mind day by day plays lightly over the surface, or grapples earnestly with the substance, of a thousand topics. But the spiritual self is, to all intents and purposes, dead; and neither boisterous animal spirits nor intellectual fire can galvanise it into life. The spiritual senses do not act: the spiritual world is as if it did not exist. The eye of that soul is closed; it sees in spiritual truth only diseased imaginations or needless scruples. Its ears are closed: Christ and His Apostles are to it only like any other talkers in the Babel of human tongues. Its mouth is closed: it never speaks to God in prayer, or to man in faith and love. Its hands and feet are tightly bandaged in the grave-clothes of selfish habit; it cannot rise; it cannot engage in works of benevolence and mercy for the love of God; it must lie on, in the darkness and putrefaction of its spiritual tomb; while death, as the Psalmist says, gnaweth upon it.[b] And a great stone has been rolled to the door of its sepulchre; the deadweight of corrupt and irreligious opinion which bars out from it the light and air of heaven, and makes its prison-house of death secure. How is such a spell and encumbrance of death to be thrown off, if no help, no motive quickening power come from on high? Even if angels should roll away the stone, how can life itself be restored, unless He Who is its

[a] Eph. iv. 24.  [b] Ps. xlix. 14.

Lord and Giver shall flash into this dead spirit His Own quickening power, and bid it see, and hear, and walk, and work, and feel, and rejoice in its returning life, and go forth to brace its strength, and assert its liberty?

Yes, this is the deepest common point between Christ's Resurrection and the conversion of souls: both are wrought by the same Divine Artist. And of the two works, the soul's conversion is the greater triumph of His Power; since the matter of a dead body cannot, like the perverse will of a dead soul, hinder the energy of life-giving grace. Can we go further, and trace God's creative Hand in any common points of likeness between the Risen Life of Jesus Christ upon the earth, and the newness of life of a regenerate or penitent Christian?

II.

Speaking roughly, then, there are three characteristics of the Risen Life of our Lord which especially challenge attention, as corresponding to certain features of the new life of Christians.

1. Of these the first is its reality. The Resurrection of Jesus Christ was the real resurrection of a really dead Body. The piercing of our Lord's side,[a] to say nothing of the express language of the Evangelists, implied the truth of His Death.

And being thus truly dead, He really rose from the dead. As St. Luke says, "He showed Himself alive after His passion by many infallible proofs."[b] Men have thought to effect a compromise between their own unbelief and the Apostolical language, by saying that Christ rose in the hearts of His disciples. It has been said that the

[a] St. John xix. 34.  [b] Acts i. 3.

idea entertained by the disciples of the character and work of their Master was too bright and glorious a thing to be buried in His grave, and that when the first agony of grief was past, the Crucified One presented Himself again to their imaginations arrayed in even more than His ancient beauty. But, supposing a process of imagination such as this to have taken place in the case of one or two minds, is it reasonable to suppose that it can have taken place in a great many minds and at the same time? Are men frequently able so to persuade themselves of the truth and reality of the unreal and the untrue, as to stake everything, to work and to die for their persuasion of its truth and reality? Certainly St. Paul had no shadow of doubt that the Body of Jesus literally rose from His grave.[a] How did St. Paul come to believe that? A modern writer, who denies the Resurrection because he denies that any miracle is possible—a position which is really atheistic—frankly admits that he is entirely unable to account for St. Paul's conviction; nor can that conviction be really accounted for, except by our supposing that it was warranted by fact. And as it was not the idea of Christ that rose, but Christ Himself; so when He rose, it was not as a phantom. "He truly rose again from death, and took again His Body, with flesh, bones, and all things appertaining to the perfection of man's nature."[b] Had it been only a phantom that hovered around the precincts of the Sepulchre, or in the upper chambers of Jerusalem, or on the hill-sides of Galilee, it would assuredly have been found out. It would have been found out by the keen-sighted love of the Magdalene, or by the three holy women, or by the eager, searching anxiety of Peter, or by the disciples on the Emmaus road, or by the ten gathered at night in the upper chamber. In our day

[a] 1 Cor. xv. 3, 4, 11, 15, 17, 20.    [b] Art. III.

probably men would be as little disposed to believe in a risen phantom as in a real resurrection. It was not so eighteen centuries ago; and our Lord was pleased to provide especially against this particular mistake. When the eleven at Jerusalem supposed that they had seen a spirit, and cried out for fear, "Behold," He said, "My hands and My feet, that it is I Myself; handle Me, and see; for a spirit hath not flesh and bones, as ye see Me have."[a] With the same motive, He asked for and ate on this occasion a piece of a broiled fish, and of an honeycomb.[b] And when St. Thomas had protested that he at least would not believe that the Resurrection was real unless he could test it by his senses of sight and touch, our Lord deigned to satisfy him. "Reach hither thy finger, and behold My hands; reach hither thy hand, and thrust it into My side: and be not faithless, but believing."[c] We know the result. The nearer men came to the Risen Jesus, the more satisfied they were that He had risen indeed. Undoubtedly when risen, His Body possessed new qualities of subtlety and splendour, which had not belonged to It before the Resurrection: He vanished out of sight at Emmaus;[d] He appeared at Jerusalem in the midst of the disciples when the doors were shut.[e] But these higher endowments did not destroy the reality of the Resurrection: the Body Which rose was the Body Which had been crucified. It had been sown in dishonour; It was raised in glory: It had been sown in weakness; It was raised in power.[f] It was the same Body, but glorified.

So it is with the soul: its newness of life must be, before all things else, real. What avails it to be risen in the imagination and good opinion of others, if in fact we still lie in the tomb of sin? What profits it to be like the

[a] St. Luke xxiv. 39.    [b] Ibid. 42.    [c] St. John xx. 27.
[d] St. Luke xxiv. 31.    [e] St. John xx. 19.    [f] 1 Cor. xv. 43.

Angel of the Church of Sardis, in having a name that we live, while yet we are dead?[a] Were it not better for us, if we are dead, that men should think and speak of us as being what we are? Is it well for a dead soul to be periodically galvanised by unmerited flattery into awkward mimicries of the language and action of the Christian life? And, even if our new life be not altogether imagined for us by others, what is the value of the mere ghost of a moral renewal; of prayers without heart, of actions without a religious motive, of religious language far in advance of our true convictions and feelings? Shadowy phantoms of a renewed life stalk through the world and the Church: they have a spiritual picturesqueness in the distance; they are often so like the real, that, as though we were visiting wax-works, we find it hard to distinguish between the living and the dead. There is the phantom-life of imagination; when a lively fancy has thrown around the history, or practices, or literature, or services of religion, the charm of an absorbing interest, without, however, touching religious principle! There is the phantom-life of strong physical feeling; when occasional bursts of religious passion are mistaken for discipline and surrender of the will. There is the phantom-life of sheer good nature; when, although much is done for the public service, there is no inward reference to God and His Law. There is the phantom-life of good taste; when it is simply taken for granted that certain religious proprieties belong to a particular social position. Phantoms these—the corpse which they represent still lies on in its sepulchre. Phantoms! for they melt into thin air, when some harder stress of service or of sorrow is laid upon them. They may not challenge investigation with the "Handle Me and see" of the Risen Jesus: they could not bear that

[a] Rev. iii. 1.

probing of the wounded hands and of the pierced side which was invited in the upper chamber. To come near them, it may be, is to be disillusionised: it is to experience the reverse of that which the Queen of Sheba expresses at the court of Solomon; it is sadly to learn that distance, reputation, our own wishes or fancy, had lent enchantment to a form which in itself was without substance and reality.

Brethren, the first lesson which the Risen Christ teaches the Christian is reality, genuineness. Try to feel more deeply than you talk; try to act as you feel in your best and highest moments. Do not in your new life, dally with old thoughts, old associations, old and known sources of danger,—the grave-clothes which are left in the tomb of sin,—the bandages which fetter the liberty of a risen life. For "Christ our passover is sacrificed for us: therefore let us keep the feast, not with the old leaven, nor with the leaven of malice and wickedness; but with the unleavened bread of sincerity and truth."[a]

2. A second characteristic of Christ's Risen life,—it lasts. Jesus did not rise, that, like Lazarus, He might die again. "I am He"—so ran the message to St. John in Patmos—"That liveth, and was dead; and, behold, I am alive for evermore, and have the keys of hell and of death."[b] "For evermore." No new life upon the earth to be followed by a death of pain and shame, no new victory over the tomb awaited Him. Sin was conquered once for all. Christ's triumphant life in the glory of God the Father could not again be exchanged for a state of suffering. "Christ being raised from the dead dieth no more; death hath no more dominion over Him. For in that He died, He died unto sin once: but in that He liveth, He liveth unto God."[c]

[a] 1 Cor. v. 7, 8.    [b] Rev. i. 18.    [c] Rom. vi. 9, 10.

So with the new life of the Christian. It should be a resurrection once for all. I say, "it should. be." God's grace does not put force upon us. What He is to do in us and for us depends in fact upon ourselves. The Christian must "reckon himself to be dead indeed unto sin, but alive unto God, through Jesus Christ our Lord." [a] And if this seems hard to flesh and blood, he will remember that we have forces at command which are able to cope with flesh and blood; that if "the Spirit of Him That raised up Jesus from the dead dwell in us, He That raised up Christ from the dead shall also quicken our mortal bodies by His Spirit That dwelleth in us." [b] If Christ, the Risen Christ, be in us, the body is dead because of sin, but the spirit is life, because of righteousness. [c] Have these words of the Apostle lost their force? Surely not: numbers of Christian hearts will thankfully attest their undying power. They will say with David, "As for me, I am like a green olive-tree in the house of God: my trust is in the tender mercy of God for ever and ever." [d] They will say with St. Paul, "Therefore having been justified by faith, we have peace with God through our Lord Jesus Christ, by Whom also we have access by faith into this grace wherein we stand." [e]

Does this mean that the Christian escapes all sin whatever; that his life is a literal and absolute transcript of the Life of the sinless Christ? On the contrary, "in many things we offend all." [f] "If we" Christians "say that we have no sin, we deceive ourselves, and the truth is not in us." [g] But the new life of the Christian is like the Risen Life of Christ in this; that it is at least "undefiled and innocent from the great offence." [h] It escapes from those capital and deadly falls whereby the soul forfeits life

---

[a] Rom. vi. 11.  [b] Rom. viii. 11.  [c] Rom. viii. 10.  [d] Ps. lii. 9.
[e] Rom. v. 1, 2.  [f] St. James iii. 2.  [g] 1 St. John i. 8.  [h] Ps. xix. 13.

and liberty, and is consigned once more to the chambers of the dead.

Are we then to suppose that the Christian is guaranteed against any such falls by the gift of a grace which cannot but insure his safety? Certainly not. In giving us His grace, God does not annihilate our moral freedom: our probation does not end at baptism, or at conversion. There is no such thing in the kingdom of grace as a talismanic insurance against eternal loss. Even St. Paul feared lest after all his years of service he might fail at last. "I keep under my body, and bring it into subjection; lest that by any means, when I have preached to others, I myself should be a castaway."[a]

What is certain is that, once risen with Christ, we need die no more. On His side God will certainly be true. We have but to look to Him; to cling to Him; to watch, suspect, keep a tight hand upon ourselves. We have a moral, as distinct from a material, assurance of continued perseverance in spiritual life. Nothing from without can avail to destroy our life, if it be not seconded from within. "I am persuaded, that neither death, nor life, nor angels, nor principalities, nor powers, nor things present, nor things to come, nor height, nor depth, nor any other creature, shall be able to separate us from the love of God, which is in Christ Jesus our Lord."[b]

Many of us may have heard of the great French monarch who reigned two centuries ago, going through his Lenten and Easter duties with even passionate fervour, and then falling back in the later spring into his old debaucheries. Certainly it was a hideous libel upon the teaching of Christ's Resurrection. Yet what if, with far fewer and slighter temptations than his, we too, on a less historical and public scene, repeat his experiences! Do

[a] 1 Cor. ix. 27.     [b] Rom. viii. 38, 39.

not numbers of Christians complain that their new life is so insecure and feeble that they seem to tremble, day by day, upon the brink of another moral sepulchre? Who can marvel at this, or at much besides, if they persistently haunt the infected precincts, and breathe the atmosphere of corruption, in the perilous hope that a half-voluntary death may yet be followed by a fresh spiritual resurrection? Surely "Christ being raised from the dead dieth no more." If our new life is to be like His, we may not doubt His grace and His power, but also we may not tamper with that which cannot be consented to without forfeiting it.

3. A third note of Christ's Risen Life. Much of it—most of it—was hidden from the eyes of men. They saw enough to be satisfied of its reality. But of His eleven recorded appearances, five took place on a single day: and there is accordingly no record of any appearance on thirty-three days out of the forty which preceded the Ascension. Certainly St. Luke implies that our Risen Lord was constantly seen by His Apostles at other times, when He communicated to them the laws of His future kingdom.[a] But, allowing for these undescribed appearances,—Christ's Risen Life, as a whole, is veiled in silence and mystery. After the Resurrection His visible presence is the exception rather than the rule. If we omit the walk to Emmaus, and to the Mount of the Ascension, there are no records of His movements in detail; nothing like the journeyings of the days of the Ministry. He seems to belong already to another world. He is now in one place, now in another; here, in a secret gathering in Jerusalem, there, on the shore of the Galilean lake. He appears and He is gone; He vanishes and He is heard of elsewhere;

[a] Acts i. 3.

# The Model of our New Life.

His disciples cannot trace His steps, yet they are ever prepared for Him; a Stranger, they think, will meet them by the way, Whom yet they know; or, out of the clear air into which they gaze will presently appear the outline of His loved and glorious Form, and a Voice of blessing and comfort will fall on their ears—a Voice which could be none but His.

By all this the Apostles were gradually educated for the future which was before them. The great forty days were a time of transition from one relation towards Christ our Lord to a new and distinct relation. It was a gentle passage from the everyday, active, and uninterruptedly Visible Presence of the days of Christ's ministry to the days of His Invisible Presence in the Pentecostal Kingdom; of that Presence which was to last to the end of time,[a] and which we enjoy at this hour.

And yet we cannot help asking, What was the Risen Christ doing during these long absences from His disciples? Ah! what? Who can doubt? Certainly He needed not strength, as we need it; but communion with the Father was His glory and His joy. And can we here fail to see a lesson and a law for all true Christian lives? Of every such life, much, and the most important side, must be hidden from the eyes of men. It is a matter of the first necessity to set aside some time in each day for secret communion with Him, in Whose presence we hope to spend our eternal future. Doubtless our business, our families, our friendships, our public duties, have their claims. In many a life, such claims may leave only a scanty margin for anything beyond. But where there is a will there is a way: and time must be made for secret earnest prayer, for close self-questioning, for honestly examining all that touches our present condition,

[a] St. Matt. xxviii. 20.

and our tremendous destinies, for planting our foot, humbly, yet firmly, upon the threshold of Eternity. Alas! for those who shrink from solitude, who live only on the surface of life, who find in the uninterrupted whirl of pleasure or of business a refuge from the solemn, yet friendly, voice that speaks in the soul's inner chambers. Alas! for those who know so little of the true source of our moral strength, as to see in such earnest communion with God only the indulgence of unpractical sentiment; and thus fail to connect these silent hours with the beauty and vigour of many of the noblest and most productive lives that have ever been lived in Christendom.

Does not the forest tree, while flinging trunk and branches high towards the heavens, strike its roots, for safety and for nourishment, ever deeper into the soil beneath? And is not this parable of nature interpreted by the highest lesson of grace; by the example of our Lord and Saviour in the days of His Resurrection glory?

What multitudes of men and women day by day throng the aisles of this Cathedral between its services, to marvel at the genius of our great English architect, or to gaze at the memorials of the famous dead! Would that of these some at least might be found to use it as being what it is, a House of Prayer, a place of welcome retreat from the torrent of care and business which surges unceasingly around its walls! Would that here too, men to whom time is money, might, in view of their eternity, come apart for a short while, to claim high fellowship with their Risen Lord; to brace themselves for their work, their sufferings, their unknown future; for all that may be in store for them between the moment which is passing, and that other inevitable moment, of such unspeakable solemnity to each and all of us, when this world will be already fading from their sight!

In these three respects, then, at least, the true Christian life is modelled upon the Resurrection. It is sincere and real: it is not like a taste or a caprice, for it lasts; it has a reserved side, apart from the eyes of men, in which its true force is nourished, and made the most of. Each Easter, we may trust, some additions are made from the ranks of indifference, or from the ranks of sin, to that band of servants of the Risen Jesus, whose lives are modelled on His. God grant that it may have been so this year! We sorely need such reinforcements to the Christian army, for the sake of the Church and of the country. It is by really risen lives that languishing Churches are invigorated, and that a visible advance in society of moral corruption and decay, ever pregnant with coming disaster, is most surely arrested. And this is the day of the Resurrection, when all who sleep in sin are bidden with a solemnity that is ever new to rise from the dead that Christ may give them light,[a] when all who have risen are warned to keep their eye upon His life Who is the Model, as He is the Lord, of Christians.

For this first Resurrection is not, as Hymenæus and Philetus thought, the only one.[b] It will be followed by another, and our place in that second and literal rising from the dead depends upon our share in this. "Blessed and holy is he that hath part in the first Resurrection: on such the second death hath no power."[c] Time is passing: each year, as it escapes us, adds, to use St. Cyprian's beautiful phrase, to "our store in Paradise." Since this day last year, it may be, many of us have parted with those, to part with whom has been to change the whole face of life, and to make the present more unlike the past than it ever, we feel, can be unlike the future. The sorrows of life would be more than we could bear, if in very

[a] Eph. v. 14.    [b] 2 Tim. ii. 17, 18.    [c] Rev. xx. 6.

deed we had no future; if there were really nothing to uphold us beyond a few broken lights playing fitfully, as if in cruel mockery, upon the walls of our earthly prison-house. But our sorest losses matter not, if, as we know, death is but the gate of Life, and Christ the true Monarch of that happier world which lies beyond it. Only may He, by His supernatural grace, endow us poor sinners, in this present life, with some rays of the moral and spiritual lustre of His Own glorious Resurrection, and so hereafter "change our vile bodies, that they may be fashioned like unto His glorious Body, according to the mighty working whereby He is able even to subdue all things unto Himself."[a]

[a] Phil. iii. 21.

# SERMON XXI.

## SEEKING THINGS ABOVE.

### COL. III. I.

*If ye then be risen with Christ, seek those things which are above, where Christ sitteth on the right hand of God.*

THE Resurrection of our Lord Jesus Christ from the grave speaks both to the understanding and to the heart, but it speaks, first of all, to the understanding. In days like ours, when the minds of men are much exercised about the grounds of faith, the Resurrection has come into the same sort of prominence in Christian teaching that it occupied in the very first days of the Christian Church. It is the great occurrence which beyond any other in human history proves that Christianity is from God. Christ Himself appeals to it as the certificate of His claims: His Apostle stakes the whole case of Christianity upon its literal truth: " If Christ be not risen, our preaching is vain; your faith is also vain."[a] But the Resurrection has a moral and devotional aspect too: it is at once the pattern of a true Christian life, and the force which invigorates it. " Like as Christ was raised from the dead by the glory of the Father, even so ye also should walk in newness of life."[b]

[a] 1 Cor. xv. 14.      [b] Rom. vi. 4.

According to St. Paul, those great mysteries of our Lord's Life, His Death, His Burial, His Resurrection, are not to be looked at as merely events external to Christians, which took place in a distant country, and in an age long past; they were repeated in the soul of each sincere convert who sought Christian Baptism. First of all, the old sinful nature was crucified: "We are crucified with Christ, that the body of sin may be destroyed, that henceforth we should not serve sin."[a] Next, the soul was "buried with Him in Baptism;"[b] hidden away, as it were, in the tomb of Christ from the associations of its old life; living a life that was hidden with Christ in God. Thirdly, the soul was raised to a new level of faith and practice, of thought and feeling, which is called "newness of life." The likeness of Christ's Death was to be followed by the likeness of His Resurrection:[c] the power of His Resurrection was to assert itself in a movement ever victorious and upward, whereby the soul, while yet on earth, incessantly sought its true and eternal home. "If ye then be risen with Christ, seek those things which are above, where Christ sitteth on the right hand of God."

Risen with Christ! What a life does not the expression suggest for us, poor sinful men! The Apostle, it seems, thinks of Christians as leading a life like that of our Lord during the forty days that elapsed between His Resurrection and His Ascension into heaven. He had left His tomb, and He was seen again and again by Apostles and disciples, and friends and brethren. And yet between each appearance there were long intervals, during which He was withdrawn from sight, and preparing for the last triumphs of the Ascension. They who had seen Him never knew when He might not without warning appear again; on the sea-shore, or in

[a] Rom. vi. 6.  [b] Rom. vi. 4.  [c] Rom. vi. 4, 5.

# XXI]  Seeking things above.  39

the private chamber, He might show Himself without visibly approaching them. He was waiting still on earth until He had given His last instructions, and had completed the due measure of proofs that He was in truth alive. But He was but pausing. His eye was ever upwards; He was seeking "things above;" the "throne on the right hand of the Majesty on high,"[a] the manifested "glory which He had with the Father before the world was."[b] And Christians who have part in His Resurrection-life will be looking onwards and upwards too. They too will seek things above; and they will prosecute this search by a triple effort; an effort of the understanding, an effort of the affections, and an effort of the will.

## I.

"Seek those things that are above." This is the business, first of all, of the understanding; of the understanding of a Christian who has risen with Christ.

Among certain words which of late years have come to be employed in a narrow and inaccurate sense, there is the word "thinker." It is so used as to imply that only those men think at all, who bring their reasoning faculties to bear on the solution of abstract problems, and who give proof of this by their lectures or their books, or by some one of the customary means of securing intellectual notoriety. If this restricted use of the word were correct, the thinkers would certainly constitute a very small and select class indeed: but in truth it would be just as reasonable to confine the thinkers to this restricted class, as to say that a working man is only a man who works with his hands and muscles, and not a man

[a] Heb. i. 3.   [b] St. John xvii. 5.

who works with his brains. All human beings, who are in possession of their faculties, are, in some degree, and very seriously, thinkers. Thought is not only or always the exercise of reasoning power: it observes, it contemplates, it measures, it examines, as well as, and before, it, properly speaking, reasons; nay, in a large number of human beings it never gets beyond these earlier processes, and yet it would not be true to say that they do not think. In truth the understanding is in action whenever any object is presented to it; and some object is present to every understanding during each of its waking moments. This is not the less true because the understanding often apprehends that which is before it in a confused and indistinct manner; or because it apprehends several objects at once, with the result that they present to it a blurred and indefinite whole. It is with the eye of the mind as with the eye of the body. If I walk down a London street, my eye rests upon a great number of human beings, and on a great variety of inanimate objects; and the successive images are not less real because they succeed each other so rapidly, and no one is distinguished from the rest without some deliberation and effort. So it is with the mind. It is not bereft of thought, or, as is contemptuously said, vegetating, because it is not keenly conscious of each step of its advance; the understanding is always resting upon something with whatever degree of deliberation; and this process is, properly speaking, thought; it is not the less thought because it does not go on to draw inferences and construct arguments any more than a limb in motion is less a moving limb, because it is not engaged in some gymnastic feat requiring both strength and practice.

We are all of us, then, properly speaking, at least in this sense, thinkers; and thus the solemn question arises,

XXI]     *Seeking things above.*     41

"What do we think about?" What are the objects on which our thought rests, when it is free and at our disposal? For with many of us, during a great part of the working day, there is, of course, no choice as to the direction of our thoughts. We are obliged to throw them as completely as we can into our business, if we mean to get through it; if we mean to satisfy our employers or our consciences, and to do our duty by those who depend on our conscientious industry. To give your mind to what you have in hand is the first condition of all good work: and we may be very sure that when St. Paul was a tent-maker,[a] he did give his whole mind to the work of making tents, as if there was, for the time being, nothing else to be done in the wide world. But then there is a fixed hour at which business ends; and you regain, with the liberty of movement, the liberty of thought. What do you habitually think about, when there are no demands upon you, when you are necessarily alone, when neither friends nor books put in a claim which has to be attended to? What do you think about, when you make no effort to think, when thought follows its own course, as if it were a natural force; in the hours of solitude, in the hours of darkness? The question is not unimportant. For the instinctive direction which thought takes at such times may tell us much about our real selves; about the path along which we are travelling towards eternity; about the judgment which is already forming with respect to us in the Mind of God.

Is it not the case, brethren, with many of us, that at such times thought is occupied with much which, to say the least, does not guide it heavenward? It is almost at the mercy of the first claimant. It is weighted with the importunity of sense; it is dissipated or distorted by the

[a] Acts xviii. 3.

exigencies of passion; it is darkened by resolute avoidance of the Face or even of the idea of God. What mean those long periods, in lives which were surely destined for better things, in which thought persistently haunts questions and subjects which a higher judgment condemns; in which it beckons

> " foul shapes in dream intense,
> Of earthly passion ;"

in which it eagerly welcomes some work of fiction which, under the pretence of describing an historical period, suggests almost at every page that which it does not dare describe? What mean those long hours, or days, or months of sullen moodiness; in which the mind broods with desperate self-degradation over some trifling or imagined wrong; in which, as it surveys some real or supposed opponent, no excellence is recognised, and no failure unnoticed or unexaggerated; in which life is embittered for all around, but for none half so terribly as for the man himself whose thought is thus discoloured by selfish hate? Or what shall we say of those minds, too numerous, alas! in our day, who only raise themselves above the mire and dust of earth to think of God as the capricious or heartless Master of their destinies; who trace Him everywhere in life as " an austere man, reaping where he had not sown, and gathering where he had not strawed;"[a] who would with their own hands paint clouds over the Face of the All-Merciful, and then complain that He is what they themselves have endeavoured to make Him?

It is sometimes supposed that, if thought is only active, it must needs be good : that it is only when it stagnates that it breeds the deadly mischiefs which degrade the soul; that

[a] St. Matt. xxv. 24.

thought in motion is like running water, ever transparent and ever pure. Far be it from any of us to refuse honour to those who by vigorously exerting their reason honour the Creator in using one of the noblest of His gifts: but do not let us suppose that, because they so far escape a merely animalised existence, they necessarily raise either themselves or others. For thought may be exercised upon subjects which assuredly degrade it, and which therefore degrade it in the very ratio of its activity. The more resolutely a thinker thinks who believes that all that exists is really resolvable into matter and force, the more surely must his thought be itself materialised: the harder he works the deeper he buries himself in the thick folds of matter: nay, perhaps he even ends by proving to himself that the conditions under which, and the results with which, he thinks are such as to make any thinking at all a waste of energy.

Easter then is surely a summons to thought: and it bids thought rise heavenward with the rising Christ. The Resurrection is not merely a symbol; it is the warrant as well as the pattern of this mental resurrection. By rising from the grave Jesus Christ has made it possible for man to seek things above, as never before. Before He rose men had thought and written about another world; sometimes under the guidance of the earlier Revelation which was made to Israel, sometimes by the light of the natural reason, which was the guide to the peoples of heathendom. But at best the veil was only half withdrawn: there was no clear light, no working and recognised certainty, nothing that would stand the wear and tear of discussion, of passion, of trouble, of life. Men hoped and guessed; but Nature with its sullen uniformities was too much for them. When thought would rise to the world beyond, Nature seemed to frown discouragement, and thought shrank back and buried itself, with pathetic despair, in the dust of earth. But Jesus rose from the grave in which they had laid Him, and all was changed. His Resurrection was a sensible interference from a higher world with the laws and rules of this: it broke in upon the stern order of decay and death, which thus became a foil to its own immense significance; it proved to the very senses of men that there is a life beyond the grave, and a heaven, into which they whom we name the dead may really enter. And it bade thought rise with the rising Christ; not merely into the new and glorious earthly life which preceded the Ascension, but also into that world beyond the stars into which He passed in order to prepare a place for us.

Seek then in thought those things which are above. Seek the conversation of the wise and the instructed; study the masterpieces of literature; make the most of whatever enlarges and ennobles the conception of nature and of human life. In all the higher and purer regions of thought, you are nearer Christ, even though His Name be not uttered. "Whatsoever things are true, whatsoever things are honest, whatsoever things are just, whatsoever things are pure, whatsoever things are lovely, whatsoever things are of good report; think of these things."[a] Even if they do not bear His Name they are assuredly His. But, as you seek, let your cry be ever Excelsior. Rest not in the highest earthly excellence. Be not satisfied until you have struggled beyond literature, beyond science, beyond Nature, into that world which human thought may enter under the guidance of Revelation; into that kingdom of heaven, which, since the Redeemer died and rose, has been opened to all believers, and in which He, the King of Glory, sits, ceaselessly

[a] Phil. iv. 8.

adored by tens of thousands of the highest intelligences, and ennobling human thought even by the distant sight of transcendental truth. "Seek those things which are above, where Christ sitteth on the right hand of God."

## II.

"Seek those things which are above." This is the business, not merely of the understanding, but of the affections.

The affections are a particular form or department of desire: and desire is the strongest motive power in the soul of man. Desire is to the soul what the force of gravitation is to a material body. Thus it is that when we have ascertained the objects upon which desire is set, we know the direction that a soul is taking. If these objects are in heaven, the soul is moving upwards and heavenward: if they are on earth, the soul follows; it is sinking downwards. " Where your treasure is, there will your heart be also."[a] Desire is the raw material which is fashioned on the one hand into covetousness, or ambition, or sensuality, and on the other into the love of God: it becomes of this or of that complexion according to the object it pursues. Thus, St. Augustine has finely said, " Whithersoever I am being borne, it is love that bears me:" " Quocunque feror, amore feror." "If I am borne upward, it is by the Love of the Highest Good: if I am carried downward, it is by corrupt or perverted desire ; by desire which has attached itself to false or unworthy objects, but which nevertheless overmasters my movement as a spiritual being." In this sense St. James says that " desire, when it is finished, bringeth forth sin :"[b] sin is the act whereby perverted desire attains its object. Desire

[a] St. Matt. vi. 21.      [b] St. James i. 15.

was indeed meant to attach the soul to God, the Highest Good, by a spiritual attraction that should keep it, though in its freedom, true to its centre, just as the planets move ever round their central sun. And sin resembles those catastrophes which might result if it were conceivable that a planet should leave its orbit and dash wildly into space, amid stars and worlds which it could only approach as the messenger of disorder and ruin. Sin is the product of unregulated desire: and in the right control and direction of desire lies the wellbeing of human life.

Now, as has been said, the affections are a particular department of desire. God gives to every human being a certain measure of affection. No man is altogether, at first, without this precious gift. It is dealt out by us, partly to those whom Providence has appointed to receive it; to a father and a mother, to brothers and sisters, to those loved ones whom our earliest memories associate with home. It is also expended on objects which in our freedom we choose to be its recipients. For we may spend our natural store of affection as we will. We may squander it on the pleasures of sense, or we may compress it into high self-sacrifice. But spend it as we will, we cannot both spend and keep it; we do not spend it twice. When it first flows forth from the pure open heart in the early morning of life it seems to defy exhaustion. But since the being who loves is finite, the supply is really limited. And the despair of those who have given their best or their all at the bidding of some unlawful pleasure is to find, while life is yet young, but all too late, that the heart may be like a dried-up spring, from which the stream of love will no longer flow. One of the notes of the degraded heathen in St. Paul's day was that they were without natural affection.[a] One of the notes which

[a] Rom. i. 31.

he foresees in the apostate Christians of the last days is that they too will be without natural affection.[a] Already the world is a great exhibition of hearts which have spent their store of love, and cannot escape from the wasting fever which preys upon the very force that feeds it; ay, that "wasting fever of the heart," which is almost worse than the moral death of which, if unassuaged, it is the assured presentiment.

"Seek then," with your affections, as with your understanding, "things above." As truth is the prize of the understanding, so beauty is the prize of the heart. Let the Eternal Beauty woo and win your hearts. Earth has less beauty than truth to offer you. In that higher world there are many objects, many beings well worthy of enthusiastic love; pure intelligences that stand before the Most Holy, strong in a rectitude which has been proved and has endured. In that world, we may be very sure, there are sights and sounds, things and beings, which eye hath not seen, nor ear heard, neither hath it entered into the heart of man to conceive.[b] But there is One above all others, Who has claims such as no other can have on the affections of the human heart. How He lived on earth, and what He said and did, and how and why at last He died, we know from His Gospel. None other such as He has worn the human form; none other has invited and drawn towards Himself the unstinted homage of millions of hearts, who love Him better and more perfectly as they know Him more. For to love Him is to love a Being Who sustains love; Who responds to it by pouring in new supplies, that both replenish its source and enhance its volume: "the love of God is shed abroad in our hearts by the Holy Ghost that is given unto us,"[c] and thus "grace" is with all them that love our Lord Jesus

[a] 2 Tim. iii. 3.   [b] 1 Cor. ii. 9.   [c] Rom. v. 5.

Christ in sincerity.[a] And for this among other reasons did He rise from His grave, that He might draw the affections of man upward, from earth to heaven, and so might lead them to gravitate surely towards Himself; the only Being in loving Whom the heart can never incur risk of exhaustion or of disappointment.

### III.

"Seek those things which are above." Here is, lastly, a command addressed to that sovereign faculty, the will.

We need not discuss the question whether the will is a distinct faculty of the soul, or whether it is merely desire informed and guided by intelligence; in other words, a result of the combined action of the two powers which we have already considered. For, practically speaking, nothing depends on the settlement of this question one way or the other. We know what the will is in each one of ourselves, whatever may be the true analysis of its ingredients. We know that there is at the centre of our being a power which rules all others, which chooses, and refuses, which precipitates and holds back; a power which, while professing obedience to reason, not seldom arranges its premises and even settles its conclusions, and which gives play to affection or restrains it, almost at discretion; a power in which every soul recognises the seat of empire, if man be indeed master of himself, and not the slave of necessity or of nature. Yes; it is not reason, it is not feeling, it is will which in the last resort rules the soul, and by which therefore the great question of its destiny must be decided. And therefore it is to the will that the Apostle says; O ruler of man, "seek those things that are above." Grant that the will is weakened by an inheritance

[a] Eph. vi. 24.

of moral disease, this weakness has been corrected at least in those who are risen with Christ. He has washed them with His Blood, and poured into them, by His Spirit, His justifying and invigorating grace, so that they can do as they list, if they only have the heart and loyalty to do it. "I can do all things," says St. Paul, "through Christ that strengtheneth me."[a] Away with the faint-hearted and false notion that religious effort is after all an affair of temperament! Natural disposition may make things easy or difficult: but it cannot either prompt or arrest the onward upward movement of a free because regenerate will. We Christians seek things above or things below, at our discretion: we have been made masters of ourselves by Christ; and we cannot shift the responsibility which attaches to us, by putting it upon the very circumstances which are placed within our control.

"Seek those things that are above." Never in our busy human life is this advice unneeded, but surely it is especially to be borne in mind by Christians at a time like the present, when all thoughts and hearts are full of the stirring and eventful incidents of a great struggle between political parties.[b] Far be it from me to say that for those who take part in such a struggle as we have been witnessing there are not high and noble ends to be pursued; claims of justice, promptings of conscience, requirements of principle which do certainly ennoble it, and which all the higher natures that engage in it keep before their eyes, whatever be the dust and tumult that surrounds them. But for the majority of men, is it not too often otherwise? Personal antagonisms, disappointed or gratified ambitions, the excitement of mere change, the satisfaction of envy or of discontent;—these, from the nature of the case, do

[a] Phil. iv. 13.
[b] Preached in the middle of the General Election, April 1880.

largely enter into every such contest. And most men who are deeply committed to it, and who observe narrowly what takes place within themselves, would confess that on such occasions it is easier to lose moral ground than to gain it. At any rate, it must be well for us Christians to recall at a time like this the Apostolic warning: "Seek those things which are above."

Serious as are the issues when a great people has taken into its hands the task of deciding upon the control of its future destinies, they are infinitely little when placed in the light of the Eternal World. What shall we think of all that is passing now, when we look back on it, one hundred, or fifty, or twenty, or ten, or five years hence, from our place beyond the veil? It will only interest us so far as it has borne upon our personal discharge of a single duty. Our highest wisdom, even now, is to look beyond it, into the heights and depths of that future and unending Life, which is the true goal of our existence; and which, if we are indeed risen with Christ, we shall assuredly seek more earnestly and constantly than anything else or less that can engage our attention.

# SERMON XXII.

## FAITH'S CONQUEST OF THE WORLD.

1 St. John v. 4.

*This is the victory that overcometh the world, even our faith.*

OUR Lord's triumph over death naturally leads us to think of its more striking consequences; and among these the conquest of human nature by the Religion of the Cross was certainly not the least. Just as in the famous song, after the Deliverance from Egypt, which Moses and the children of Israel sang, and to which Miriam responded,[a] the thought passes almost at once from the discomfiture and ruin of Pharaoh to the already foreseen conquest of Canaan; just as in the twenty-second Psalm, which is in fact a picture of the Passion, David, after noting the relief of the Ideal Sufferer, adds that "all the ends of the world shall remember themselves, and be turned unto the Lord, and all the kindreds of the nations shall worship before Him:"[b] so in the New Testament accounts of our Lord's Death and Resurrection, and of the events which followed, the same order is observed. The great conquest of death on Easter morning is quickly

[a] Exod. xv. 1-22.  [b] Ps. xxii. 27.

followed by the slow but progressive victory of the Apostles over the opposition and prejudices of an unbelieving world. And the instrument whereby this victory was secured is precisely stated: it is the faith of Christians. This faith is spoken of indeed, not merely as the means of victory, but as already in itself a victory over human blindness and prejudice: "This is the victory that overcometh the world, even our faith."

There are many words and phrases in the Bible which have lost their force by being misapplied or vulgarised; and "the world" is one of these. At certain periods of life, all men speak of "the world" as something with which *they* have nothing to do, and which does not understand them. They have spent their whole time and strength in the pursuit of honours, or of wealth, or of pleasure. But in the hour of trouble, of failure, of disgrace, they talk of the hard judgments of the world, of the world's want of sympathy, of the falseness and fickleness of the world, just as if they had never had any part in the habits of life and thought which breed these qualities. Again, persons who belong to a very small clique or sect do sometimes bring themselves to think of all other Christians as making up the world in the sense of St. John; and thus it has come to pass that in consequence of this misuse, the expression, notwithstanding its high authority, at least in its original sense, has been tacitly discredited. Too often we think of "the world" as representing no serious and undoubted reality, but only different objects of a capricious condemnation, varying with the persons who may happen to name it. The "world," it has been suggested, is a religious term suited to express dissatisfaction with those sections of the community with which the speaker does not happen to be in sympathy. Thus the word is either dropped or is retained in a sense

XXII]   *Faith's Conquest of the World.*   53

which is anything but condemnatory; one might suppose at times that it had somehow been transfigured since the days of St. John. We talk commonly of the religious world, the Christian world, even of the clerical world; and when these adjectives are wanting, the world seems to be a thing of at least neutral tint; the ideas which attach to it in the New Testament have disappeared; and we all speak of our place in it, and of our deference and duties towards it, without suspecting that, as St. John says, it is something not to be acquiesced in, but to be overcome.

I.

Now the first question before us is, What did St. John mean by the "world"?

The old Greeks had employed the very word which St. John here uses, to describe the created universe, or this earth, in all its ordered beauty: and the word often occurs in this sense in Holy Scripture. When, for instance, St. Paul says, that "the invisible things of God from the creation of the world are clearly seen,"[a] he plainly means by the world the material universe. When St. Paul tells the Athenians of "God That made the world and all things therein,"[b] or when St. Peter, describing the flood, says, that "the world that then was, being overflowed with water, perished,"[c] both Apostles are thinking of this earth; this corner of God's universe which is the home of us men. But neither of these senses can belong to the word in the passage before us. This material world is not an enemy to be conquered; it is a friend to be reverently consulted, that we may know something of the Eternal Mind That framed it; "The

[a] Rom. i. 20.    [b] Acts xvii. 24.    [c] 2 St. Pet. iii. 6.

heavens declare the glory of God, and the firmament sheweth His handy-work;"[a] and "the earth is the Lord's, and the fulness thereof."[b] How could faith possibly be the victory that overcometh such a world as this? The natural world is itself a revelation of God; it is not faith's foe, it may well be faith's support.

Does St. John then mean by the world the entire human family; the whole world of men? We find the word, undoubtedly, used in this sense, also, in the Bible. When our Lord tells His disciples, "Ye are the light of the world;"[c] or when He says, that the field in which the Heavenly Sower sows His seed is the world;[d] or when He cries, "Woe to the world because of offences;"[e] or "I am the Light of the world;"[f] or "I speak to the world those things which I have heard of Him;"[g] He means human beings in general. And this sense is even more apparent in St. Paul's description of the public estimate of the Apostles: "We are made as the filth of the world, and are the offscouring of all men unto this day"[h]—where "all men," for so it should be rendered, and "the world" are clearly parallel expressions. And the Pharisees, as reported by St. John, use the word "world" in this sense of "everybody;" when, referring to our Lord's popularity, they cry, in their vexation, "Behold, the world is gone after Him."[i] This use of the word is popular as well as classical: it is found in Shakespeare and Milton; but it is not St. John's meaning in the present passage. For this world, which thus comprises all human beings, included the Christian Church and St. John himself. Whereas the world of which St. John is speaking is plainly a world with

[a] Ps. xix. 1.  [b] Ibid. xxiv. 1.  [c] St. Matt. v. 14.
[d] Ibid. xiii. 38.  [e] Ibid. xviii. 7.  [f] St. John viii. 12.
[g] Ibid. viii. 26.  [h] 1 Cor. iv. 13.  [i] St. John xii. 19.

which St. John has nothing to do; a world which is hostile to all that he has at heart; a world to be overcome by every one that is born of God, by St. John himself, and by the Christians whom he is addressing.

In this passage, then, the world means human life and society, so far as it is alienated from God, through being centred on material objects and aims, and thus opposed to God's Spirit and His kingdom. And this is the sense of the word in the majority of cases where it occurs in the writings of St. John. This is the world of which our Lord said to the Jews: "The world cannot hate you, but Me it hateth."[a] This is the world of which He observed that "it could not receive the Spirit of truth."[b] This is the world with whose gift of false peace to its votaries He contrasted His Own: "My peace I give unto you: not as the world giveth, give I unto you."[c] This is the world of whose prince our Lord said, "he hath nothing in Me."[d] Respecting this world, He warned His disciples: "If the world hate you, ye know that it hated Me before it hated you. If ye were of the world, the world would love its own: but because ye are not of the world, but I have chosen you out of the world, therefore the world hateth you."[e] To this world He referred in His Intercessory Prayer: "I pray not for the world, but for them that Thou hast given Me. They are not of the world, even as I am not of the world."[f] This is the world which St. John bids us not to love;[g] which, as he proclaims, passes away, with the desires thereof;[h] which is, in its essence and active movement, the lust of the flesh, and the lust of the eyes, and the pride of life;[i] which, he says, lies, as a whole, in wickedness;[k] and which "whatsoever is born

---

[a] St. John vii. 7.  [b] *Ibid.* xiv. 17.  [c] *Ibid.* xiv. 27.  [d] *Ibid.* xiv. 30.
[e] *Ibid.* xv. 18, 19.  [f] *Ibid.* xvii. 9, 14.  [g] 1 St. John ii. 15.
[h] *Ibid.* ii. 17.  [i] *Ibid.* ii. 16.  [k] *Ibid.* v. 19.

of God overcometh." [a] This world, according to St. Paul, has a spirit of its own, opposed to the Spirit of God;[b] and there are "things of the world" opposed to "the things of God;"[c] and rudiments and elements of the world which are not after Christ;[d] and there is a "sorrow of the world that worketh death," as contrasted with a "godly sorrow unto repentance, not to be repented of;"[e] so that, gazing on the Cross of Christ, St. Paul says "that by it the world is crucified to him, and he to the world"[f]— so utter is the moral separation between them. To the same purpose is St. James's definition of true religion and undefiled, before God and the Father;—it consists not only in active philanthropy, but in a man's keeping himself unspotted from the world.[g] And there is the even more solemn warning of the same Apostle, "that the friendship of the world is enmity with God."[h]

## II.

This body of language shows that the conception of the world as human life, so far as it is alienated from God, is one of the most prominent and distinct truths brought before us in the New Testament. The world is a living tradition of disloyalty and dislike to God and His kingdom, just as the Church is or was meant to be a living tradition of faith, hope, and charity; a mass of loyal, affectionate, energetic devotion to the cause of God. The world is human nature, sacrificing the spiritual to the material, the future to the present, the unseen and the eternal to that which touches the senses and which perishes with time. The world is a mighty flood of

[a] 1 St. John v. 4.    [b] 1 Cor. ii. 12.    [c] *Ibid.* vii. 33.
[d] Col. ii. 8; Gal. iv. 3.    [e] 2 Cor. vii. 10.    [f] Gal. vi. 14.
[g] St. James i. 27.    [h] *Ibid.* iv. 4.

thoughts, feelings, principles of action, conventional prejudices, dislikes, attachments, which has been gathering around human life for ages; impregnating it, impelling it, moulding it, degrading it. Of the millions of millions of human beings who have lived, nearly every one probably has contributed something, his own little addition, to the great tradition of materialised life which St. John calls the world. Every one too must have received something from it. According to his circumstances the same man acts upon the world, or, in turn, is acted on by it. And the world, at different times, wears different forms. Sometimes it is a solid, compact mass; an organisation of pronounced ungodliness. Sometimes it is a subtle, thin, hardly-suspected influence; a power altogether airy and impalpable, which yet does most powerfully penetrate, inform, and shape human life.

When the Apostle St. John spoke of the world, he was no doubt thinking of it generally as an organisation. The world of the Apostolic age was the Roman society and Empire; with the exception of the small Christian Church. When a Christian of that day named the world, his thoughts first rested on the vast array of wealth, prestige, and power, whose centre was at Rome. He thought of all that had made Egypt, and Assyria, and Babylon, and Tyre, to be what they had been, brought together on a larger and more splendid scale. He thought of the fleets in the Mediterranean; of the legions on the Euphrates and the Danube; of the great company of officials who administered the provinces and cities of the Empire; of the merchants whose enterprises were carrying them even beyond the limits of the Roman rule; of the numerous and powerful literary class, which set itself to educate taste, and to inform and control opinion; of the immense slave population which ministered to the comfort and luxury of these masters of men; and, above all, at the summit of the whole, of the Cæsar of the day, throned in a splendour and majesty, which seemed to other men even to transcend the limits of human existence. He thought of this complex yet organised mass of elegance, of brutality, of power, of degradation, of intelligence, of wealth, of hideous misery, which had been built up by the labour and suffering of an imperial race, during five centuries of vicissitude and effort; and then his thoughts turned to the source and centre of this great organisation, to the Empire city, to Rome. Rome was the very core and essence of the world. To Rome all the streams of human effort converged; from Rome they radiated; within Rome were the minds and energies which impelled and controlled the vast machine of government; at Rome was to be found the representative ability and the representative vice of the complex whole. When two Apostles sought a name with religious significance for Rome, they at once thought of that older seat of empire, which, in pride, and wealth, and oppressiveness, and ungodliness, was foremost in an earlier age of the world's history. Both St. Peter in his First Epistle,[a] and St. John in the Revelation,[b] salute Pagan Rome as Babylon; as the typical centre of organised worldly power among the sons of men, at the very height of its alienation from Almighty God.

The world then of the Apostolic age was primarily a vast organisation. But it was not a world that could last. "After these things I saw another angel come down from heaven, having great power. And he cried mightily with a strong voice, saying, Babylon the great is fallen, is fallen. . . . And I heard another voice from heaven, saying, Come out of her, my people, that ye receive not of her plagues. For her sins have reached unto heaven,

[a] 1 St. Pet. v. 13. [b] Rev. xviii. 2.

## XXII]  Faith's Conquest of the World.    59

and God hath remembered her iniquities."[a] Alaric the Goth appeared before Rome; and the city of the Cæsars became the prey of the barbarians. The event produced a sensation much more profound than would now be occasioned by the sack of London. The work of a thousand years, the greatest effort to organise human life permanently under a single system of government, the greatest civilisation that the world had known, at once so vicious and so magnificent, had perished from sight. It seemed to those who witnessed it as though life would be no longer endurable, and that the end had come.

But before the occurrence of this catastrophe, another and a more remarkable change had been silently taking place. For nearly three hundred years the Church had been leavening the Empire. And the Empire, feeling and dreading the ever-advancing, ever-widening influence, had again and again endeavoured to extinguish it in a sea of blood. Among the great persecutors are the noblest as well as the most degraded of the Emperors: Nero, Domitian, Trajan, Hadrian, Marcus Aurelius, Septimius Severus, Maximinus, Decius, Valerian, Diocletian. Diocletian, who came last, was the most implacable; and Diocletian failed. After Diocletian came Constantine. But from the year of the Crucifixion, A.D. 29, to the Edict of Toleration, A.D. 313, there were 284 years of almost uninterrupted growth, promoted by almost perpetual suffering; until at last, in St. Augustine's language, the Cross passed from the scenes of public executions to the diadem of the Cæsars.

Yes! by this wonderful change the Empire had become Christian; and when it sank beneath the blows of the barbarians, the Christian Church, and it alone, remained

[a] Rev. xviii. 1, 2, 4, 5.

erect. But meanwhile what had become of the world; the world of St. John? Had it ceased to be? Was it banished utterly beyond the frontiers of triumphant Christendom? Or had it taken a new form? had it ceased to be an organisation, only to become a spirit, a temper, a frame of mind, a settled habit of thought and feeling more subtle, penetrating, and deadly than the organised world that had preceded it?

Yes! so indeed it was. The world had passed within the conquering Church. The world which early Christian writers such as Tertullian saw without the Christian fold, St. Bernard, and others long before him, detected within it. Even in St. Augustine's day the world had crowded, almost with a rush, within the Church. Emperors like Honorius, provincial governors like Marcellinus, successful generals like Bonifacius, were Augustine's fellow-Christians. The world now to a great extent used Christian language, it accepted outwardly Christian rules. And in order to keep this world at bay, some Christians fled from the great highways and centres of life, to lead the life of solitaries in the Egyptian deserts; while others even organised schisms, like that of the Donatists, which, if small and select, relatively to the great Catholic Church, should at least be unworldly. They forgot that our Lord had anticipated the new state of things by His parables of the Net[a] and of the Tares;[b] they forgot that whether the world presents itself as an organisation or as a temper, a Christian's business is to encounter and to overcome it. The great question was and is, how to achieve this; and St. John gives us explicit instructions. "This is the victory that overcometh the world, even our faith."

[a] St. Matt. xiii. 47-52.   [b] *Ibid.* xiii. 24-30, 36-43.

## III.

This is, I say, the question for us of to-day, no less than for our predecessors in the Faith of Christ. For the world is not a piece of the furniture of bygone centuries, which has long since perished, except in the pages of our ancient and sacred books. It is here, around and among us; living and energetic, and true to the character which our Lord and His Apostles gave it. It is here, in our business, in our homes, in our conversations, in our literature; it is here, awakening echoes loud and shrill within our hearts, if, indeed, it be not throned in them. Now, as of old, its essence is passionate attachment to the material and passing aspects of human life; it is forgetfulness of the immaterial and imperishable realities. Do you want to know whether you love the world or not? You need not love it because you are fond of natural objects, and spend much time in studying them scientifically; they may well lead you up to God. You need not love it, if you have a true love of your fellow-creatures, and lose no opportunity of doing them any service that lies in your power; this is not a temper which our Lord would condemn. But supposing, for instance, you belong to the middle classes in society, are you, above all things, anxious for a fortune, or for a social position which is at present denied you? Do you spend much time and thought on the question how to make money, and how to get on in social life? Do you experience disappointment when others succeed; when they attain to wealth or to honours which you think are rightfully your own? Do you think slightingly of those who are below you, while you make great efforts to stand well with those who are above you? Does a slight cause you keen distress, and a little flattery, whether sincere and deserved or not, great satisfaction? Do you measure men, not by what they are in point of character, but by their titles and incomes; by what they are called or have? and do you convey this fatal estimate of life to those who are in contact with you? If so, be your position what it may, you are in league with the world. It has its grip upon you; and its prince is your ruler more entirely than you think. And be sure, that if you do not break away and overcome it, it will drag you deeper and deeper down; it will dim the eye of your soul till you see no spiritual truth distinctly; it will chill your heart till you feel no pure and generous affection stir within it; it will unnerve your arm, and make your will falter, for all action that is unselfish and high-minded; at least when the time for action comes. And therefore, "whatsoever is born of God overcometh the world;"[a] as a man fighting for his life, a Christian conquers this passion for materialised existence; he conquers it not as a pastime, but as a condition of his spiritual safety.

Is the world-temper to be overcome by mental cultivation?

We live in days when language is used about education and literature, as if of themselves they had an elevating and transforming power in human life. In combination with other and higher influences, mental cultivation does much for man. It softens his manners; it tames his natural ferocity. It refines and stimulates his understanding, his taste, his imagination. But it has no necessary power of purifying his affections, or of guiding or invigorating his will. In these respects it leaves him as it finds him. And, if he is bound heart and soul to the material aspects of this present life, it will not help him to break his bonds. No doubt there are fine things in great writers about the

[a] 1 St. John v. 4.

unsubstantial and fugitive character of this life and its enjoyments. But we read; we admire; we assent; and we pass on; perhaps, with the observation that it is a striking passage. The illusion that there is a sort of moral or even sacramental force in literary pursuits, would never be cherished by any who have considered the history of literature. Polite learning is no monopoly of Christians; when St. John wrote, it could hardly be said to be possessed by them at all. Had Christians been dependent on their cultivation in St. John's days, they certainly would have had a poorer chance of conquering the world than had the Stoics, who were, some of them, very polished and cultured indeed.

Is the world then to be overcome by sorrow, by failure, by disappointment; in a word, by the rude teaching of experience?

Sorrow and failure are no doubt to many men a revelation. They show that the material scene in which we pass our days is itself passing. They rouse into activity from the depths of our souls deep currents of feeling; and we may easily mistake feeling for something which it is not. Feeling is not faith; it sees nothing beyond the veil. Feeling is not practice; it may sweep the soul in gusts before it, yet commit us to nothing. Feeling deplores when it does not resist; it admires and approves of enterprises which it never attempts. Consequently, self-exhausted, in time it dies back; leaving the soul worse off than it would be, if it had never felt so strongly; worse off, because at once weaker and less sensitive than before. It is piteous to think how many a disappointment, many a failure, many a sorrow, ends like this. If illuminated by faith, it might have raised the sufferer from earth to heaven; but it has left him an enfeebled cynic, who has indeed found out much about the world that he knew not before, but who is much less able than he was before to overcome it.

Certainly, if the world is to be overcome, it must be, as St. John tells us, by a power which lifts us above it; and such a power is faith. Faith does two things which are essential to success in this matter. It enables us to measure the world; to appraise it, not at its own, but at its real value. It does this by opening to our view that other and higher world of which Christ our Lord is King, and in which His saints and servants are at home; that world which, unlike this, will last for ever. A country lad may think much of the streets and homes of the little village in which he was brought up, until he has seen London. But when, after his first visit to this great city, he returns to his rural home, he learns to take a more modest and more accurate view of its architectural merits. The first step to overcoming the world is to have satisfied ourselves that all here is insignificant by comparison with that which will follow it. And faith opens our eyes to see this; to see things as they really are; to understand not only the origin of life, but also the true end of life, and the means whereby that end may be reached. When "the eyes of a man's understanding are thus enlightened that he may know what is the hope of his calling, and what the riches of the glory of his inheritance among the saints,"[a] faith enables him to take a second step. Faith is a hand whereby the soul lays actual hold on the unseen realities; and so learns to sit loosely to, and detach itself from that which only belongs to time. Especially are we nerved to overcome the world by faith in our Lord and Saviour, true God and true Man, for us men, Born, Crucified, Risen, Ascended, Interceding; Who gave His life for us on the Cross; Who gives it to us by His Spirit, and in His

[a] Eph. i. 18.

Sacraments. It was not natural courage in the women and children, who yielded up their lives for Jesus Christ in the first ages of the Church, that made them more than conquerors; it was that they saw and held fast to Him, Whose very Name their persecutors cast out as evil. It is not good taste, or common sense, or ripe experience, or culture and refinement, which will enable any man now-a-days to conquer the strong and subtle forces which play incessantly around his soul, and which will drag him downwards with fatal certainty, if he cannot counteract them. Only when we are one with Him against Whom the world did its worst, and Who bent His head in death, ere by His Resurrection He overcame it, can we hope to share the promise of sitting with Him on His throne; even as He Himself also overcame, and is set down with the Father on the Father's throne.[a]

[a] Rev. iii. 21.

# SERMON XXIII.

## THE RAISER OF THE DEAD

PHIL. III. 20, 21.

*The Lord Jesus Christ: Who shall change our vile body, that it may be fashioned like unto His glorious body, according to the working whereby He is able even to subdue all things unto Himself.*

HERE we have one of those clear glimpses into the world beyond the grave, of which, after all, there are not many in the New Testament, and each of which is so dear to the faith and hope of a Christian. St. Paul had been speaking of some Christians whose interest was altogether centred in earthly things. Of these persons he says that their end in another life is destruction; that their god, or object of devotion in this life, is their lower appetites, or, as he puts it, with Apostolical plainness, their belly; and that their glory, or subject of thought and conversation, is that which will hereafter be their shame. In contrast with this way of passing life, St. Paul describes the life of Christ's true servants. Their conversation, he says, or their citizenship, is in heaven. They have not yet reached their country; they are only on the way to it; but already, before they touch its shores, they have been invested with its rights of citizenship, in consideration of the commanding merits and self-sacrificing generosity of their Leader. They are in the position of emigrants for whom the friendly government of a colony should provide beforehand a home and civic duties. Heaven, then, as being already their country, naturally occupies a first place in their thoughts; but they cannot set foot in it until a great change, a new and unimaginable experience, has passed over them. It is upon this change, and upon the Person of Him Who is to effect it, that their eyes are continually fixed while the present scene lasts. "We look for the Saviour, the Lord Jesus Christ: Who shall change our vile body, that it may be fashioned like unto His glorious body, according to the working whereby He is able even to subdue all things unto Himself."

Such a subject, my brethren, even if the daily lesson did not suggest it, connects itself naturally enough with Eastertide. Christ did not rise, as He did not die, only for Himself. He rose for our justification.[a] In this present life we share His righteousness, when He gives us His new nature. But the virtue of His Resurrection is not exhausted on this side the grave. It secures to us a bodily resurrection in glory, at some distant epoch, when all that now meets the eye shall have passed away. This is the last and most magnificent of the gifts of our great and Risen Redeemer; "He shall change our vile body, that it may be fashioned like unto His glorious body, according to the working whereby He is able even to subdue all things unto Himself."

And death is throughout life so constantly dogging our footsteps that such a subject as this can never be uninteresting. How near any one of us might be to it, we may have noted only in yesterday's paper. There we

[a] Rom. iv. 25.

read how a man whose devotion to geological science during many years has long since won for him a European reputation, and the beauty and simplicity, and, let me dare to add, the religious sincerity of whose character, have commanded the affectionate respect of a very wide circle of cultivated friends, passed two days since, by what we should call the most natural of accidents, out of the very midst of his intellectual interests into the world of the dead. None who knew the late Professor Phillips,[a] and understand the place he held in the world of thought as an honest and truthful student of Nature, while firmly believing in man's spiritual destiny, will regard his death as other than a serious loss to the religion, as well as to the higher learning, of this country.

I.

What is the nature of this change referred to in the text?

Observe St. Paul's way of describing the human body in its present stage of existence: "our vile body," or, as it would be more exactly rendered, "our body of humiliation."

The human frame appeared to Greek artists the most exquisite thing in nature: it was the form which seemed to them most nearly to unveil a Divine Beauty to the eye of sense. We know from their sculptures which have come down to us how fondly they studied it: they have left in stone the splendid record both of their genius and of their enthusiasm. How impossible it is to imagine the phrase, "our vile body," upon the lips of the men who decorated the Parthenon! Such a phrase belongs to another and a totally distinct world of feeling and of

[a] John Phillips, M.A., F.R.S., Professor of Geology at Oxford.

thought. It implies that the man who uses it has seen deeper and higher than the realm of sense. The Greek knew only this visible world, and he made the most of it. The Hebrew had had a revelation of a higher Beauty; and when men have come into contact with the Eternal, they sit lightly to the things of time. The Greek was occupied with the matchless outline of the human form. The Hebrew could not forget that his bodily eye rested after all on a perishable mass of animated clay; he could not but think of what was coming, of the decaying texture and substance of the flesh, of the darkness and corruption of the grave. So Isaiah: "All flesh is grass, and all the goodliness thereof as the flower of the field: the grass withereth, the flower fadeth."[a] So Job: "Man that is born of a woman hath but a short time to live, and is full of misery. He cometh up as a flower, and continueth not."[b] So the Psalmist: "As soon as Thou scatterest them they are even as a sleep, and fade away suddenly like the grass. In the morning it is green, and groweth up: but in the evening it is cut down, dried up, and withered."[c] So, quite in the Old Testament spirit, St. James: "What is your life? It is even a vapour, that appeareth for a little time, and then vanisheth away."[d] It is in the same sense that St. Paul says "our body of humiliation." The phrase embodies the mind of both Testaments: the body is destined to disease and death. Prophets and Apostles do not write as artists; they are thinking of the eternal realities.

Not that this phrase implies any one-sided depreciation of the body, such as we meet with, for instance, in heathen ascetics. For Christianity here keeps a middle way between two opposite errors, which have distorted man's thought when he endeavours, apart from Revelation, to

[a] Isa. xl. 6, 7.
[b] Job xiv. 1, 2.
[c] Ps. xc. 5, 6.
[d] St. James iv. 14.

form a just estimate of his own being. On the one hand, the body has seemed to be the whole man, just as it does to our modern materialists; as though life must cease altogether with death, or after death be so attenuated into a purely shadowy existence as to lose all the importance of reality. On the other hand, the body has been treated as a mere incumbrance, having no organic relation to the complete life of man; as the soul's prison-house; as the chain which ties noble spirits down to the soil of earth; as the mere instrument of a being who is complete without it, and who is not free until he has escaped from it. The moral effect of the first of these opinions is to encourage unbounded sensual indulgence, while it can be had, since such indulgence has no consequences in an after world, in which continued existence is held to be so enfeebled or so improbable. The moral effect of the second of these opinions is to encourage suicide; since, if the alliance between soul and body is so disadvantageous and unnatural, the sooner we put an end to it the better.

Between these opposite exaggerations Revelation holds a middle course. According to the teaching of the Bible and the Church, although not always according to the teaching of particular persons who have professed to be guided by the Bible, the body is essential to man's completeness, whether in this or a future life. Pope's Ode to Immortality is conceived in the sense of Plato, not in that of the New Testament. According to Revelation, death is the disturbance of that union of soul and body which constitutes the complete man. Death therefore introduces a morbid condition of existence; a strictly abnormal separation of the two constitutive parts of our being; and this irregular interruption of the true life of man ends at the Resurrection, when man re-enters upon the original completeness of his existence. The body then, in the revealed doctrine about man, has all the honour which can belong to it, as a necessary part of man's nature. Although the body is not the seat of man's consciousness, it is the soil into which his conscious being strikes and takes root. We know not whether in this life the human spirit can work independently of the body,—of the brain. It may be so on extraordinary occasions, such as was St. Paul's ecstasy into the third heaven. As a rule it certainly is not so. The body asserts its importance, constantly, imperiously. Madness is a disturbance inflicted on the soul by a diseased brain; and, in lesser ways, the body of every man forces his spirit to share its weakness. "The corruptible body" presseth down the soul;[a] not merely staying the hand and silencing the voice, but impoverishing or arresting thought, and chilling affection, and paralysing will. So intimate and awful is the embrace, which, during this stage of our being, links soul and body together!

And yet, masterful as the body is, it is not the governing element in man's nature. Mark the phrase: "our body of humiliation." Man is something higher, nobler, than the animal form with which he is so intimately identified that it is part of himself. Man, in the eye of Revelation, as in reality, lives on the frontier of two vast and mysterious worlds; the world of pure spirits, and the world of animal existences. By his spiritual nature, or soul, he belongs to the ranks of angelic intelligences; they rise above him in tier beyond tier of being, upwards towards the awful Throne of the Everlasting Father. By his bodily frame man belongs to the world of animal existences. They stretch away beneath his feet, some of them with such powers of association and instinct as to suggest the shadow of a spiritual nature, down to the point at which, amid the zoophytes, animal life sinks by scarcely

[a] Wisdom ix. 15.

perceptible gradations into the lines of vegetable existence. Alone among the creatures man occupies this frontier post in nature ; having a body on the one hand, and being on the other a conscious spirit. And from the point of view of his higher, that is, his spiritual existence, his body seems to him a body of humiliation. It falls under all kinds of limitations and disabilities from which pure spirit is exempt. It can move, but only under the conditions of any other animal, and less swiftly and freely than most. It comes into existence through physical causes, which are indeed those which obtain throughout the animal world : it is subject to diseases, and finally to death, just as are lower creatures. As the Preacher says : " That which befalleth the sons of men befalleth beasts ; even one thing befalleth them : as the one dieth, so dieth the other ; yea, they have all one breath ; so that a man hath no pre-eminence above a beast: for all is vanity. All go unto one place ; all are of the dust, and all turn to dust again."[a]

Such is the physical frame of man in this present life. It is a body of humiliation. And we Christians should regard it as only a degrading incumbrance, to be treated like an ill-mannered stranger who had forced himself upon us, whom we could not well get rid of, yet wished to keep in his place ; if it were not that a flood of glory has been shed on it ; and that it has great prospects, a splendid future, in store for it. We Christians know that our nature as a whole has been ennobled as well as invigorated by the Son of God. Bending, in the immensity of His love, from the throne of heaven, He has taken it upon Him in its integrity, body and soul alike, and joined it by an indissoluble union to His Own Eternal Person. That Body Which was born of Mary, Which lived on

[a] Eccles. iii. 19, 20.

## XXIII]  *The Raiser of the Dead.*  73

this planet for thirty-three years, Which was spat upon, buffeted, scourged, crucified, Which underwent the anguish and the coldness of death, and was raised again in glory —That Body exists somewhere in space, at "the right hand of God the Father Almighty" (so our poor human language struggles to express the unimaginable truth), and thereby confers on all who are partakers of human flesh and blood a nobility of which our race can never be deprived. " Forasmuch as the children were partakers of flesh and blood, He likewise Himself took part in the same."[a]

Certainly He has ennobled us; and yet while life lasts how great is the interval between us and Him! How unlike to ours is the Body of glory Which rose from the tomb on Easter morning; in its indescribable beauty, in its freedom of movement, in its inaccessibility to decay, in its spirituality of texture! "His glorious Body!" exclaims St. Paul. His greatest gift is yet to come. We shall die as do the creatures around us; whether by violence or by slow decay. But He will gather up what death has left, and will transfigure it with the splendours of a new life. He will change our body of humiliation that it may be fashioned like unto the Body of His glory. Sown in corruption, it will be raised in incorruption. Sown in dishonour, it will be raised in glory. Sown in the extremity of physical weakness, it will be raised in superhuman power. Sown a natural body, which is controlled on every side by physical law, it will be raised, a true body still, but belonging to the sphere of spirit.[b]

Most difficult indeed it is to the imagination to understand how this poor body, our companion for so many years, nay rather, part of our very selves, is to be first wrenched from us at death, and then restored to us, if we

[a] Heb. ii. 14.      [b] 1 Cor. xv. 42-44.

will, transfigured by the glory of the Son of God. Little indeed can we understand that inaccessibility to disease, that radiant beauty, that superiority to distance and material obstructions when moving through space, that spirituality, in short, which awaits but which will not destroy it.

> "Heavy and dull this frame of limbs and heart,
>   Whether slow creeping on cold earth, or borne
> On lofty steed, or loftier prow, we dart
>   O'er wave or field: yet breezes laugh to scorn
>
> Our puny speed, and birds, and clouds in heaven,
>   And fish, like living shafts that pierce the main,
> And stars that shoot through freezing air at even—
>   Who would but follow, might he break his chain?"

Such is Nature's whisper: but Faith replies :—

> "And thou shalt break it soon. The grovelling worm
>   Shall find his wings, and soar as fast and free
> As his transfigured Lord—with lightning form
>   And snowy vest; such grace He won for thee.
>
> When from the grave He sprang at dawn of morn,
>   And led through boundless air thy conquering road.
> Leaving a glorious track, where saints new-born
>   Might fearless follow to their blest abode" [a]

## II.

And thus we are anticipating this question: What is the ground of the great Christian expectation of a glorified body in a future life? How shall we get it?

To this the Apostle would answer, "According to the working whereby He is able even to subdue all things unto Himself." Everything of course depends on that. St. Paul had no doubt that Jesus Christ, crucified some

[a] *The Christian Year:* Twenty-third Sunday after Trinity.

thirty years before, was living and reigning while he himself was writing to the Philippians. St. Paul knew that Jesus Christ had actual jurisdiction over all things on earth and in heaven. As God, He always had such power; it belonged to His Eternal oneness with the Father. It had been conferred on Him as Man. "All power is given Me in heaven and in earth."[a]

With those who do not take our Lord Jesus Christ at His word, St. Paul's words about Him would of course have no weight. If He is not God, if He does not wield Divine powers through His exalted Manhood, it is idle to discuss the probabilities of a future which depends altogether upon His practical omnipotence. But if He is God,—and His words about Himself are morally worthless, or worse than worthless, on any other supposition,— if His acts and character sufficiently warrant His words; then this phrase, "the working of His power," covers all the ground. We are in the presence of Omnipotence.

It seems to you, you say, very strange that the various elements of a human frame resolved into dust many centuries ago should be re-collected, re-animated, endowed with a new and more glorious life. What has become of the particles? They have been absorbed, and re-absorbed into other bodies. They have passed through animals and vegetables. They have been incorporated with distinct substances, and detached again. By this time they are scattered in a thousand directions; they are whirling round and round in the never-ceasing fated cycle of destruction and reconstruction, of growth and decay, which makes up the vast life of the Universe.

How are the ingredients which have belonged to a single body to be rescued from this subsequent and oft-repeated appropriation; how are they to be re-collected,

[a] St. Matt. xxviii. 18.

re-arranged, re-incorporated, ere the promised reconstruction and transfiguration can be achieved? It is a bundle of impossibilities, you say; it is a miracle which costs too much.

Certainly it is an astonishing exertion of superhuman Power which is under consideration. But surely it is not more than any reasonable believer in God would assent to upon sufficient evidence of His declared will. No man can believe in God, without believing in an act of power, compared with which the resurrection of the dead is a trivial incident. To believe in God is to believe in the original creation of all things out of nothing. To admit that matter, that any single particle of matter, is eternal, is to deny the solitary Eternity of God; it is, in other words, to part with an essential condition of belief in God. Certainly, if matter is eternal, we are still face to face with a mystery at least as formidable as the first Article of the Christian Creed. But then there is nothing to relieve its darkness.

If a reasonable man believes in God, he cannot escape belief in creation out of nothing: and who that has ever tried to think out what these words mean would object to anything that God has promised, on the score of its being miraculous? Creation is, after all, the great miracle. It is the miracle of miracles; and the man who believes it will not question God's word merely because the results to which it is pledged are what we call miraculous. By the very act of believing in God he believes in an initial miracle, compared with which all that can possibly follow is insignificant.

### III.

Such a faith as this in the Resurrection, when it is sincerely entertained, ought to have practical consequences. If, at death, we parted company with the body for good and all, if the soul was the only part of our being which had a future in store for it, then it would not matter what was done, either in life or in death, with the perishing husk. But if this body of humiliation is the heir to a splendid destiny, we shall treat it, both in life and in death, as princes are treated who live in expectation of a throne; we shall treat it with all the care and honour which its prospects demand.

*a.* Hence, first, respect for the human body after death[a] is a natural result of Christian belief that the inanimate form lying before us is not utterly gone for ever; that it certainly has a future. We may not say that respect for the dead has no place in Heathendom. There are vague instincts, corresponding to guesses, which man in a natural state makes about his destiny; there are vague apprehensions of ghostly powers who might do an ill turn to the irreverent; there are superstitions which prompt respect for the dead. But Christianity has made this feeling a rule; has given it reason and permanence by the great glowing faith in the Resurrection. Just as the Body of the Lord Jesus, after His human soul had parted from It, and had descended into the region of the imprisoned dead,[b] was carefully wrapped in linen and laid in a tomb until the morn of Easter,[c] so ever since have the bodies of departed Christians been looked upon with some portion of the faith and love of Nicodemus and Joseph; for they too, we know, will rise. We are not handling a lump of decaying matter, which has lost its interest for ever, and which will presently be resolved into its chemical constituents, to be recombined no more.

[a] Acts viii. 2 ; St. Aug. *De Civ. Dei*, xii. 13.
[b] 1 St. Pet. iii. 18, 19.     [c] St. Matt. xxvii. 59, 60.

It lies before us, indeed, a body of humiliation, but one day it is to be fashioned like the glorious Body of the ascended Son of God. And we feel and act towards it accordingly.

Many who hear me will be aware that of late, in this and other countries, a controversy has been going on upon the question whether it would not be better to burn our dead than to bury them in the soil. Here in England an accomplished physicist has urged with great ability the arguments which may be produced for Cremation. He insists that the practice of burying, even in large suburban cemeteries, is, and is likely to become, increasingly dangerous to the public health. He refers to the evidence which was collected in the course of the inquiries which preceded the prohibition of intramural burial. He maintains that the old dangers will repeat themselves as the population spreads around and beyond our modern burying-places in the suburbs of the Metropolis.

If it could be shown that the dead could not be buried anywhere in the soil, without involving harm or danger to the living, we should, undoubtedly, be right in entertaining this proposal. The bodies of the dead would rise just as easily and certainly out of the ashes that had been placed in an urn, as out of the decomposed contents of any vault in this Cathedral, or of any grave in a country churchyard. The mighty power of Christ would not work less effectively in the one case than in the other. But, on the other hand, ought anything short of a proved necessity, such as motives of convenience or economy, to warrant a serious departure from the immemorial practice of Christendom? Cremation does not represent a new and unthought-of improvement upon the custom of the world. Remember that when Christianity appeared upon the scene the Pagan world very generally burned its dead. The Church deliberately substituted burial for cremation; and we may not lightly distrust the instinct of our first fathers in the faith. Jesus Christ was buried, not burned. We cannot think of the burning of His Sacred Body without a shudder. And as He is, so are we in this world.[a] Surely to a believer in the Resurrection it is more welcome to leave our dead in the soil, as in the hands of God, than to hasten, or anticipate, by the violent operation of a furnace, His wonted treatment of the body for which He has so great a future in reserve.

β. But secondly, much more important is our duty towards the body during this present life. That duty may be explained in two words: guard it and train it. You who are well off, do what you can for the bodies of the poor. They too will rise. And keep your own "in temperance, soberness, and chastity." Keep it from all that would bar its entrance to the presence of Christ. Keep it from those mischiefs which have their seat in it; since, as St. Peter says, they war, not merely against the physical constitution, but against the soul,[b] with which the body is so closely linked. Every one that hath the Resurrection hope in him "purifieth himself, even as Christ is pure."[c] Do not forget how the sinful body may, even here, be made clean by Christ's Body, as the soul may be washed with His most precious Blood;[d] do not neglect that glorious Sacrament which, if worthily received, "preserves body and soul unto everlasting life."[e] And train the body too. Train it, not merely as a Greek athlete,

[a] 1 St. John iv. 17.   [b] 1 St. Pet. ii. 11.   [c] 1 St. John iii 3.
[d] Communion Service : Prayer of Humble Access.
[e] Communion Service : Words of Administration.

or as a beautiful animal, in the hope of an earthly prize;[a] but train it as a destined partaker in those scenes of transcendent joy and worship, which are described in the Apocalypse.[b] "Present your bodies," says the Apostle, "a living sacrifice;"[c] in work, and in that best of work, in worship. Worship, bodily reverence as well as spiritual communion, is a preparation for heaven. The body which is never reverent, which never bends in adoration before the Being of beings, is not likely to be joined to a soul that has learned to hold real communion with the Infinite. In such matters Christian instinct is better than argument; and when Eternity is once treated as a practical reality, we are not far from agreeing as to how to bear ourselves among the things of time.

[a] Cor. ix. 25.  [b] Rev. v. 13, 14.  [c] Rom. xii. 1.

# SERMON XXIV.

## THE LORD'S DAY.

REV. I. 10.

*I was in the Spirit on the Lord's Day.*

WHAT is the meaning of this expression,—" the Lord's Day"?
Does it mean "the Day of Judgment," and is St. John saying that in an ecstasy he beheld the last judgment of God? Undoubtedly " the day of the Lord " is an expression often applied to the Day of Judgment both in the Old and New Testaments. But such a meaning would not serve St. John's purpose here. He is thinking of the date of his great vision, not yet of the scene to which it introduced him. And just as he says it was in the isle of Patmos, thus marking the place, so he says that it was on the Lord's Day, thus marking the time. Whatever the Lord's Day may mean, it cannot mean the Day of Judgment.

Does it then stand for the annual feast of our Lord's Resurrection from the dead; as we should now say, Easter Day? That day, as we know from the Epistle to the Corinthians, was observed in Apostolic times.[a] It was

[a] 1 Cor. v. 7, 8.

the feast which the Corinthians were to keep, "not with the old leaven, nor with the leaven of malice and wickedness, but with the unleavened bread of sincerity and truth."[a] But it could hardly have served for a date, because, in the Apostolic age, as for some time after, there were two different opinions in the Church as to the day on which Easter ought properly to be observed. If the Lord's Day, in this passage, had meant Easter Day, it would not have settled the date of the Revelation without some further notice of the exact time of year.

Does the phrase then mean the Sabbath-day of the Mosaic law? God calls the Sabbath, by the mouth of Isaiah, "My holy day,"[b] and the language of the Fourth Commandment, "The seventh day is the Sabbath of the Lord thy God,"[c] might well justify the expression. But there is no instance in the New Testament of an allusion to the Sabbath, except by its own name, the Sabbath. If St. John had meant the Sabbath, or seventh day of the week, he would certainly have used the word Sabbath. He would not have used another word which, in the days of the Apostles, and ever since, the Christian Church has applied, not to the seventh day of the week, but to the first.

There is indeed no real reason for doubting that by the Lord's Day St. John meant the first day of the week, or, as we should say, Sunday. Our Lord Jesus Christ made that day in a special sense His Own, by rising from the dead on it, and by connecting it with His first six appearances after His Resurrection. On the first Lord's Day, He appeared five times. After the lapse of a week, on the next Lord's Day, He appeared to the Eleven, having during the interval, so far as we know, remained out of sight. The Day of Pentecost, on which the Holy

[a] 1 Cor. v. 8.    [b] Isa. lviii. 13.    [c] Exod. xx. 10.

Ghost came down from heaven, and created the Church of Christ, also fell on a Lord's Day; seven weeks after the Day of the Resurrection. And from this time we find scattered hints of its observance, as when St. Paul spent a week at Troas, in the course of his third missionary journey. "Upon the first day of the week," we are told, "the disciples came together to break bread," that is, to partake of the Holy Communion; "and Paul preached unto them." So when St. Paul is giving directions to the Corinthians for a collection of money on behalf of the poor members of the Church in Palestine, he writes, "Upon the first day of the week let every one of you lay by in store, as God hath prospered him, that there be no gatherings when I come."[b] This passage shows that the first day in the week was then recognised as a natural day for especial religious efforts; and it is here connected with what we should call a weekly offertory. St. Paul tells the Corinthians that he had already given a similar order to the Galatian Churches.[c]

When, then, some years afterwards, we find St. John an exile at Patmos, saying that he was in the Spirit on the Lord's Day, we know what he means. The day was already observed by Apostolic Christians as the weekly festival of the Resurrection. No doubt, on that very day, St. John had held communion with his Lord and Master in the Sacrament of His love. Nay, it is possible, as has been conjectured, that it was during that awful service that he was in the Spirit, in a state of inspired trance or ecstasy; so that as the veil of sense dropped away, he saw "the invisible things," and "the things that shall be hereafter,"[d] under such forms as were needed for the purpose of translation into the thought and language

[a] Acts xx. 7.
[c] 1 Cor. xvi. 1.
[b] 1 Cor. xvi. 2.
[d] Rev. i. 19.

of man. It is the last mention of the day in the New Testament. And, after Pentecost, it is the greatest.

The Lord's Day, then, of the Christian Church is the weekly commemoration of the great event which is annually celebrated at Easter. And, therefore, Easter is a fitting time for considering the character of the day, and the uses to which it should be put by Christians.

What are the principles which are recognised in the observance of the Lord's Day by the Church of Christ?

I.

The first principle embodied in the Lord's Day is the duty of consecrating a certain proportion of time, at least one-seventh, to the especial service of God.

This principle is common to the Jewish Sabbath, and to the Christian Lord's Day. "Remember that thou keep holy the Sabbath-day"[a] means for us Christians, "Remember that thou keep holy one day in seven." Keep the day holy; consecrate it. So the precept runs. It is the same word in the original as that which is used when the consecration of the priests,[b] of the altar,[c] of the first-born,[d] of the people of Israel,[e] of the finished Temple,[f] are severally prescribed. Such consecration implies two things; a separation of the thing or person consecrated from all others, and the communication to him, or it, of a quality of holiness or purity. The first idea predominates in the remarkable order to sanctify Mount Sinai by hedging it round and making it inaccessible.[g] The second predominates in the other cases referred to. The two ideas meet in the case of the Sabbath, or of the Lord's Day.

[a] Exod. xx. 8.
[b] Exod. xxviii. 41; xxix. 1; xl. 13-15.
[c] Exod. xxix. 36; xl. 10.
[d] Exod. xiii. 2.
[e] Exod. xix. 10, 14.
[f] 1 Kings viii. 64.
[g] Exod. xix. 12, 13.

The day is to be unlike other days, and it is also to be marked by positive characteristics which shall proclaim its dedication to God.

To this idea of the especial consecration of a section of time, it is objected that in a true Christian life all time is consecrated. Life, as a whole, is owed to the Creator; the whole of time is not less His due than the whole service of mind, and soul, and strength. How, it is asked, can there be any deliberately unconsecrated time in the life of a true disciple of Him " Who died for us, that whether we wake or sleep we should live together with Him;"[a] Who "died for all, that they which live should not any longer live unto themselves, but unto Him Which died for them, and rose again"?[b] Does not this consecration of a section of time ignore the existing obligation to a service which knows no limits but the limits of strength and life?

The answer is that the larger obligation of love is not ignored because the smaller one of duty is insisted on. Human life being what it is, it is easy to do nothing by undertaking to do everything. Certainly the whole life of a Christian should be a consecrated life: God is not to be forgotten in the week because He is especially remembered on Sunday. But a duty which is always obligatory is likely to be recognised when certain definite times for recognising it are insisted on. All a Christian's time is properly consecrated time; but practically, in many cases, none would be consecrated unless an effort were made to mark a certain proportion of it by a special consecration. The case is parallel to that of prayer. Our Lord says that men ought always to pray, and not to faint.[c] The Apostle says, " Pray without ceasing."[d] And the life of a

[a] 1 Thess. v. 10.
[b] 2 Cor. v. 15.
[c] St. Luke xviii. 1.
[d] 1 Thess. v. 17.

good Christian is, no doubt, a continuous prayer; the spirit of prayer penetrates and hallows it; each duty is intertwined with acts of the soul which raise it above this earthly scene to the Throne and presence of Christ. But, for all that, in all Christian lives stated times of prayer, private as well as public, are practically necessary, if the practice of prayer is to be consistently maintained. Yet morning and evening and mid-day or other devotions are perfectly consistent with recognition of the Apostolic and Divine sayings, that prayer should be incessant in a Christian life. And in like manner the especial consecration of one day in seven does not involve an implied rejection of the rights of Jesus Christ over all Christian time. It is like those small payments known to the law, which do not profess to give an equivalent for that which they represent, but only technically to acknowledge a much larger claim; it implies that all our time belongs to God, although, considering our weakness, He graciously accepts a prescribed instalment or section of it.

And, apart from its importance in the life of the servants of God, the public setting apart of a certain measure of time to God's service is a witness to His claims borne before the world, and calculated to strike the imaginations of men. Such an observance makes room for the thought of God amid the pressing importunities of business and enjoyment. Like a great cathedral, it is a public attestation of what is due to God; addressed to the senses, and making itself felt in the common habits of men. From this point of view, our English Sunday, whatever may be said about mistakes in the detail of its observance, is a national blessing. It brings the existence and claims of God before the minds even of those who do not make a good use of it. And religious foreigners have not seldom told us that it fills them with envy and admiration; and that we shall do well to guard that which, once lost, is certain to be wellnigh, if not altogether, irrecoverable.

II.

A second principle represented in the Lord's Day is the periodical suspension of human toil. This is closely connected with that of the consecration of time. In order to make the day, by this prohibition, unlike other days; in order to make room for the acknowledgment of God on it; ordinary occupations are suspended. Here again we have a second principle common to the Jewish Sabbath and to the Christian Lord's Day. "Six days shalt thou labour, and do all that thou hast to do."[a] But of the seventh day it is said, "In it thou shalt do no manner of work; thou, and thy son, and thy daughter, thy man-servant, and thy maid-servant, thy cattle, and the foreigners who live with thee."[b] In the Old Testament a variety of particular occupations are explicitly forbidden on the Sabbath; sowing and reaping,[c] gathering wood and kindling a fire for cooking,[d] holding markets,[e] every kind of trade, pressing grapes,[f] carrying any sort of burden.[g] In a later age the Pharisees added largely to these prohibitions. They held it unlawful to pluck an ear of corn in passing through a corn-field,[h] or to assist and relieve the sick;[i] although they ruled that an animal which had fallen into a ditch might be legally helped to get out,[k] and that guests might be invited to an entertainment,[l] and that a child of eight days old might be circumcised.[m] There

[a] Exod. xx. 9.    [b] Exod. xx. 10.    [c] Neh. xiii. 15.
[d] Num. xv. 32-36; Ex. xxxv. 3.    [e] Neh. x. 31; xiii. 16-18.
[f] Neh. xiii. 15-20.    [g] Jer. xvii. 21, 22.    [h] St. Mark ii. 23, 24.
[i] St. Matt. xii. 10; St. John ix. 14-16.    [k] St. Matt. xii. 11.
[l] St. Luke xiv. 1.    [m] St. John vii. 22, 23.

were thirty-nine Rabbinical prohibitions on the Sabbath, of which one limited a Sabbath-day's journey to two thousand cubits, and another forbade killing even the most dangerous vermin, while a third proscribed the use of a wooden leg, or a crutch, or a purse. These, and other prohibitions, illustrate the tendency of mere law to become, sooner or later, through excessive technicality, the caricature and the ruin of moral principle. And it was against these Pharisaic perversions of the Sabbath that our Lord protested by act and word; reminding His countrymen that the Sabbath was made for the moral good of man, and not man for the later legal theory of the Sabbath.[a] But the broad principle of abstinence from labour, however misrepresented in the later Jewish practice, was itself sacred; and it passed into the Christian observance of the Lord's Day. We see this plainly in notices of the observance in the early times of the Christian Church. They show that the general rule of the Fourth Commandment with regard to work, modified by our Lord's teaching respecting duties of charity and necessity, was held to apply to the Christian Lord's Day. Thus Tertullian, writing at the end of the second century, calls the day both Sunday and the Lord's Day; says that it is a day of joy and that to fast on it is wrong; yet adds that "business is put off on it, lest we give place to the devil."[b] And thus when, under Constantine, the Imperial Government had acknowledged the faith of Christ, and Christianity made itself felt in the principles of legislation, provision was very soon made for the observance of the Lord's Day. Even four years before the Council of Nicæa, Constantine issued an edict ordering the judges, the town populations, the artists and tradesmen of all kinds, to cease from labour on the Lord's Day. He allows agricultural labour to go on, if the safety

[a] St. Mark ii. 27.   [b] Tert. *de Orat.* c. 23.

## The Lord's Day.

of crops or the health of cattle depends on it. And when we examine the Codes of the Emperors Theodosius and Justinian, in which the experience and traditions of the great Roman lawyers are combined with, and modified by, the softening influences of Christianity, we find that the observance of the Lord's Day is carefully provided for. Works of necessity, whether civil or agricultural, are allowed; others are forbidden. Public spectacles of all kinds and the games of the circus are suppressed.[a] And the great teachers of the Church in the fourth and fifth centuries did what they could to second the imperial legislation by exhorting the faithful to abstain from works or sights which profaned the Holy Day of the Christian week.

This insistance on a day of freedom from earthly labour is not inconsistent with a recognition of the dignity and the claims of labour. On the contrary, it protects labour, by arresting the excessive expenditure of human strength; and it raises and consecrates labour by leading the workman's mind to acknowledge the Source and Support of his exertions.

When, in the first French Revolution, there prevailed a fanatical eagerness to show how well the world could get on without Christianity, some important experiments were made on this very subject. And the general result was to prove that the abstinence from labour on one day in seven is enacted in the interests of labour itself. Especially is this the case at a time like our own, when men live and work at high pressure; when capital demands quick returns for outlay; when competition is keen, and the place of a man who faints for a moment at his post is at once occupied by a stronger rival, who stands

[a] Cod. Theod. l. xv. t. 5, de Spectac. c. 2; Cod. Just. l. iii. t. 12, de Fer. c. 3.

hard by, watching his opportunity. It is sometimes asked why this abstinence from labour should be dictated to us; why each man cannot make a Sunday for himself, when his strength or health demands it. The answer is, Because, in a busy, highly-worked community, unless all are to abstain from work, none will abstain; since, in point of fact, none can afford to abstain. This is the principle of the Bank holidays · the State comes in to do for labour four times a year, on a small scale, what the Church does on a large scale every week ; it essays to make a general rest from work possible by an external sanction. And this is the principle which inspires an excellent movement lately set on foot for the early closing of houses of business. Unless, in deference to the authority, whether of law or public opinion, all employers of labour consent to close their business at an earlier hour, none can afford to do so. If the sanction of the Sunday rest from toil were to be withdrawn, it would, in a civilisation like ours, go hard, first with labour, and then, at no distant interval, with capital. The dignity and obligation of labour is sufficiently recognised in the precept : " Six days shalt thou labour, and do all that thou hast to do ;" and the health and happiness and moral wellbeing of the labourer is secured by a seventh day, in which the labourer is to " do no manner of work."

### III.

Thus the Sabbath and the Lord's Day agree in affirming two principles; the hallowing a seventh part of time, and the obligation of abstinence from servile work on one day in seven. But are the days identical? May we rightly call the Lord's Day the Sabbath ? These questions must be answered in the negative. The Lord's Day was never identified with the Jewish Sabbath before the rise of Puritanism in the seventeenth century. The Puritan Divines had a remarkable knowledge of the contents of Holy Scripture; but, when reading it, they seem to have had no eye for its perspectives. They had broken away to a very serious extent from the old Church interpretation, which would have saved them from some of their mistakes; and there was, in that age, no criticism sufficiently educated to replace even imperfectly the guidance which they had lost. Accordingly, in their anxiety to secure a strong Scriptural sanction for the observance of the Lord's Day, they said that the Lord's Day was in fact the Jewish Sabbath, and that all that is said in the Old Testament about the Sabbath applies to it. Thus, without suspecting it, they took up about the Sabbath exactly the position which the Judaizers in Galatia took up about circumcision. They said that a purely Jewish ordinance was a necessary element of the Christian life; and if St. Paul could have appeared in the seventeenth century, or afterwards, to Christians who had made such a mistake as this, is it not likely that he would have repeated with modifications his old exclamation.[a] 'O my well-meaning but foolish English friends, who hath bewitched you, that you should revive a Jewish observance in the midst of Christendom?'

Observe that the Jewish Sabbath and the Christian Lord's Day, while agreeing in affirming two principles, differ in two noteworthy respects.

First, they differ, as has already been implied, in being kept on distinct days. The Sabbath was kept on the last day of the week: the Lord's Day is kept on the first. "The seventh day," and no other, "is the Sabbath of the Lord thy God."[b] When then the Christian Church keeps its weekly holy day on the first day of the week, it does

[a] Gal. iii. 1.    [b] Exod. xx. 10.

much more than change the day. Had the motive of the observance remained the same, this change in a Divine law would have been unpardonable. The change was made because there was an imperative reason for making it.

For the Lord's Day and the Sabbath Day differ, secondly, in the reason or motive for observing them. The Sabbath is the weekly commemoration of the rest of God after creation. "Remember that thou keep holy the Sabbath-day. For in six days the Lord made heaven and earth, the sea, and all that in them is, and rested the seventh day: wherefore the Lord blessed the seventh day, and hallowed it."[a] Israel was the people to whom God had revealed the mystery of creation; that master-truth by which human thought is saved now as of old from the sin and folly of confounding God with His works. The Sabbath was the weekly commemoration of the finished work of God. It brought before the mind of the Jew the ineffable majesty of the Great Creator, between Whom and the noblest work of His hands there yawns an impassable abyss. Thus the Sabbath observance, apart from its directly sanctifying effect upon individual life, was the great protection to the Jews against the idolatry with which they came in contact in Egypt, in Phœnicia, in Babylon, and against the Greek modes of thought which tried them so sorely at Alexandria and in Palestine under the Macedonian kings of a later time.

The Christian motive for observing the Lord's Day is the Resurrection of Christ from the dead. That truth is to the Christian Creed what the creation of the world out of nothing is to the Jewish. The Lord's Day marks the completed Redemption, as the Sabbath had marked the completed Creation. The Resurrection is also the funda-

[a] Exod. xx. 8, 11.

# XXIV]  *The Lord's Day.*  93

mental truth on which Christianity rests; and thus it is as much insisted on by the Christian Apostles as is God's creation of all things by the Jewish prophets. Not, of course, that the creation of all things by God is less precious to the Christian than to the Jew: but it is more taken for granted. In Christian eyes, the creation of the world of nature is eclipsed by the creation of the world of grace; and of this last creation, the Resurrection is the warrant. The Resurrection is commemorated, as St. Irenæus points out, on the first day of the week, when God brought light and order out of darkness and chaos.[a] It is the risen and enthroned Lamb Who says, "Behold, I make all things new:"[b] and therefore if "any man be in Christ, he is the new creation; old things are passed away, behold, all things are become new."[c] Of this new creation, the Lord's Day is the weekly festival, as being the festival of the Resurrection.

In a remarkable passage of the Epistle to the Colossians, St. Paul connects the keeping of the Jewish Sabbath by Christians with that of the new moon. "Let no man judge you . . . in respect of an holyday, or of the new moon, or of the Sabbath days."[d] In St. Paul's eyes the Jewish Sabbath was just as much part of the discarded system of the ceremonial law, as was the observance of the new moon. The Christian Lord's Day stands on different ground: It is sometimes, indeed, loosely called the Christian Sabbath; but the epithet Christian implies that it is no longer the Sabbath in the Jewish sense any more than " the Israel of God," about which St. Paul writes to the Galatians,[e] is the same thing as the Israel of David or of Ezra. The Jewish Sabbath stands in the same relation to the Lord's Day as does Circumcision to Christian Baptism; as does the

[a] Gen. i. 3, 4.   [b] Rev. xxi. 5.   [c] 2 Cor. v. 17.
[d] Col. ii. 16.   [e] Gal. vi. 16.

Paschal Lamb to the Holy Communion; as does the Law to the Gospel. It is a shadow of a good thing to come.[a] It is only perpetuated by being transfigured, or rather it is so transfigured as to have parted with its identity. The special consecration of a seventh part of time, the abstinence from labour, remains. But the spirit and governing motive of the day is changed. Christians stand no longer at the foot of Sinai, but by the empty tomb in the garden outside Jerusalem. And here a third and last principle, which is embodied by the day, comes into view.

### III.

This third principle is the public worship of God. The cessation of ordinary work is not enjoined upon Christians only that they may while away the time, or spend it in aimless self-pleasing, or in something worse. The Lord's Day is the day upon which our Lord Jesus Christ has a first claim. On this great day every instructed Christian thinks of Him as completing the work of our Redemption; as vindicating His character as a Teacher of absolute truth; as triumphing over His enemies; as conquering death in that nature which had hitherto always been subject to its empire; as designing, now that He has overcome the sharpness of death, to open the kingdom of heaven to all believers.

"Morn of morns, and day of days."

It is unlike any other in the week; and the sense of this finds its natural expression in prayer and praise.

The Sabbath, too, had its special religious observances. There was a "Holy Convocation" on it; a meeting together of the people for a religious purpose. The usual

[a] Heb. x. 1.

morning and evening sacrifices were doubled. The shewbread, one of the types of the Blessed Sacrament, was changed. In the days after David, a new course of priests and Levites commenced its ministrations. And when Jews lived far from the Temple, they met together in the synagogues, to hear the Law and the Prophets read to them, and to listen to exhortations which were based on these sacred words.

In the Church of Christ the first duty of a Christian is, like the Holy Women and the Disciples, to seek to hold converse with our Risen Lord. A well-spent Lord's Day should always begin with that supreme act of Christian worship, in which we meet Jesus verily and indeed; the only public service known to the early and Apostolic Church; the Most Holy Sacrament of the Body and Blood of our Redeemer.

What the practice of our fathers in the faith was within a few years after the Apostles had gone to their rest, we learn from the celebrated letter of the cultivated heathen governor, Pliny, to his Imperial master, Trajan: "The Christians," he says, "are accustomed to meet together on a stated day, before it is light, and to sing hymns to Christ as God, and to bind themselves by a Sacrament, not for any wicked purpose; but never to commit fraud, theft, or adultery, never to break their word, nor to refuse, when called upon, to deliver up any trust."[a] This was his impression as a heathen, looking at the Sacred Service from without, and gathering its nature from Christian language about it which he imperfectly understood. How Sunday was kept by Christians about the year Anno Domini 140 is very fully described by an eminent convert from Paganism, Justin Martyr. He says that on that day there was an assembly of all Christians who

[a] Plin. *Ep.* 97.

lived either in town or country; that the writings of the Apostles and Prophets were read; and that prayer was offered, and alms were collected, and the Holy Sacrament of our Lord's Body and Blood was celebrated.[a] As we descend the stream of time, illustrations become more numerous. But in the early Church of Christ it was taken for granted that a Christian would observe the Lord's Day, first of all, by taking part in that solemn Sacrament and Service which the Lord had Himself ordained. A Christian of the first or second century would not have understood a Sunday in which, whatever else might be done, the Holy Communion was omitted; and this great duty is best complied with as early in the day as possible. When the natural powers of the mind have been lately refreshed by sleep, when as yet the world has not taken off the bloom of the soul's first self-dedication to God, when thought, and feeling, and purpose, are still bright and fresh and unembarrassed; then is the time, for those who would reap the full harvest of grace, to approach the Altar. It is quite a different thing in the middle of the day; even when serious efforts are made to communicate reverently. Those who begin their Sundays with the Holy Communion know one of the deepest meanings of that promise, "They that seek Me early shall find Me."[b]

Not that it is wise or reverent to suppose that all the religious duties of a Sunday can be properly discharged before breakfast, and that the rest of the day may be spent as we like. No Christian whose heart is in the right place will think this. Later opportunities of public prayer and of instruction in the faith and duty of a Christian will be made the most of, as may be possible for each. Especially should an effort be made on every Sunday in

[a] S. Justin. *Apol.* I.      [b] Prov. viii. 17.

the year to learn some portion of the Will of God more perfectly than before; some truth or aspect of His Revelation of Himself in the Gospel; some Christian duty, as taught by the example or the words of Christ. Without a positive effort of this kind a Sunday is a lost Sunday: we shall think of it thus in eternity. Where there is the will to seek truth and wisdom there is no difficulty about the way: books, friends, sermons, are at hand. We have but to be in earnest, and all will follow.

When the religious obligations of Sunday have been complied with, there are duties of human brotherhood which may well find a place in it: kind deeds and words to friends, visits to the sick, acts of consideration for the poor, are in keeping with the spirit of the day. Above all, it should be made a bright as well as a solemn day for children; first solemn but then and always bright, so that in their after-life they may look back on the Sundays of childhood as its happiest days. And in itself there would be no harm if, for those who live in towns, museums and picture-galleries could be open on Sundays, just as the fields and the gardens are open to those who live in the country; for Art, like Nature, is to each one of us what we bring to it. The danger of such proposals is that, to realise them, Sunday labour must be employed, in some cases on a very considerable scale; and this would too easily lead the way to its employment for other and general purposes, and so to the abandonment of an essential characteristic of the Lord's Day.

Among the thoughts which Sundays, more than other days, bring back to us, is the memory of those whom we have known and loved, and who have passed away. We do well to make the most of these thoughts: they are sent us from above to enable us to prepare to follow. Some perhaps who hear me are thinking to-day of those brave men whose bones were laid two days ago in the vaults of this Cathedral.[a] They died in the service of their country: the accomplished engineer, the gallant sailor, the Arabic scholar, whose acquirements were of such an order that probably not more than half a dozen men in Europe could even do them justice. They died at the call of duty. And their example is treasured in the memory of a grateful country. We buried them on Friday, looking, as Christians should, to His Cross Who redeemed them; and now Sunday sheds upon their new-made graves the light and comfort of the Resurrection.

But, as I have said, the atmosphere which a true Christian breathes, on Sunday especially, is above all an atmosphere of worship. He may think it right and reverent to say little. But the day says to him from its early dawn, "Lift up thy heart," and his answer is, "I lift it up unto the Lord."[b] He knows that he has indeed "come unto Mount Zion, and to the city of the Living God, and to an innumerable company of angels, and to the general assembly of the Church of the Firstborn whose names are written in heaven, and to Jesus."[c] The invisible world, with all its beauty and all its awe, is around him, and he is able to keep earthly preoccupations at bay, and to surrender himself to the influences which stream down upon him from the Throne of the Redeemer. He is, in his way, like St. John, in the Spirit, and sees the higher and everlasting realities, and measures earth against heaven, and time against eternity, and man, so poor and weak, when at his best and strongest, against the Almighty and Everlasting.

[a] Professor Edward Henry Palmer, Captain Gill, and Lieutenant Charrington. Cf. Besant's *Life and Achievements of E. H. Palmer*, pp. 328, 329.
[b] Communion Service. [c] Heb. xii. 23, 24.

## The Lord's Day.

Sundays such as these are to many of us like shafts in a long tunnel; they admit at regular intervals light and air. And, though we pass them all too soon, their helpful influence does not vanish with the passing. It furnishes us with strength and light for the duties which await us, and makes it easier to follow loyally the road towards our eternal home which God's loving Providence may have traced for each of us. Let us endeavour, while we may, to make the most of these hours of grace and mercy, and to lead others to do so ; in the solemn conviction that as each such day passes one more decisive step has been taken, of whatever kind, in the direction of a destiny, which, once fixed by death, is fixed irrevocably.

# SERMON XXV.

## THE LORD OF LIFE.

St. John xiv. 19.

*Because I live, ye shall live also.*

THIS saying of our Lord's in the supper-room, like so much else which He uttered there, is only to be fully understood in the light of His Resurrection and Ascension into heaven. When He said, "Because I live," He had death immediately before Him. He was taking the measure of death; death was to be no real interruption of His ever-continuing Life. Death, with all its physical and mental miseries, was only an incident in His Existence. Already He sees the Resurrection beyond, and He exclaims, "I live." It was not possible, as St. Peter says, that He, the Prince of Life, should be holden of death;[a] and He treats death as an already vanquished enemy, which cannot have any lasting effect upon His indestructible Life.

And further, this Life of His, thus inaccessible to permanent injury, enduring beyond the Cross and Grave, is the cause of ours. "Because I live, ye shall live also." He describes what is impending: "Yet a little while, and the

[a] Acts ii. 24.

world seeth Me no more." He would be hidden away in the tomb. "But ye see Me."[a] His disciples would see Him; first with their bodily eyes, during the forty days after His Resurrection, and next with the eyes of faith, throughout all the ages, until He comes to judgment. And thus "Because I live, ye shall live also." Assured of the enduring continuity of His Life, the disciples might be certain of their own. Because He lives after His Resurrection, after His Ascension, in the Life of Glory, therefore His disciples, in some sense, will live also.

### I.

Here let us observe, first of all, what our Lord's words do not mean.

They do not mean that the immortality of the soul of man is dependent upon the Redemptive Work, or upon the Glorified Life of Christ. Man is an immortal being, just as he is a thinking and feeling being, by the original terms of his nature. God has made him immortal, whether for weal or woe. Whether a man is redeemed or not, whether he is sanctified or not, he will exist for ever. God might have given him a soul subject to annihilation. But God has given him a soul which is indestructible. And this quality of the soul of man is just as much a part of man's nature as are the limbs of his body or the faculties of his mind.

Of late we have heard something of a phrase new to Christian ears, "conditional immortality." We are told that man is not immortal by the terms of his nature, that he may become immortal if he is saved by Christ. Unredeemed man, the man who dies in a state of nature, so we are told, becomes extinct, if not at death, yet very

[a] St. John xiv. 19.

shortly afterwards, when anything that may survive death will fade away into nothingness. This, it is said, is more in keeping with what we see around us than the old Christian doctrine that every human being must necessarily exist, in whatever condition, for ever. Everything around us changes, decays, passes away, and this dissolution of all the organised forms of matter seems, it is suggested, to forewarn man of his own approaching and complete destruction; unless, indeed, some Great and Superhuman Power should take him by the hand, and confer on him the gift of immortality which, in virtue of his own nature, he does not possess. Some of the persons who talk and think thus forget that the New Testament treats man as a being who will live after death whether in happiness or in misery. And others forget that, before our Lord came, the best and most thoughtful men in the heathen world were satisfied of this truth; as indeed any of us may be who will consider how generally unlike the spirit or soul of man is to any merely material creature. Let us dwell for a while on some considerations which go to establish this unlikeness between spiritual and material beings.

1. The first is that the spirit or soul of man knows itself to be capable, I do not say of unlimited, but certainly of continuous, development. However vigorous a tree or an animal may be, it soon reaches a point at which it can grow no longer. The tree has borne all the leaves, buds, flowers, fruits, that it can. Its vital force is exhausted; it can do no more. The animal has attained, we will suppose, to the finest proportions of which its species is capable; it has done its best in the way of strength and beauty, and the limit has been reached; it can do no more. With the soul of man, whether as a

thinking or feeling power, it is otherwise. Of this, we can never say that it has certainly exhausted itself. When a man of science has made a great discovery, or a man of letters has written a great book, or a statesman has carried a great measure or series of measures, we cannot say—"He has done his all; he is exhausted." Undoubtedly in man the spirit is largely dependent on the material body which encases it: "the corruptible body," so says ancient Hebrew wisdom, "presseth down the soul."[a] As the body moves towards decay and dissolution, it inflicts something of its weakness and incapacity upon its spiritual companion, the soul. But the soul constantly resists and protests against this, asserting its own separate and vigorous existence. The mind knows that each new effort, instead of exhausting its powers, really enlarges them, and that, if only the physical conditions necessary to continued exertion in the present state of things are not withdrawn, it will go on continuously making larger and nobler acquirements. So too with the heart, the conscience, the sense of duty. In these too there is no such thing as finality. One noble art suggests another: one great sacrifice for truth or duty prompts another. The virtuous impulse in the soul is not, like the life-power of a tree or an animal, a self-exhausting force. On the contrary, it is always, even more consistently than thought, moving forward, conceiving of and aiming at higher duties, and understanding more clearly that, advance as it may, it will not reach the limits of its activity. "Be not weary in well-doing"[b] is the language of the Eternal Wisdom to the human will. But never has it been said to the body of man or animal, or to tree or flower, "Be not weary of growing or thriving." For organised matter, in its noblest forms, differs from spirit

[a] Wisdom ix. 15.  [b] 2 Thess. iii. 13.

in this, that it does reach the limits of its activity; and then it enters on the path of decay and dissolution.

2. A second consideration is this. The spirit or mind of man is conscious of and values its own existence. This is not the case with any material living forms, however lofty or beautiful. The most magnificent tree only gives enjoyment to other beings; it never understands that it itself exists; it is not conscious of losing anything when it is cut down. Poets may fondly treat it as an object of their pity or sympathy; but it has no interest in its own perfection. An animal does indeed feel pleasure and pain. But it feels each sensation as each sensation comes; it never puts them together: it never takes the measure of its own life, and looks on it, as if from outside, and as a whole. The animal lives wholly in the present. It has no memory. Now and then some object, which it has met before, rouses in it a sense of association with some past pleasure or pain: but that is all. Practically the animal has no past. Nor does it look forward. The future is a blank to it: it forecasts nothing. It does not expect the pains or the pleasures of its coming existence; it has no anticipations even of death, except such as its senses may immediately convey to it. How different is it with the conscious, self-measuring spirit of man! Man's spirit lives more in the past and in the future than in the present, exactly in the degree in which it makes the most of itself. Man, as a spirit, reaches back into the past; reviews it; lives it over again in memory; turns it to account in the way of experience. Man, as a spirit, reaches onward into future time; gazes wistfully at its uncertainties; maps it out; provides for it; and, at least conditionally, disposes of it. Man, as a spirit, rises out of and above the successive sensations which make up to an animal its

whole present life; he understands what it is to exist; he understands his relation to other beings and to Nature; he sees something of the unique grandeur of his being among the existences around him. And then withal he desires to continue his existence beyond the present, into the future which he anticipates; into a very distant future, if he may. The more his spirit makes of itself, of its powers and resources, the more earnestly does it desire prolonged existence. Thus the best of the heathens have enjoyed a clear presentiment of a life beyond the grave. These men, of high thoughts and noble resolves, could not understand, that because material bodies were perishing around them, therefore conscience, reason, will, the common endowments of humankind, must or could be extinguished too. These men longed to exist, ay, after death, that they might continue to make progress in all such good as they had begun in this life; in high thoughts and in excellent resolves. And with these longings they believed that they would then exist, after all in this life was over. The longing was itself a sort of proof that its object was real; for how was the existence of the longing to be explained, if all enterprise in thought and in virtue was to be abruptly broken off by the shock of death? At any rate, in this longing, and in the power of self-measurement out of which it grew, the spirit of man discovered its radical unlikeness to the lower forms of life around it. It became familiar with the idea of a perpetuated existence, under other conditions, beyond the grave.

3. A third consideration, of much weight, which pointed towards the natural immortality of man, was this. Unless a spiritual being is immortal, such a being does, in one very important respect, count for

less in the Universe than mere inert matter. For matter has a kind of immortality; at any rate, so far as our observation goes, it does not perish; it only changes its form. We speak commonly of the growth and destruction of living things of trees, and animals. But we must be careful how we use any such word as destruction, if we mean more than destruction of form; or any such word as growth, if we imagine any real addition to the sum-total of matter in the Universe. Existing matter may be combined into new forms of life; and these forms may be dissolved, to be succeeded by new combinations of the same matter. Within the range of our experience, no matter ceases to exist; it only takes new shapes, first in one being, and then in another. The body of the dead animal nourishes the plant, which in turn supplies nourishment for and is absorbed into the system of another animal. This animal, in turn, is resolved into its chemical elements by death, and the cycle begins afresh. It is possible that the predicted destruction of the world at the Last Day will be only a rearrangement of the sum-total of matter which now makes up the visible Universe. It is possible that forms will change, beyond all power of imagination to conceive, but that there will be no real increase or diminution of existing material. Certainly every serious and consistent believer in God knows that there was a time when matter did not exist, and that a time may come when the Will which summoned it into existence may annihilate it. But within tracts of time, so vast as to strain and weary the mind which attempts to contemplate them, matter has a practical immortality; an immortality which would place the spirit of man at a great relative disadvantage if man's spirit ceased to exist at or soon after death. If man's spirit naturally perishes, the higher part of his nature is much worse off than the chemical ingredients of his body, or of the bodies of the animals around him; since these certainly do survive in new forms. Observe that man's spirit cannot be resolved, like his body, into form and material; the former perishing while the latter survives. Man's spirit either exists in its completeness, or it ceases to exist. The bodily form of William the Conqueror has long dissolved into dust. The material atoms which made up the body of William the Conqueror during his lifetime exist sómewhere now under the pavement of the great church at Caen. But if the memory, and conscience, and will of the Conqueror have perished, then his spirit has ceased to be. There is no substratum below or beyond these which could perpetuate existence; there is nothing spiritual which survives them. For the soul of man,—your soul and mine,—knows itself to be an indivisible whole; a something which cannot be broken up into parts and enter into union with other minds and souls. Each man is himself: he can become no other. His memory, his affections, his way of thinking and feeling, are all his own: they are not transferable. If they perish, they perish altogether; there are no atoms which survive them, and which can be worked up into other spiritual existences. Thus the extinction of an animal or vegetable is the extinction of that particular combination of matter, not of the matter itself: but the extinction of a soul, if it were possible, would be the total extinction of all that made it to be what it was. In the natural world, destruction and death are only change. In the spiritual world, the only possible analogous process would mean annihilation. And therefore it is a reasonable and very strong presumption that spirit is not, in fact, placed at such disadvantage when compared with matter; and that, if matter survives the dissolution of organic forms, much more must spirit survive the dissolution of the material forms with which it has been associated.

These are the kind of considerations by which thoughtful men, living without the light of revelation, might be led to see the reasonableness, the very high probability, of a future life. They are not demonstrations which compel belief in man's immortality;—to minds of a certain order they may seem poor and inconclusive. But they have led many a noble soul, before now, up to the very gates of the Church of God. Do not let us think scorn of them as "mere philosophy;" do not let us forget that God teaches men up to a certain point through reason and nature and conscience, just as beyond it He teaches us through His Blessed Son. This teaching of nature is presupposed by Christianity. And it is no true service to our Master Jesus Christ to make light of this elementary teaching of God by reason and conscience, with the view of heightening the effect of Christ's work for man. At the same time, it is true that, outside the Jewish Revelation, the immortality of man was not treated by any large number of men as anything like a certainty. Jesus Christ assumed it as certain in all that He said with reference to the future life. And it is the Resurrection of Jesus Christ,—the tangible fact of His real survival of the collapse and sharpness of His Own death,—which has in this, as in so many other ways, opened the kingdom of heaven to all believers. What has been may be; what has been forbids the thought that it could not be. And thus the Christian Faith has brought "immortality to light"[a] through the Gospel. Christianity did not create immortality for man, but brought it to light as a fact of his nature, imperfectly apprehended until Christ died and rose from the dead. Christ our Lord does not make any one human being immortal any more than He

[a] 2 Tim. i. 10.

invests any one with reason, or conscience, or will. Immortality, like these other gifts, is part of the outfit of man's nature; but then our Lord has poured a flood of light upon its meaning and reality.

And what a solemn fact is this immortality of ours, dimly apprehended by reason, and made certain by Revelation! What an unutterably solemn fact; that every single person in this vast congregation will live, must live, in some sphere or other, for ever! At this moment each of us has, or rather is made up of, memory, will, and conscience; each of these is altogether his own. A hundred years hence no one of us will be still in the body: we shall have passed to another sphere of being. But we shall subsist, each one with memory, will, and conscience intact, and utterly separate from any other living being. And ten thousand years hence, or if the imagination can take in these vast tracts of time, ten million years hence, it will be still the same. We shall still exist, each one with his memory, will, and conscience intact, separate from all other beings in our eternal resting-place.

II.

And this brings us to consider what Christ's words do mean: what is the kind of life which we Christians do or should live, because Christ our Saviour lives it.

Clearly, my brethren, something is meant by "Life" in such passages as this, which is higher than and beyond mere existence; not merely beyond animal existence, but beyond the existence, the mere existence, of a spiritual being. We English use "life," in our popular language, in this sense of an existence which is not merely dormant or inert, or unfruitful, but which has a purpose and makes the most of itself. And the Greeks had an especial word to describe the true life of man, his highest spiritual energy; a word to which our Lord, either in language, or probably by some modulation of His voice, must have used an equivalent in the Syro-Chaldee dialect which He actually employed. This is the word employed, when our Lord says, "I am the Life;"[a] and when St. Paul says, "Christ Who is our Life."[b] And thus in the present passage our Lord does not say, "Because I exist, ye shall exist also;" but, "Because I live, ye shall live also." This life is existence in its best and highest aspects; the existence of a being who makes the most of his endowments; who consciously directs them towards their true object and purpose; in whom they are invigorated, raised, transfigured, by the presence of a new power,—by grace.

This enrichment and elevation of being is derived from Christ our Lord: He is the Author of our new life, just as our first parent is the source of our first and natural existence. On this account St. Paul calls our Lord the Second Adam;[c] implying that He would have a relation towards the human race, in some remarkable way resembling that of our first parent. And, in point of fact, He is the parent of a race of spiritual men, who push human life to its highest capacities of excellence, just as Adam is the parent of a race of natural men who do what they can with their natural outfit. The Second Adam! Remember that title of our Lord Jesus Christ. As natural human existence is derived from Adam, so spiritual or supernatural life is given to existing men by Christ. "As we have borne the image of the earthly, we must also bear the image of the Heavenly."[d]

When our Lord was upon earth He communicated His Life to men, by coming in contact with them. What

[a] St. John xiv. 6.  [b] Col. iii. 4.
[c] 1 Cor. xv. 45.  [d] Ibid. 49.

is said of Him on one occasion, and in reference to a particular miracle, is true of His whole appearance upon the earth:—"virtue went out of Him."[a] A common way of describing this is to say that He produced an impression deeper and more lasting than has any who has ever borne our form. Certainly He did this. He acted, He spoke. And His looks and gestures and bearing were themselves vivid and effective language. And men listened and observed. They had never seen or heard anything like it. They felt the contagion of a Presence, the influence of Which they could not measure; a Presence from Which there radiated a subtle, mysterious energy, which was gradually taking possession of them they knew not exactly how, and making them begin to live a new and a higher life. What that result was upon four men of very different types of character we may gather from the reports of the Life of Christ which are given us by the four holy Evangelists.

But at last He died, and rose, and disappeared from sight. And it is of this after-time that He says, "Because I live, ye shall live also." How does He communicate His life when He is out of the reach of our senses; and when the creative stimulus of His visible Presence has been withdrawn?

The answer is, first, By His Spirit. What had been partly visible was now to be wholly an invisible process. The Spirit of Christ, that Divine and Personal Force, whereby the mind and nature of the Unseen Saviour is poured into the hearts and minds and characters of men —was to be the Lord and Giver of this Life, to the end of time. "He shall take of Mine, and shall show it unto you."[b] "If any man have not the Spirit of Christ, he is none of His."[c] "But if any man be in Christ," through

[a] St. Luke vi. 19.   [b] St. John xvi. 15.   [c] Rom. viii. 9.

being baptized into the one Spirit, "he is the new creation. Old things are passed away; behold, all things are become new."[a]

And, secondly, the means whereby the Spirit of Christ does especially convey Christ's life are the Christian Sacraments. The Sacraments are the guaranteed points of contact with our Unseen Saviour; for in them we may certainly meet Him and be invigorated by Him as we toil along the road of our pilgrimage. Ah! if the Sacraments were only symbols of a grace withheld, only memorials of an absent Christ, they would have no legitimate place in the religion of our Lord. They would be on a par with the dead ceremonies of the Jewish law. They would belong appropriately to that old religion of mere types and shadows which, since the coming of Christ our Lord, has given place to a religion in which all is real. Certainly, in thus bestowing on us the Life of Christ, the Divine Spirit is not, as the old phrase has it, "tied to Sacraments:" for the Spirit of God fills the world, and turns persons and words and circumstances to account in His dealings with the soul of man. But Sacraments are chartered means of grace. And, such being our Lord's appointment, if we mean to live "because Christ lives," we cannot do without them. We could do without a purely symbolical washing in water, but "except a man be born of water, and of the Spirit, he cannot enter into the kingdom of God."[b] We could do without bread and wine eaten in memory of an absent Christ Who died many centuries ago; but "except ye eat the Flesh of the Son of Man, and drink His Blood, ye have no life in you."[c] And if we cannot understand how rites so simple should convey to us transcendent blessings and powers which come straight from the Heart of the in-

[a] 2 Cor. v. 17.  [b] St. John iii. 5.  [c] Ibid. vi.

visible world; is this wonderful when we understand so little of the lower forms of life, of those simple yet most mysterious processes of nature which surround us on every side? What is life in the animal? what is it in the tree? why should food support it in the one case, and moisture in the other? Our commonplace and our scientific answers to these questions only reveal to us a world of mystery;—a world, the frontiers of which we know by heart, but the real nature of which is beyond us.

It is this new Life, thus bestowed by Christ our Lord, which makes it a blessing to have the prospect before us that we shall individually exist for ever. It is these new thoughts and affections and dispositions which come from Him, and which are, in fact, His Own, by which an endless existence can be raised to the level of Eternal Life. What this life is in its highest form we read in the records of that One Life, ideal and yet most real, Which was once lived on earth, and Which is described in the Gospels. What it may be, we see in those great saints and servants of His, who, since the coming of Christ, have lived from age to age, and have shown to the world, by their patience and heroism, how much His grace can make of our poor, frail, fallen humanity. What it is too often, we know in ourselves. We know how vast is the interval between the way in which we think, and express ourselves, and act, and the actions and language and thoughts which are set before us in the Gospels.

Why is our Christianity thus poor and feeble and depressed and disappointing? Why is it so unequal to its great traditions in the past, to the anticipations which, in our higher moments, we cherish for the future? Before our eyes is the same Ideal as That Which has shone upon all the generations of Christendom. We have the same hopes and fears, the same warnings and encouragements, as any of Christ's servants in days gone by. May it not be that we modern Christians have not seldom practically forgotten the fact that the true Life of man comes from Him alone Whose Name we bear? May it not be that we trust to our own energy, or common sense, for a power and for results which faith and love must receive from the pierced Hands of an Invisible Saviour? "Because I live, ye shall live also." We rely wholly on His Death for the pardon of our sins, and we do well. But He has more to give us than this. We must not rest content with half His Gospel. If He died for our sins, He "was raised again for our justification."[a] "If, when we were enemies, we were reconciled to God by the death of His Son, much more, being reconciled, we shall be saved by His Life."[b] Let us be up and doing. Let us look to the sources of our true outfit for the eternal world, and let us make the most of them. Our immortality is certain. But what sort of immortality is it to be? That is a question before which all else that concerns us fades away into insignificance. It can only be satisfactorily answered by the soul which hastens to draw water from the Wells of salvation;[c] which, having heard the pardoning words, "Thy sins, which were many, are forgiven thee,"[d] kneels on, in persevering love, at the feet of the Divine Master; receives from Him the invigorating Gift which is needful for the Life Eternal; and, as the closing scene draws nigh, knows more and more clearly the truth of the gracious promise, "Because I live, thou shalt live also."

[a] Rom. iv. 25.     [b] *Ibid.* v. 10.
[c] Isa. xii. 3.     [d] St. Luke vii. 47.

# SERMON XXVI.

## THE VICTORY OF EASTER.

### 1 St. John v. 4.

*That which is born of God overcometh the world: and this is the victory that overcometh the world, even our faith. Who is he that overcometh the world, but he that believeth that Jesus is the Son of God?*

THE leading idea of Easter is Victory: victory over death; victory over sin, which is the cause of death; victory won by the Great Conqueror rising from His grave, and by His servants, who, at an immeasurable distance, tread in His footsteps here, and will reign with Him hereafter. Hence the selection of the passage of Holy Scripture before us as the Epistle for the First Sunday after Easter. The phrase, "overcometh the world," occuring as it does, after St. John's manner, not less than three times within the compass of two verses, opens to our view a subject in harmony with the season; while it also suggests considerations which the welcome presence in this Cathedral of some of the highest representatives of the Law renders appropriate to-day.[a]

[a] Preached before the Judges, the Lord Mayor, and the Corporation of London.

## I.

And here the first point to be decided is the precise meaning of the expression, "the world." Perhaps we feel that a certain haziness and indefiniteness attaches to it. And it is therefore to the purpose to observe that the word is used in the New Testament, and especially in St. John's writings, in three distinct senses.

By "the world" is meant, first of all, this visible Universe, or at least this particular globe on which we live. The Greeks called the Universe, Cosmos, on account of the beauty of order which is observable throughout it; but our word "world," in ordinary language, is restricted generally to the planet which is our home. And when our Lord, referring to the literal sun, says, that a man who walks by daylight stumbles not, because he seeth the "light of this world,"[a] He means by "world" this earthly abode of man. When, in His great Intercessory Prayer, He glances back at "the glory which I had with Thee before the Cosmos was,"[b] He means the visible order of things, the created Universe. When St. John says, that if all the unrecorded things which Jesus did were to be written—every one,—he, the Evangelist, supposes that "even the world itself could not contain the books that should be written,"[c] it is plain that, whether he is thinking of the planet or the Universe, he is at any rate thinking of physical nature. He is thinking of surface, and space, and cubic feet; in short, of the material Cosmos. It is needless to say that the "world" in this sense is not a thing to overcome, any more than is the sea or the atmosphere. In this sense the "world" suggests no moral con-

[a] St. John xi. 9.  [b] *Ibid.* xvii. 5.  [c] *Ibid.* xxi. 25.

demnation, nothing of the nature of a moral estimate or judgment of any kind. And we have only not to abuse it, but to make it subserve His glory Who made it and us. It is a palace in which we men pass our lives; such is our Creator's will and bounty. It is a visible revelation, as His Apostle has told us, of the invisible order and beauty of His Uncreated Life.[a] Our duties towards it, are study, if possible; in any case, reverent sympathy and admiration. For it is our Maker's handiwork, and "the works of the Lord are great," whether in the material or moral world; "sought out of all them that have pleasure therein. His work is worthy to be praised and had in honour;" although it is "His Righteousness,"—the necessary moral qualities of His Nature,—which "endureth for ever."[b]

By the "world" again is meant, as in our every-day language, so in the speech of the New Testament, the sum-total of all living men; human life in its completeness. It is the "world" in this sense into which our Lord "came," so Holy Scripture speaks, at His Incarnation. Into the material Universe, He Who being Divine was already present with all His works, could not come by anything of the nature of a local transfer of His Presence. When visibly present among men He spoke of Himself as "the Son of Man Which is in heaven;"[c] that is, as being also the Eternal Son of God. But into the world of collective human life He could and did come, by taking our nature upon Him; by being, as St. Paul speaks, "born of a woman, and made under the law;"[d] by robing Himself in a created Form, and so entering into and subjecting Himself to the conditions of human society and life. In this sense our Lord says, "I came forth from the Father,

[a] Rom. i. 20.  [b] Ps. cxi. 2, 3.
[c] St. John iii. 13.  [d] Gal. iv. 4.

and am come into the world: again, I leave the world, and go to the Father;"ᵃ and Martha confesses at Bethany, "I believe that Thou art the Christ, the Son of God, Which should come into the world."ᵇ Every man, St. John says, who comes into this world is lightened by the true Light of it,ᶜ at least in respect of his reason. And when we are told that God "loved the world,"ᵈ that Christ is "the Saviour of the world,"ᵉ and "the Light of the world,"ᶠ and "the Bread Which giveth life unto the world;"ᵍ that He will judge the world,ʰ and that He desires that the world should believe in His being sent from heaven;ⁱ the "world" clearly means the whole human family. The Almighty and Everlasting God hateth nothing that He has made, as He originally made it; and as it exists in His creative thought; and humanity, despite its corruptions and its crimes, is the object of His love and condescensions. This human world, too, by and of itself, is no more a thing to overcome than is the material Universe: the great human family, of which we all are members, is not an enemy towards which we owe no other duties than war and victory. Misanthropy is not a Christian virtue; man, as man, is entitled to our best respect, care, affection, enthusiasm: "Honour all men;"ᵏ "Do good unto all men;"ˡ "Be patient towards all men;"ᵐ —these are the Apostolic rules of duty to the world in the sense of collective humanity. It cannot therefore be the world in this sense to which the text refers.

There is a third sense of the word "world," to which our Lord introduces us by saying that "this is the con-

ᵃ St. John xvi. 28.     ᵇ *Ibid.* xi. 27.     ᶜ *Ibid.* i. 9.
ᵈ *Ibid.* iii. 16.      ᵉ *Ibid.* iv. 42.    ᶠ *Ibid.* viii. 12.
ᵍ *Ibid.* vi. 33.       ʰ *Ibid.* xii. 31.   ⁱ *Ibid.* xvii. 21.
ᵏ 1 St. Pet. ii. 17.    ˡ Gal. vi. 10.       ᵐ 1 Thess. v. 14.

demnation, that light is come into the world, and men loved darkness rather than light, because their deeds were evil."[a] Here it is clear that "the world" and "men" are equivalent expressions, and yet that especial stress is laid upon the sin which taints and warps human life. Human society as it actually is; as alienated from God; as formed upon and as fostering principles which are incompatible with His honour; as estranged from the life of God by the ignorance that is in men—is in this third sense "the world." "This present evil world"[b] is the full designation which Scripture gives it. It is said to give a false peace of its own, utterly unlike that true peace which Christ gives to His servants. "Peace I leave with you, My peace I give unto you: not as the world giveth, give I unto you."[c] It has a keen instinct, which at once detects and persecutes the holiness which exposes its real character: "The world cannot hate you," said Jesus Christ to the Jews, "but Me it hateth, because I testify of it, that the works thereof are evil."[d] If the world hates the disciples, they know that it hated their Lord before it hated them.[e] If indeed they were of the world, the world would love his own; but because they are not of the world, but Christ has chosen them out of the world, therefore the world hateth them.[f] The world is spiritually blind: "it cannot receive the Spirit of truth, because it seeth Him not, neither knoweth Him."[g] The contrast between the true disciples of Jesus Christ and the world, considered as corrupt human society, appears further in our Lord's prediction of a coming time, in which "the disciples shall weep and lament, but the world shall rejoice;"[h] and in His Intercessorial Prayer, "O

[a] St. John iii. 19.  [b] Gal. i. 4.  [c] St. John xiv. 27.
[d] Ibid. vii. 7.  [e] Ibid. xv. 18.  [f] Ibid. xv. 19.
[g] Ibid. xiv. 17.  [h] Ibid. xvi. 20.

righteous Father, the world hath not known Thee: but I have known Thee, and these have known that Thou hast sent Me."[a] The world is accordingly in this sense constantly connected in Scripture language with the energetic presence of sin. It is the sin of the world which, the Baptist tells us, the Lamb of God takes away.[b] When the Comforter comes, according to Christ's prediction, "He will reprove the world of sin."[c] Indeed St. John goes so far as to say that "the whole world lieth in wickedness,"[d] and so is contrasted with the Apostolic Church, which " knows that it is of the truth."[e]

Accordingly the phrase being " of the world," has a very serious significance in the mouth of our Lord and of the Beloved Disciple. Our Lord says of His Apostles that "the world hath hated them, because they are not of the world, even as I am not of the world."[f] The man who "is of the world" has a moral and spiritual relationship to the temper, feelings, character of the average mass of men. The world inspires and moulds him; it governs his sympathies, and forms his thoughts. He is a product of it; he is born, morally and mentally, of it. Thus St. John, when speaking of some men who were undoing God's work at Ephesus in his day, said, "They are of the world, therefore speak they of the world, and the world heareth them."[g] On the other hand, he bids Christians "love not the world, neither the things that are in the world." And then he gives as a reason, "If any man love the world, the love of the Father is not in him. For all that is in the world, the lust of the flesh, and the lust of the eyes, and the pride of life, is not of the Father, but is of the world."[h]

---

[a] St. John xvii. 25.    [b] Ibid. i. 29.    [c] Ibid. xvi. 8.
[d] 1 St. John v. 19.    [e] Ibid. iii. 19.    [f] St. John xvii. 14.
[g] 1 St. John iv. 5.    [h] Ibid. ii. 15, 16.

This then is the world which we have to overcome; not the beautiful Universe wherein we live; not humanity with all its burden of sorrow, and all its capacity for greatness; but human life viewed as it exists apart from God. The "world" of St. John's Epistle is general society, thinking, feeling, acting, without any reference to the Being Who made it; making itself as completely its own ruler, its own end, its own reward, as if He did not exist. In this sense the "world" is not easy to overcome. It is not a thing of yesterday: it is a tradition of many ages, of many civilisations, which, after flowing on in the great current of human history, has come down, charged with the force of an accumulated prestige, even to us. To this great tradition of regulated ungodliness each generation adds something; something of force, something of refinement, something of social or intellectual power. The world is Protean in its capacity for taking new forms. Sometimes it is a gross idol-worship; sometimes it is a military empire; sometimes it is a cynical school of philosophers; sometimes it is the indifference of a *blasé* society, which agrees in nothing but in proscribing earnestness. The Church conquered it in the form of the Pagan Empire. But the world had indeed had its revenge when it could point to such Popes as were Julius II., or Alexander VI., or Leo X.; to such Courts as were those of Louis XIV. or Charles II.; for it had throned itself at the heart of the victorious Church. So now between the world and Christendom there is no hard and fast line of demarcation. The world is within the fold, within the sanctuary, within the heart, as well as without. It sweeps around each soul like a torrent of hot air, and makes itself felt at every pore of the moral system. Not that the world is merely a point of view, a mood of thought, a temper or frame of mind, having no actual, or as we should say, no objective existence. It has an independent existence. Just as the kingdom of God exists whether we belong to it or no, and yet, if we do belong to it, is, as our Lord has told us, within us [a] as an atmosphere of moral power and light;—so the world, the kingdom of another being, exists, whether we belong to it or no, although our belonging to it is a matter of inward motives and character. The world penetrates like a subtle atmosphere in Christendom, while in Heathendom it is organised as a visible system. But it is the same thing at bottom. It is the essential spirit of corrupt human life, taking no serious account of God, either forgetting Him altogether, or putting something in His place, or striking a balance between His claims and those of His antagonists. And thus friendship with it is "enmity with God," [b] Who will have our all. And a first duty in His servants is to free themselves from its power, or, as St. John says, to overcome it.

## II.

How is the world to be overcome?

Among many answers to this question, I notice only one to-day. There are men who answer, 'By scrupulous obedience to the laws of the land. Conform to the ideal of conduct prescribed by law. Avoid what the law condemns; do what the law prescribes; and you have conquered the world. This is the highest practicable ideal of human life. Not merely is the good man the good citizen: the good citizen is also necessarily the good man.'

Now there are two main reasons against acquiescing in this.

First, what is human law? It is in theory always, and generally in fact, the application of moral truth, of

[a] St. Luke xvii. 22.  [b] St. James iv. 4.

justice, to the relations which exist between human beings. It is a digest of so much applied morality as society wants in order to secure itself against insurrectionary selfishness and passion. But it is only a part of, an extract from, morality. It is not the whole. Those parts of the moral law which cannot be violated without danger to the social fabric are enforced. The statute-book and the letter of the Sixth and Eighth Commandments are fairly at one. But other Commandments are not enforced, although they are just as truly parts of the Divine Law as are the precepts which protect life and property. Governments say that they do not want those other Commandments of God in order to secure the preservation of society. But then it is plain that to obey human law is not the same thing as to obey the law of God. Human law gives us one standard of conduct; the law of God another. Human law insists upon honesty and respect for life and person; the law of God upon charity and purity as well. To obey human law scrupulously is perfectly consistent with disobedience to vital features of the law of God. Obedience to human law is so far from implying victory over the world, that it only involves that exact amount of obedience upon which the world itself insists.

Again, human law is only a rule of outward conduct. It does not reach to the region of motive. As the old maxim says, " De occultis non judicat;" it concerns itself with that which meets the eye, and falls upon the ear. Outward propriety, as distinct from inward rectitude, is all that it can hope to enforce, and is enough to serve its purpose.

But does such outward propriety involve victory over the world? May it not consist with thoroughly bad motives which, in the sight of the All-seeing Ruler of the Universe, have the value of finished acts, and which have only not become visible because they lacked the opportunity of circumstance? Does not this outward conformity to law leave the root of evil within us untouched, as it was untouched in the case of those Pharisees who cleansed the outside of the cup and platter in all departments of conduct,[a] but were within what our Lord described with such trenchant severity? The Pharisees, and the society to which they, more than any others, gave the tone, constituted the "world" of the Gospel history. But if obedience to law had been the secret of vanquishing it, they would have been among its most distinguished conquerors.

No; if the world is to be overcome, it will not itself furnish us with the secret of victory. It will, no doubt, disguise its empire. It will lead us, if necessary, to that particular point on the road to freedom which may half satisfy our aspirations, without compromising its own power. But if we would conquer it we must lay hold on something outside and independent of it; upon a vision of truth, upon a motive to exertion which altogether transcends its sphere.

Hence "this is the victory that overcometh the world, even our faith." Faith is the hand by which the soul lays hold upon a Truth, a Power, a Being higher and more beautiful than any which are obvious to sense. Thus the soul gains a support in its struggle for emancipation and victory which is equal to its needs. "Who is he that overcometh the world but he that believeth that Jesus is the Son of God?" Believe that He is only the son of man; the wisest, if you will, and the best of men; yet the requisite force is lacking. For practically you only assent to a fact which is bounded by the frontier of human existence. But believe that Jesus is the Son of God; that

[a] St. Matt. xxiii. 25.

His Life was that of God manifest in the flesh;<sup>a</sup> that His Death was that of the Everlasting Son, purchasing His Church with His Own Blood;<sup>b</sup> that His Mercy and His Power are alike boundless; and that He helps and befriends us, by His Spirit and Sacraments on earth, and by His Majestic Intercession in heaven; and life is irradiated by a new idea of its solemnity and its blessedness. Reason, indeed, can teach us to despair of the world, when she leads us to some grave, such as are many around you here, and points to the worthlessness of wealth and honours, which must fade so soon and so entirely. But Faith does not teach only the negative side of the lesson. Faith insists that Redemption by the Son of God makes life worth living, and thus enables us to rate the world at its true value.

### III.

That this is so, is plain if we consider how the world acts upon us, one by one. For the world is very jealous of any appearance of revolt against its authority. And it has at command a machinery which is well calculated to repress the first symptoms of disaffection.

1. It acts, first, secretly, but most powerfully, by public opinion. Public opinion is the intellectual arm of the world. It is exactly the same in no two countries; in no two centuries; it might be true to say, in no two following years. It has its leading and its subordinate organs. There is a public opinion in nations, in particular places, in particular classes and circles. Between these there are many and startling contradictions; and yet there is unity. There is unity of temper; unity as to the general

<sup>a</sup> 1 Tim. iii. 16.   <sup>b</sup> Acts xx. 28.

principles to be kept in view, amid differences as to detail. Penetrating the differences of different classes, countries, interests, there is a common opinion in each age, in each country, which is sufficiently consistent with itself, and sufficiently powerful to make itself felt as the voice of the world; the voice which the mass of men at once utter and obey.

Do I say that it is a duty on the part of every Christian to contradict the whole public opinion of the country and the age in which he lives? Certainly not. In the worst times, in the lowest civilisations, public opinion necessarily affirms some truth. And when the Church of Christ has more or less influence in leavening society; when society calls itself Christian, and sets store upon the designation; it is clear that public opinion must, from the nature of the case, affirm a great deal of truth. This being certain, a depreciation of or contempt for all public opinion as such is evidently misleading: it is a sure sign of folly or fanaticism. But much more misleading is entire submission to it. Whatever be its authority in pronouncing upon material interests, it is no safe guide in dealing with spiritual questions. For it represents not the highest, purest, most disinterested thought of the time on these subjects; as also it certainly does not represent the lowest and most degraded. It is essentially a middle term; a compromise between sublime truth and wild error, between lofty goodness and downright selfishness. And its very moderation, whereby it so exactly represents the world, is an element of its power.

To do justice to public opinion, and yet to be independent of it, a man must have hold on a higher criterion and test of truth. We are the slaves of the human until we are in communion with the Divine. Years often will pass in a man's life, until some turn of events, some danger to truth or right, reveals his hold on the Invisible to himself and to the world. At such times it is that men take their sides, and show what they are. On the one side they whisper,—' Don't you see which way the current is flowing? Be prudent, and don't quarrel with your bread and butter.' On the other they proclaim, in trembling accents of humble thankfulness, "We know that the Son of God is come, and hath given us an understanding that we may know Him that is true;"[a] "We ought to obey God rather than men."[b]

2. The world acts upon us, secondly, by ridicule. Ridicule is often the voice of public opinion irritated at resistance to its empire. And it may be an instrument of terrible power.

Many men who would pass through the fire for what they believe to be right cannot face a sneer. They have abundant physical courage; the courage of animals with strong nerves. They have little moral courage; the courage of men with sensitive consciences and strong wills. Moral courage is indeed a higher courage than physical courage. It is more difficult to sustain: it gets much less encouragement from the results of victory. Yet why should ridicule be so formidable? What is a sneer, in most cases, but the confession that an argument is not at command? As Dr. Johnson said, you cannot refute a sneer. But this is because there is nothing solid to refute. The cleverest things in an infidel writer like Voltaire are sneers; they are not arguments. But they did their work upon two-thirds of the French people none the less powerfully for that. Until a man has learned to estimate ridicule at its true value, he has not a chance of overcoming the world; whether it be the world of a public school, or the world of

[a] 1 St. John v. 20.   [b] Acts v. 29.

a business establishment, or the world of a learned profession, or the great world which includes all these, of mixed and common English life.

And the best antidote to ridicule is devotion to a friend. Ridicule tells powerfully against fancy theories: its shafts fall powerless on loyal hearts. Laugh at a new social or political doctrine, and you may rend it to pieces more readily than by argument. Laugh at men whose hearts have been won by a character of great strength and beauty, and you will be hoarse with laughter without injuring anybody. Now Faith reveals to Christians a Living Person, Who is the object of their enthusiastic love. And in the depth of that love there is a store of moral power which the ridicule of the world cannot touch.

3. The world acts upon us, lastly, by persecution. In the first ages of the Church, when the world was confessedly Pagan, it made great use of this instrument for enforcing its supremacy. It imprisoned and killed Christians, from the days of Nero to the days of Diocletian. It persecuted by social exclusiveness, by inflicting loss of property and position, by bloody tortures, by death. The mildest forms of persecution are all that are now possible in this country. But if a man is deprived of advantages which he would otherwise have enjoyed; if he is met by a cold bow or a vacant stare, when he expects a cordial greeting; if he feels that he is under a ban, because he has dared to obey his conscience, when obedience is unwelcome or unpopular; he is, to all intents and purposes, persecuted. And if he can stand this persecution patiently, calmly, silently, so much the better. " Blessed are they which are persecuted for righteousness' sake: for theirs is the kingdom of heaven." [a]

[a] St. Matt. v. 10.

But how is he to stand it? "By seeing Him that is invisible,"[a] so the Apostle answers. Who that has had to undergo a painful operation does not know the support that is given by holding the hand of a sympathising friend until it is all over? And faith places the hand of the persecuted in the Hand of Christ. "Fear not," He says, "for I am with thee: I have called thee by thy name; thou art Mine."[b] It is thus that the world, when doing its worst, is vanquished. Thus was it vanquished by young and weak and friendless men and women and children in the first ages of the Church, who were "strong in faith:" thus is it vanquished now by every one who resolves for Christ's sake to live a life of high duty and self-denial, amid opposition and under difficulties.

It is faith in the Son of God, Who of His unspeakable mercy took our flesh, and died, and rose again for us, that enables us to rise to a higher, purer, truer conception of what life is and means, and so to overcome the world. Human law cannot do this. But law, in a Christian land, makes the task easier. Law is the cover, the fence which shelters the infant life of religion, and protects its tender growth from violence and outrage. And religion in turn reinforces law. Religion makes obedience to law welcome, "not only for wrath, but also for conscience' sake:"[c] it arrests at the fountain-head those passions which, in their unrestrained indulgence, are at war with law. Law and religion work on the same side, and in parallel lines; law punishes that which religion would prevent. Religion does much more work in the conscience than is necessary for the purposes of law; but, excepting under circumstances which are happily exceptional, law, when prosecuting its stern errands of justice, can appeal to the sanction of religion.

[a] Heb. xi. 27.   [b] Isa. xliii. 1.   [c] Rom. xiii. 5.

For the complete wellbeing of man, nothing can be more untoward than a collision between the behests of the religious conscience and the public administration of justice. The Roman magistrates and the martyrs whom they sentenced in the first ages of the Church, ought in the interests of humanity to have been on the same side. For if human life is protected by order, it is only permanently enriched by sacrifice; and as prevention is better than cure, so the motives which make crime unwelcome or impossible are more powerful agents than the strong arm which punishes its perpetrators. Law, in short, cannot overcome the world: it can only regulate its course. If men would rise above it they must gaze on Him Who overcame it when He died upon the Cross and rose from the Grave, and Who permits His true servants to lay hold on His pierced Hands, and to share in His glorious victory.

# SERMON XXVII.

## THE GOOD SHEPHERD.

St. John x. 11.

*Jesus said, I am the Good Shepherd.*

PERHAPS no one Gospel, during the whole course of the Church year, speaks to us more directly, more persuasively, than that which is appointed for to-day. The Sunday of the Good Shepherd,[a] as in some parts of Christendom this day has been called, has an interest for us, "the sheep of His pasture,"[b] which need not be insisted on.

### I.

In the first eighteen verses of the tenth chapter of St. John there are three distinct allegories. First comes the allegory of the Shepherd; next that of the Door; lastly that of the Good, or Beautiful, or Ideal Shepherd. These, I say, are allegories rather than parables. An allegory differs from a parable, as a transparency might differ from a painting on canvas. In the parable, the narrative has a body and substance, so to call it, of its own; it has a value which is independent of its application or interpre-

[a] The Second Sunday after Easter.     [b] Ps. c. 2.

tation; it often lends itself to more interpretations than one. In the allegory, the narrative suggests its one obvious interpretation step by step; narrative and interpretation are practically inseparable; it is impossible to look steadily at the picture presented to the mind's eye by the allegory, without perceiving the real persons and events to which it refers, moving almost without disguise behind it. One illustration of this occurs in the allegory of Sarah and Hagar, which St. Paul interprets for us in the Second Lesson of this afternoon.[a] And another will be supplied as we proceed with the passage before us.

In order to understand the three allegories, we must remind ourselves that in the East a sheepfold is not a covered building, but a simple enclosure of some extent, surrounded by a wall or palisade. Within this enclosure are collected many flocks of sheep, which have wandered far and wide during the day under the care of shepherds. The shepherds lead them to the enclosure or fold at nightfall; and during the night a single herdsman, here called the porter, keeps the gate, and guarantees the safety of the collected flocks. In the morning the various shepherds return to the fold to claim their respective flocks at the hand of the night-porter: they knock at the gate of the enclosure and he lets them in. Then each for himself separates his own flock from the others with which during the night they have been intermixed; each again leads his sheep forth to the day's pasturage.

Our Lord's three allegories place us face to face with the pastoral life of the East at three different periods of the Eastern day. In the first, the allegory of the Shepherd, it is still the freshness of the early morning. The dew is on the ground: the shepherds are returning to the fold to claim their flocks, which have been assembled

[a] Gal. iv. 21-31.

within it during the night. If a robber endeavours to lead away some of the sheep, he must find entrance into the fold in some dishonourable way. He does not attempt the door, where he knows that he will be recognised and arrested. He climbs over some other part of the enclosure. He comes for no good purpose; he comes only to kill and to destroy. The porter only opens the gate to the regular shepherds: the shepherd calls his own sheep by name, and they know his voice. He leads them forth from the fold: he does not drive, he walks before them: they follow him, because they know him and trust him.

The second allegory is that of the Door. Here we are in the hot noontide of the Eastern day. The fold which is here implied, without being mentioned, is not that in which the sheep were collected during the night. It is a day-enclosure, to which, during the hours of burning sunshine, the sheep may retire for rest and shade, and out of which they may wander at will to seek for pasture. In this allegory there is no mention of a shepherd: he has disappeared. The most important feature is the door of the mid-day fold. The door of this fold is the guarantee of safety and of liberty to the sheep. "I am the Door," says our Lord: "by Me if any man enter in, he shall be saved, and shall go in and out, and find pasture."[a]

In the third allegory, that of the Good Shepherd, we have reached the evening. Already the shadows are lengthening upon the hills, and the shepherds have collected their flocks to lead them to the night-enclosure. As the darkness gathers, the flock is attacked by wolves who lie in ambush for it. The Good Shepherd, who loves his sheep with a personal affection, throws himself between his imperilled flock and their cruel enemy, and in doing so sacrifices himself: "he giveth his life for the

[a] St. John x. 9.

sheep."[a] This allegory of the Good Shepherd is not a mere repetition of the first allegory of the Shepherd, although they both refer to One Person and One only. The shepherd who knocks at the door in the early morning is contrasted with the thief and the robber who climbs into the fold some other way. The Good Shepherd who gives his life for his flock at nightfall is contrasted with the hireling or mercenary, who flies at the approach of the wolf, and sacrifices his flock to his own personal safety.

II.

The question arises, What would our Lord's hearers have been meant, in the first instance, to understand by this language? And we must look for an answer in what was actually going on at the time, in Judæa, before the very eyes of the Speaker. When our Lord spoke of a fold, every religious Jew would think of the commonwealth or Church of Israel. In the pastoral language of the Prophets the old Theocratic nation was the fold of the Lord Jehovah. When our Lord spoke of a shepherd, every religious Jew would think of the expected Messiah. In the twenty-third Psalm David applies the figure to the Lord Jehovah as the guardian of his own life: "The Lord is my Shepherd: therefore can I lack nothing. He shall feed me in a green pasture, and lead me forth beside the waters of comfort."[b] But in Ezekiel[c] and Zechariah[d] Jehovah is announced as destined to appear once more to His people, as the Shepherd of Israel. In Zechariah especially, the Shepherd of Israel is represented as making a last effort to rescue the sacred flock from slaughter. But he only attaches to himself the poorest of the flock,

[a] St. John x. 11.
[c] Ezek. xxxiv. 1-22.
[b] Ps. xxiii. 1, 2.
[d] Zech. xi. 3-12.

and after a month's toil receives thirty pieces of silver, that is, the wages of a labourer of the lowest class, as he breaks his staff and leaves the flock that will not be saved from bad shepherds. The whole of this instructive but difficult passage[a] was, we may reverently conjecture, especially before our Lord's Mind when He was pronouncing these allegories. He was Himself, in His Own thought, the Shepherd of prophecy, Who had come to the gate of the Jewish commonwealth to discover and lead forth His Own sheep. But who was the porter? Among various explanations, there is one answer which would have occurred to those who heard our Lord, and who knew the history of their own time; and it cannot but occur to any careful student of St. John's Gospel. The porter is St. John the Baptist. It was to the Baptist, as last and greatest of the prophets, keeping in the wilderness the gate of God's ancient fold, that Christ came at the beginning of His Ministry, as the Gospel dawn was breaking on the earth. It was from among the Baptist's followers that Christ received His first disciples. "John bare Him witness;"[b] this is the burden of the references to the Baptist in the last Gospel. And who were the thieves and robbers, who had not come into the fold through the gate? Pre-eminently, we cannot doubt, the Pharisees, who had established their great authority among the Jewish people by much hypocrisy and violence. They had not entered by the gate; their influence was not based on the old Mosaic Law, but on bad traditions which had grown up around it, and which they beyond others had fostered. And the Baptist, when he encountered them, as St. Matthew tells us, had not kept terms with them: they were "a generation of vipers," whom he warned to flee from

---

[a] Compare Pusey, *Minor Prophets*, pp. 568 *sqq.*
[b] St. John i. 15.

the wrath to come, and to bring forth fruits meet for repentance.<sup>a</sup>

The whole scene of the first allegory is laid at the commencement of Christ's Ministry. In the second He has led out His Own from the old Jewish fold into the pastures of the new kingdom. There is no shepherd mentioned here: Christ is the Door. The new fold, of which He is the Door, is the Gospel enclosure, in which His Person is everything: through Him the sheep go forth for pasture and retire within for safety. Here again He contrasts Himself with the Pharisees as thieves and robbers: the image of the Door melts away into His living Person. In the third allegory, the last days of His Ministry, which were already present when He was uttering these words, are before His Mind. The evening is upon Him: He is near His Passion. The wolf is lying in ambush for the flock; the hireling shepherd, true to his nature, flees; the Good Shepherd gives His life. Who is the wolf here? As always, the Pharisee party, which preyed upon the religious life of the people. Who is the hireling? Certainly not the Pharisee, against whom he is the natural defender. By the hireling, our Lord's hearers would have understood the Jewish priesthood. It is a mistake to suppose that the interests and views of the Pharisees and of the priesthood were identical. The Pharisees were to a very great extent a lay sect: they had obtained a preponderating influence over the religious life of the Jewish people, and had corrupted it very seriously. The priesthood ought to have held the Pharisees in check: they would have done so had they been faithful. The priesthood were not indisposed to believe in our Lord: in St. Stephen's day "a great multitude of the priests were obedient to the faith."<sup>b</sup> Even before the

<sup>a</sup> St. Matt. iii. 7, 8.     <sup>b</sup> Acts vi. 7.

Passion, "many of the chief priests believed in Jesus, but because of the Pharisees they did not confess Him, lest they should be put out of the synagogue."[a] The priests did not dare to resist the Pharisees; and Jesus was the Victim of Pharisee indignation. It was already plain what would follow. Our Lord foreknew His sufferings: but an ordinary observer of the forces which were then governing the political life of Judæa might have divined the meaning of the words, " I am the Good Shepherd : the Good Shepherd giveth His life for the sheep."

### III.

When our Lord calls Himself the Good Shepherd, is He using a title which lost its value when He ceased to live visibly upon the earth ? Or has this title any meaning for us Christians, for you and me, at the present day ?

Here we cannot but observe that, writing some forty years after the Ascension, St. Peter calls Jesus Christ, as in to-day's Epistle, the Shepherd of souls;[b] and St. Paul, the great Shepherd of the sheep.[c]

In the earliest ages of the Christian Church, when the stress of cruel persecution obliged the faithful, driven from the public places of Rome, to take refuge in the Catacombs which were burrowed out beneath the crowded streets of the Pagan city, there was One Figure above all others, which, in their dark prison-homes, Christians delighted to sketch in rude outline on the vaults under which they prayed. It was the figure of the Good Shepherd. Sometimes His Apostles were ranged on either side of Him. Sometimes the allegory was more closely adhered to, and the sheep were standing around with upturned faces, eagerly intent upon their Deliverer and

[a] St. John xii. 42.   [b] 1 St. Pet. ii. 25.   [c] Heb. xiii. 20.

Guide. Sometimes, as more especially in later Art, He was carrying a wanderer on His shoulder, or folding a lamb to His bosom, or gently leading the sick and weary of His flock. There was something in the Figure which represented the tender and active care of our Divine Master, moving, although unseen, among His persecuted flock, to cheer and to save them. And ever since those days of persecution, when Christ has been asked to bless a work of mercy for relieving the suffering, or teaching the ignorant, or delivering the captives, or raising the fallen, it has been as the Good Shepherd of the human race. The title has an attractive power that is all its own.

Not that it is easy for us at once to enter into the full meaning of this beautiful image. To do so we must know something about ourselves, and something more about the Person of our Gracious Saviour.

*a.* We must know our own weakness, our dependence, our need of a heavenly Guide and Friend. We must sincerely feel that, face to face with the eternal world and its awful Monarch, self-reliance, self-sufficiency, is a fatal mistake. An old Pagan Roman did not feel this. And therefore, in his unconverted state, he spurned the idea of having a Good Shepherd in heaven Whom it was his business to love and worship. It was humiliating to him. It was intolerable that he, with the blood of the Scipios and the Cæsars in his veins, should think and speak of himself as a sheep. To him the Christians who could do so appeared a set of poor-spirited, degraded, and contemptible people, who had never known what it was to have a part in the majesty of the Roman name. What did he want of a Shepherd in heaven? He depended on himself; he trusted himself; and if life became intolerable, he probably meant to put an end to himself. That he should be led, pastured, folded, guarded, delivered— all this was out of the question. He did not want to be placed under a sense of obligation to any one; least of all, under the sense of an obligation so utterly beyond discharge. Certainly he might have reflected that he owed the gift of existence itself to some higher Being, and that this was a debt that he could never repay. But how many of us, Christians, go through life without ever seriously thinking what it is to have been created; what it is to have a Creator; One Being to Whose bounty all that we are and have, moment by moment, is due? What wonder if, like the old Pagan Roman, we do not enter into the happiness of devotion to the Good Shepherd? Until the proud heart is broken by a sense of personal sin, and by the love of God, revealed to the soul in His beauty and in His justice, the figure of the Good Shepherd would naturally be repulsive, as inflicting upon an ordinary man some sense of personal humiliation.

β. Moreover, if we would enter into what is meant by the Good Shepherd, we must know and believe the full and awful truth about the Divine Nature of Jesus Christ.

If Jesus Christ is merely a man, how could He be, in any rational sense, a Good Shepherd to you and me? It is now eighteen centuries and a half since He left·the earth. And if we only think of Him as a departed saint, resting somewhere in the bosom of God, we have no reason whatever to attribute to Him a pastoral interest in the multitude of Christians who look up to Him, day by day, hour by hour, for help and guidance. Can we suppose that any merely created being could thus be a superintending Providence, an all-considering, all-embracing

Love, to multitudes? Yet when our Lord says, "I am the Good Shepherd," He clearly disengages Himself from the historical incidents, the political circumstances which immediately surrounded Him. He places Himself above the narrowing conditions of time: He will be to all the ages what He is to the faithful few in and about Jerusalem. It is as when He says, "I am the Light,"[a] or "I am the Way, the Truth, and the Life,"[b] or "I am the Resurrection and the Life,"[c] or "I am the True Vine."[d] All this language in the mouth of a merely human teacher would be pretentious, inflated, insufferable. We cannot conceive the best man we have ever known in life speaking of himself as the Good Shepherd of men. To do so would be to forfeit his claims to our love, our reverence, even to our respect. Why is it not so in our Lord? Because there is that in Him, beyond yet inseparable from His Perfect Manhood, which justifies His language; so that in Him it is not pretentious, not inflated, not absurd, not blasphemous, but, on the contrary, perfectly natural and obvious. We feel, in short, that He is Divine. And such sayings as "Before Abraham was I am;"[e] "He that hath seen Me hath seen the Father;"[f] "I and the Father are One,"[g]—are in the background. They explain and justify what He says about His being the Ideal Shepherd of human souls. But it is because He is also Man that such a title befits Him. Because He is no abstract Providence, but a Divine Person, Who has taken our human nature upon Him, and Who, through it, communicates with us and blesses us, He is the Good Shepherd of His people.

[a] St. John viii. 12.  
[b] Ibid. xiv. 6.  
[c] Ibid. xi. 25.  
[d] Ibid. xv. 1.  
[e] Ibid. viii. 58.  
[f] Ibid. xiv. 9.  
[g] Ibid. x. 30.

IV.

Let us reflect what this truth involves as to our relations with our Blessed Saviour.

1. As the Good Shepherd, He knows His sheep. He knows us; He knows us one by one; He knows all about each of us. "I am the Good Shepherd, and know My sheep." He knows us, not merely as we seem to be, but as we are. Others look us in the face day by day, and we them. They touch the surface of our real life; perhaps they see a little way below the surface. But "what man knoweth the things of a man, save the spirit of man that is in him?"[a] What do they know of that which passes in the inmost sanctuary of the reason, of the conscience, of the heart? Nay; do they know much of our outward circumstances; of our trials, our struggles, our exceptional difficulties, or what we deem such? Citizens of this vast metropolis, we live amid a multitude, while yet we are alone. But there is One Being Who knows all; upon Whom nothing that passes is lost; to Whom nothing that affects us is matter of indifference. To Him all hearts are open, all desires known; from Him no secrets are hid.[b] All the warps of our self-love, all the depth and corruption of our hearts, all that we might have been, all that we are, is spread out as a map before His eyes. Each moment that passes adds something which He has already anticipated; but yet the addition of new details forfeits nothing in the clearness of His comprehensive survey. It is because He knows us thus perfectly that He is able to help us, guide us, feed us, save us, if we will, even to the uttermost.[c]

[a] 1 Cor. ii. 11.
[b] Collect in the Communion Service.   [c] Heb. vii. 25.

2. While knowing us perfectly, the Good Shepherd has an entire sympathy with each of us. He is not a hard guardian, who keeps us in order without understanding our difficulties. He is touched, as the Apostle says, with a feeling of our infirmities.[a] His true Human Nature is the seat and source of His perfect sympathy; to which the image of a shepherd, if taken alone, would do less than perfect justice. Nothing that affects any of us is a matter of indifference to Him. He is not interested merely or chiefly in the noble, or the wealthy, or the intellectual, or the well-bred. Wherever there is a human soul seeking the truth, a human heart longing to lavish its affection upon the Eternal Beauty, there He is at hand, unseen yet energetic, entering with perfect sympathy into every trial, anticipating, in ways we little dream of, every danger; not indeed suspending our probation by putting us out of the way of temptation, but with each temptation also making a way to escape, that we may be able to bear it.[b]

3. For this sympathy is not a burst of unregulated affection; it is guided by perfect prudence, by the highest reason. In the days of His earthly Ministry this was especially remarkable. He dealt with men according to their characters and capacities. He did not put new cloth on an old garment, or new wine into old bottles.[c] He did not ask His disciples to imitate the austere life of the followers of the Baptist: He knew them too well. The days would come for that by and by. He did not at once unfold to them all the Truth He had to tell about His Own Divine Person, about His kingdom, about the means of living the new life. These truths would have shocked them, if prematurely announced. "I have

[a] Heb. iv. 15.  [b] 1 Cor. x. 13.
[c] St. Matt. ix. 16, 17.

many things to say unto you," He said, " but ye cannot bear them now. Howbeit, when He, the Spirit of Truth, is come, He shall guide you into all truth."[a] Those who were yet in the infancy of the Christian life were fed with milk; strong meat was reserved for others who knew more and could bear more.[b]

So it has been ever since. If we have enjoyed opportunities, or have been denied them, this has not happened by chance. The Great Shepherd of the sheep has ordered it. He has proportioned our duties, our trials, our advantages, our drawbacks, to our real needs—to our characters. We may have disputed His wisdom, or we may have made the most of it. But it is not the less certainly a characteristic of His government. "As thy days, so shall thy strength be,"[c] is a promise for all time.

4. Above all, as the Good Shepherd, Christ is disinterested. He gains nothing by watching, guarding, feeding us. He seeks not ours, but us. We can make no addition to His glory: He seeks us for our own sakes, not for His. He spent His earthly life among the villages and hamlets of a remote province, when He might have illuminated and awed the intellectual centres of the world. He spared Himself no privations in His toil for souls. So absorbing was His labour, that He had at times no leisure so much as to eat.[d] Persecutions, humiliations, rebuffs, sufferings, could not diminish the ardour of His zeal. And He crowned all by voluntarily embracing an agonising death, in order to save His flock. Once for all, eighteen centuries ago, He gave His life for the sheep. But His death is just as powerful to deliver from the jaws of the wolf as it has ever been. Self-sacrifice, such

[a] St. John xvi. 12, 13.  
[b] Heb. v. 12-14.  
[c] Deut. xxxiii. 25.  
[d] St. Mark vi. 31.

as that on Calvary, does not lose its virtue with the lapse of years: the Precious Blood is to-day as powerful to save, as, when warm and fresh, It ebbed forth from the Wounds of the Crucified. For It is, as an Apostle says, "the Blood of the everlasting covenant;"[a] and the Great Shepherd of the sheep has been raised from the dead that It may plead for us perpetually in the courts of heaven. We look up to Him on His Throne, and here in His temple we sing, day after day, that "we are His people, and the sheep of His pasture."[b] Do we mean it? We kneel day by day, and confess that we have erred and strayed from the Eternal Father's ways, which are also His, "like lost sheep."[c] Do we mean it? Have we yet returned to "the Shepherd and Bishop of our souls"?[d] Do we endeavour to know Him, as, whether we will or not, He certainly knows us? We need a Guide through the embarrassments of life: do we recognise one in Him? We need a Physician for our moral wounds; a source of strength in our temptations; a rule and measure of holiness; an arm to lean on in the valley of the shadow of death.[e] All this He is, and much more; but have we any practical knowledge of His being so? When He has fixed His eye upon us at some turning-point of life; when He has reached out His shepherd's crook, and beckoned us to follow Him, have we obeyed? No doubt faithfulness, submission, courage, perseverance, were necessary on our part. But did He not merit these very graces for us? And has He done so much for us; and shall we do nothing—nothing—for Him?

Or if this has been with us as He would wish, are we now associating ourselves with His work? As we all may join in the intercessions of the Great High

[a] Heb. xiii. 20. [b] Ps. xcv. 7. [c] General Confession.
[d] 1 St. Pet. ii. 25. [e] Ps. xxiii. 4.

Priest, so we all may work under the guidance of the Good Shepherd. How many a work of mercy in the Church of God has that gracious and tender Figure inspired, which else had been denied to poor suffering human beings! By our individual exertions, and by strengthening the hands and hearts of His ministers; by doing our best to raise their ideal and standard of work and life; by entering with sympathy and humility into cases of misery and ignorance which might well have been our own; we may all of us, laymen as well as pastors, women as well as men, simple and unlearned as well as lettered and wise, have a part in promoting among our fellows the knowledge of that Redeeming Love, which is the glory of our Divine Master Jesus, and our own only ground of hope for time and eternity.

## SERMON XXVIII.

### REVERENCE.

REV. I. 17, 18.

*And when I saw Him, I fell at His feet as dead. And He laid His Right Hand upon me, saying unto me, Fear not; I am the First and the Last: I am He that liveth, and was dead; and behold, I am alive for evermore, Amen; and have the keys of hell and of death.*

THIS is St. John's account of what happened when he saw our Lord Jesus Christ, some forty years at the least after the Ascension, in the island of Patmos. St. John had been banished there by the Emperor of the day, and, according to the tradition, was condemned to labour in the mines. But the time of persecution was to him, as it has been so often to others, a time of spiritual blessing. When exile and suffering have detached the sympathies from the world of sense, the soul looks upwards, is endowed with a keener insight, pierces the clouds, beholds, as never before, the Unseen. The vision in Bethel was enjoyed by Jacob while he was being persecuted by Esau.[a] The vision of the burning bush was vouchsafed to Moses when he was flying from the face of Pharaoh.[b] The vision of God on the chariot of the Cherubim was granted to Ezekiel when he was a captive on the

[a] Gen. xxvii. 41-45; xxviii. 10-22.   [b] Exod. ii. 15; iii. 1-22.

## Reverence. 147

banks of the Chebar.ᵃ The sight of the opened heavens, and of Jesus standing at the right hand of God, burst upon St. Stephen when he was already in the agony of his martyrdom.ᵇ St. John had reclined on the very Breast of Jesus.ᶜ But ere he could see the things invisible to sense and the things hereafter he must be sent to Patmos; as he says, "for the word of God, and for the testimony of Jesus Christ;" as "a companion in tribulation, and in the kingdom and patience of Jesus Christ."ᵈ

And this vision, with which the Book of the Revelation opens, is especially welcome to Christians in the Easter season, when we are endeavouring to realise the spiritual Presence of Christ in His Church, as suggested and secured to us by His resurrection from the dead. Let us look at it this afternoon under a single aspect; the effect it produced upon St. John. "When I saw Him, I fell at His feet as dead." It undoubtedly suggests a great many other considerations. But it teaches us one lesson, very necessary for these and for all times; the lesson, and, let me add, the secret of reverence. "When I saw Him, I fell at His feet as dead."

### I.

Every age has its moral as well as its social and political tastes; and reverence is not one of the most popular virtues at the present day. Many a man who would be anxious to be considered brave, or truthful, or even patient and benevolent, would not be altogether pleased to hear himself described as a reverent man. Probably he would not be able to assign any reason for this: it is a matter of instinct with him rather than of

---

ᵃ Ezek. i. 1-3.     ᵇ Acts vii. 54-60.
ᶜ St. John xiii. 23.     ᵈ Rev. i. 9.

deliberate judgment. Still, if he could take what we call his instinct to pieces, he would find that it embodies or reflects some such ideas as these. He would find that he is afraid of being thought reverent, because reverence is, as he supposes, a poor-spirited sort of virtue; hostile to energy, and hostile to inquiry. Reverence he imagines to be the temper of mind which readily crouches down to the falsehood which it dares not confront; which decorates fables lest it should have to examine them; which is easy-going, soft, feeble, passive. Reverence, he thinks, lives in the past, lives in the unreal, lives in sentiment; lives for the sake of existing institutions, good or bad. It is naturally fostered by their advocates, while it is the foe of active virtue in all its forms. It is the foe of strong masculine characters; the foe of improvement which is thorough and fearless; the foe of all that belongs to true human progress.

This idea of reverence is entertained by many persons who are in no degree responsible for the shape it takes, and who are quite sincere in entertaining it. They do but take in and accept and act on judgments which are floating in the mental atmosphere which they breathe. For the influence of these judgments upon themselves, until they have analysed it, they are no more responsible than they are for the water-supply of London. But, of course, originally, this atmosphere has been made what it is by various contributors and experimentalists. And among these have been some who knew quite well that, if you want to get rid of a doctrine or a virtue, the best way is boldly to caricature it. Just as the atoning virtue of our Lord's Death may be discredited if it is ingeniously represented to be at variance with the Divine Justice; just as the grace of the Christian Sacraments may be discredited by suggesting that it is akin to magical or materialising theories of God's agency; so, if it be our object to make reverence an unpopular virtue, nothing is easier than to suggest that it is merely homage to sentiment, or even homage to falsehood; that it is dramatic and unreal; that it is opposed to moral and to mental enterprise; that it is the ally of all the existing insincerities, the enemy of all the advancing truths.

You ask me, What is reverence? If we must attempt a definition, it is not easy to improve upon the saying that it is "the sincere, the practical recognition of greatness." And, when speaking thus, let us take greatness in its widest sense. There is the greatness of institutions as well as the greatness of character; greatness in the State as well as greatness in the Church; greatness in humble as truly as in splendid circumstances; greatness in the sphere of action as well as in that of thought. And each form of greatness, human or secular, not less than moral and religious, is entitled to its apportioned meed of reverence. The Highest Greatness, the Greatness from Which all other greatness proceeds, is entitled to the deepest reverence. If the recognition of such greatness is to be, not merely adequate, but sincere, it will take unwonted forms, and make exacting demands upon us.

Certainly, reverence is not the homage which weak minds pay to acceptable fictions. It would not be a virtue if it were. All virtue is based on truth. Reverence is the sense of truth put in practice. Just as humility consists in practically looking upon ourselves as we really are: so reverence consists in recognising the greatness of that which is truly great. Reverence is merely one form of sincerity; it is sincerity face to face with greatness without us; just as humility is sincerity face to face with sinfulness and demerit within us. Thus reverence is the recognition, not of a fiction, but of a fact: it is the product, not of an unhealthy sentiment, but of simple truthfulness. If an institution is seen to be not really good; if a character is obviously petty and warped; if a doctrine or a theory is discovered to be false or unsound, there is no room for reverence. The soul may not lightly confer its certificate of greatness upon an unworthy recipient: it can only do so at the cost of that which is the common basis of all the virtues—the sense of truth. It may be misled: and reverence may be yielded to unworthy characters or at idol shrines which have no real claim on it: just as men of the highest logical ability may go on reasoning throughout life from false premises. But this accidental misfortune does not destroy the real place of reverence in the human soul. Reverence is essentially the instinct of truth, recognising a greatness which claims its homage.

Nor is reverence the foe of energy. We can only imitate with a good conscience that which we revere; and reverence stimulates the energy of imitation. Accordingly, on this very account, reverence of a worthy object, the sincere recognition of real greatness, is not an excellence which may be dropped or taken up at pleasure. It is a necessary virtue, whether for a man or for a society. The man without reverence is the man who can see in God's Universe no greatness which transcends himself. He passes by all the lofty characters, all the venerable institutions, all the great doctrines, all the finest creations of man's thought, or of man's enthusiasm, and he says in effect: 'There is that in me which is as great or greater than any of these: I shall not degrade myself by owning a higher greatness than my own.' As he passes through life, a shallow cynicism is ever playing upon his features: his motto is *nil admirari*. And do you suppose that his true greatness is secured or his energy roused by this indifference or insensibility? Or is he really that, which, by refusing the tribute of reverence to any other, he practically takes himself to be?

The question need not be answered. The irreverent man is his own worst enemy. We men are so constructed that we need an ideal to look up to, as truly as we need a power on which to depend. And if the Ideal be forgotten, and we are left to ourselves; if we have nothing by which to measure our insignificance, nothing to rebuke our self-esteem, nothing to provoke and sustain our enthusiasm, nothing to admire, nothing to imitate, nothing to bow down before as utterly greater than ourselves; then, depend upon it, our whole life must perforce shrink back into its own littleness. It must be left to its narrow frontiers and its puny resources; and our want of reverence for a greatness without us will be the exact measure of our incapacity for securing it within. The great have always been reverent; and for the reason that they have looked up to and shared in a greatness higher than their own. But to aspire to greatness you must sincerely own it; to recognise nothing as really great is to aim at nothing, to achieve nothing. Nothing, let me repeat it, is more fatal to a young man's prospects of true greatness in life, than that cynical estimate of everything and everybody which destroys all his moral enthusiasms and condemns him prematurely to a self-deceiving pettiness. And what is true of a man is true of a society. The class, the race, the nation which has no ideals to admire, no institutions to revere, is doomed to narrowness, vulgarity, ruin. A great many clever epigrams have been made about hero-worship; and the worship of unworthy heroes is of course sufficiently ridiculous. But almost any hero-worship is better than none. The really pitiable thing is to revere nothing. Thoughtful Americans have said, that, amid all the material greatness of their country—and it is sufficiently astonishing—their gravest anxiety for her future is caused by the absence of reverence among all classes of her people; the absence of any sincere recognition of a greatness which may ennoble its reverers.

## II

Reverence, then, is by no means only or chiefly an ecclesiastical virtue; it is necessary to the perfection of man as man, and to the wellbeing of society. But reverence is peculiarly a creation of religion. And if we ask why religion is thus the teacher, and the Church the school of reverence, the answer is, Because religion unveils before the soul of man a Greatness compared with Which all human greatness is insignificance itself. To the eye of religious faith, over every life, every character, every institution, every ideal, there is inscribed, " God alone is Great." All other greatness is a radiation from His, and insignificant when compared with His: His is all-embracing, self-subsisting, original. All other greatness is limited : His illimitable. All other greatness fails ultimately to satisfy: His never. If the Christian's eye rests reverently upon an excellence, whether of saint, or office, or institution, beneath His Throne, it is not as on something satisfying or final: it is as on an emanation from the Source of greatness. " Every good gift and every perfect gift," however much it may win our admiration, is, we know, not self-originating, or due to human effort, but "from above, and cometh down from the Father of lights, with Whom is no variableness, neither shadow of turning."[a]

When reverence is in the immediate presence of God, it takes a new form, or it adopts a new expression. It offers

[a] St. James i. 17.

that which it offers to none other or less than God. It offers adoration. To admire a good man or a great institution, or a splendid deed, is the prompting of reverence. To admire God would be highly irreverent, since God, if we contemplate Him at all, demands much more than admiration. The least that reverence can do in the presence of boundless Power, Wisdom, and Goodness, is to prostrate before Him every created faculty. For close contact with God produces on the soul of man, first of all, an impression of awe; and this impression is deep in exact proportion to the closeness of the contact.

When St. John says that he fell at the feet of Jesus Christ "as dead," he plainly describes a collapse of all the faculties of the soul. Just as great heat or excessive cold destroys life, while moderate heat restores and moderate cold invigorates it, so it is in the spiritual world. Our spiritual capacities are finite, and they may easily be shocked or overdone. Thus it was said to Moses, " Thou canst not see My face and live."[a] Thus when Daniel, on the banks of the river Hiddekel, saw "a certain Man clothed in linen, Whose loins were girded with fine gold of Uphaz: His body also was like the beryl, and His face as the appearance of lightning, and His eyes as lamps of fire, and His arms and His feet like in colour to polished brass, and the voice of His words like the voice of a multitude," he adds, " I saw this great vision, and there remained no strength in me: for my comeliness was turned in me into corruption, and I retained no strength."[b] So when the disciples heard the words from heaven at the Transfiguration, " they fell on their face, and were sore afraid."[c] So when at his conversion there shined round about Saul of Tarsus a light from heaven on the road to Damascus, "he

[a] Exod. xxxiii. 20.  [b] Dan. x. 5-8.
[c] St. Matt. xvii. 6.

fell to the earth."ᵃ It was thus in the present instance. St. John was overwhelmed at the sight of Jesus, Whom he had known so intimately and loved so well, revealed in His awful, unearthly glory. "I saw," he says, "seven golden candlesticks; and in the midst of the seven candlesticks One like unto the Son of Man, clothed with a garment down to the foot, and girt about the paps with a golden girdle. His head and His hairs were white like wool, as white as snow; and His eyes were as a flame of fire; and His feet like unto fine brass, as if they burned in a furnace; and His voice as the sound of many waters. And He had in His right hand seven stars: and out of His mouth went a sharp two-edged sword: and His countenance was as the sun shineth in his strength. And when I saw Him, I fell at His feet as dead."ᵇ

That the general aim and effect of religion is thus to create in the human soul, first of all, an awe of the Unseen and Almighty God, is everywhere witnessed by its preachers in the Bible. The Wise Man says that "the fear of the Lord is the beginning of wisdom."ᶜ A prophet cries: "The Lord is in His holy Temple; let all the earth keep silence before Him."ᵈ An Apostle exhorts: "Let us have grace, whereby we may serve God with reverence and godly fear: for," he adds, "our God is a consuming fire."ᵉ An inspired historian says that the earliest Church at Jerusalem was multiplied, "walking in the fear of the Lord and in the comfort of the Holy Ghost."ᶠ The saints in heaven, who wonder and worship incessantly, cry, "Who shall not fear Thee, O Lord of Hosts?"ᵍ And if on earth, amid all that we are permitted to see, we are conscious with the Apostle that, after all, we only "know in part,"ʰ even this partial know-

---

ᵃ Acts ix. 4.  ᵇ Rev. i. 12-17.  ᶜ Prov. i. 7.
ᵈ Hab. ii. 20.  ᵉ Heb. xii. 28, 29.  ᶠ Acts ix. 31.
ᵍ Rev. xv. 4.  ʰ 1 Cor. xiii. 9.

ledge may deepen reverence. What we know suggests the greatness of what we do not know. "Behold, I go forward, but He is not there; and backward, but I cannot perceive Him: on the left hand, where He doth work, but I cannot behold Him: He hideth Himself on the right hand, that I cannot see Him. Therefore am I troubled at His presence: when I consider, I am afraid of Him."[a]

When reverence for God is rooted in the soul, the soul sees God in all that reflects and represents Him on earth, and yields it for His sake appropriate recognition. The father, representing His parental authority; the mother, reflecting His tender love; the powers that be in the State, ordained by God as His ministers;[b] pastors of His Church, to whom He has said, "He that despiseth you despiseth Me;"[c] great and good men, whether in past ages or our contemporaries, who shed upon the world around some of His light and love; the Bible, which embodies for all time His revelation of Himself and His will concerning us; the laws of the natural world, when they are really ascertained, as being His modes of working; the Sacraments, as channels of His grace, or veils of His Presence; all that belongs to the public worship of Christ in His temples here on earth:—these are objects of Christian reverence because they are inseparable from Him, Who is the Only Great. And ever since He took upon Him our flesh and died, He has associated the poor, the suffering, the persecuted, the lonely, with His claims to honour. "Forasmuch as ye have done it unto one of the least of these My brethren, ye have done it unto Me."[d] And if there is any one part of Christian education which is really important it is this:—to take a child by the hand and lead it through the Church, and the

[a] Job xxiii. 8, 9, 15.   [b] Rom. xiii. 4.
[c] St. Luke x. 16.   [d] St. Matt. xxv. 40.

world of nature, pointing out all that reflects God, and bidding it revere His greatness.

### III.

Let us make three observations in conclusion :—

1. Reverence is a test, a measure of faith. We do not see God with our bodily eyes: faith is a second sight which does see Him. If men see God, they will behave accordingly. We know how differently we speak of people in their presence, and when we imagine them to be quite out of the way. I do not say that this is right; but is it not almost universal? And if a man believes that God is really close to him; seeing what he is doing, hearing what he is saying, noting what he is thinking, he will surely act, speak, think, accordingly with this belief. That this is really the case is one of the very first lessons of faith. And if men are irreverent, the common-sense explanation is that they do not really believe in the omnipresence of God.

Apply this to behaviour in a church. Behaviour in church is not by any means the only province or exercise of reverence; far from it. But it is a very important one; and it is a very good test of our reverence in respect of other matters. If God is not really with us in public worship; if the promise, "Where two or three are gathered in My Name, there am I in the midst of them,"[b] does not represent a literal fact; no more senseless waste of time than the expenditure of time in Church services can well be conceived. But if He is with us; if His Presence explains and justifies all that is said and sung; must it not follow that whatever expresses our feeling of

[a] St. Matt. xviii. 20.

lowly awe at the nearness of the Most Holy, before Whom His angels veil their faces, is but the common sense of the occasion? There are, I know, some persons who maintain that real reverence,—reverence of the soul,—has nothing to do with a man's behaviour in church: that he may lounge in his seat, fold his arms, behave himself as he would not think of behaving in any lady's drawing-room, neglect the prayers, neglect the responses, sit when others kneel, look about him, devote himself to discovering who is there, while the most passionate entreaties for mercy, or the deepest expressions of awe, or the tenderest protestations of love, are rising up in Psalm or Litany towards the Throne of Christ; since all the while he may conceivably be engaged in a profoundly spiritual communion with God, which is loftily independent of the mere circumstances of attitude and attention. Brethren, I do not believe it. As a rule, if a man does not pray when others pray in church, he does not pray at all. As a rule, if a man's bodily posture is irreverent, his thoughts and feelings are irreverent too. The reason is, because the soul and body are so intimately linked to each other that the body cannot be for long in postures which are hostile to the movements of the soul. Certain postures—it is a matter of experience upon which artists and moralists are alike agreed—do correspond to certain passions, emotions, states of mind. And to keep the body by force in a posture violently opposed to a given condition of mind is to modify this condition considerably, or even to suppress it altogether. No one could for long lounge back in an easy-chair if moved by a sense of burning indignation: no one with tender affection in his heart could long maintain an expression of countenance which implied that he was entirely out of temper. He would be conscious that the contrast was ridiculous. In the same way, if a man sees God, he will behave as it is natural to behave in the presence of the Almighty. He will be too absorbed to look about at his fellow-worshippers: too much alive to the greatness and awfulness of God to care what others think about himself: he will yield to those instinctive expressions of reverence which the Creator has implanted in us by nature and refined and heightened by grace: and he will find that the reverence of the soul is best secured when the body, its companion and instrument, is reverent also. If a man feels reverent, he will kneel when others kneel. This does not apply to the sick, or the aged; but there can be no doubt about the duty of the young and the hale. To see God is to feel it to be an imperious necessity to prostrate ourselves before Him. "O come, let us worship and fall down,[a] and kneel before the Lord our Maker,"[b] is the voice of true reverence for all time.

2. Reverence begins from within. It cannot be learned as a code of outward conduct. I do not mean to say that a man may not learn up phrases, postures, proprieties of speech and proprieties of action which look like reverence, and which belong, generally speaking, to its external outfit. But if his reverence goes no deeper than this he will not deceive others, or, for any long time, even himself. He will be taken unawares and when off his guard, and then his natural irreverence will show itself. It is with reverence towards God and all that belongs to Him, as it

[a] נִשְׁתַּחֲוֶה וְנִכְרָעָה. Maurer *in loc.*, "prosternamus nos et incurvemus nos." "How impossible," said Dr. Pusey one day to a well-meaning but uninformed lady, who was objecting to reverence in church as "unscriptural formalism,"—"how impossible it would be for you to say what you do, if you knew the real meaning of the word translated 'worship' in the 95th Psalm!"
[b] Ps. xcv. 6.

is with good manners towards our fellow-creatures. The only true spring of good manners is genuine consideration for others and forgetfulness of self. Many selfish people learn up a certain amount of good manners, which they practise in public and on social occasions. But sooner or later they astonish the world by saying or doing something outrageously pompous or rude. The reason is that they have never had the true principle of good manners within them, and their attempts to keep up appearances could not be expected to succeed always or beyond a certain time. To act and speak reverently, a man must feel reverently: and if he is to feel reverently, he must see our Lord. If our Lord is merely a phrase to him, or, as we say, an abstraction, an idea, and not a real being; his outward reverence is worthless, and it will not last. If he feels what it is to be in God's presence, to speak to Him, to ask Him to do this or that, to promise Him to attempt this or that; if he has any idea of the meaning of these solemn acts of the soul, the outward proprieties will follow. It was when St. John saw Christ that he fell, as by an irresistible instinct, at His feet as dead.

3. Lastly, reverence, the deepest, the truest, is perfectly compatible with love. There are many Christians who do not understand this. Their hearts are, I doubt not, full of love to our Lord and Saviour for His gracious work of Redemption : they rejoice in Him as in their dearest Friend, Who has first washed them in His Blood, and then admitted them to His intimacy, and bade them make themselves at home in His presence. And they think, if they are to speak their minds, that to fall down before Him in His awful glory is to forfeit the liberty with which He has made them free; to go back from the

Gospel to the Law; from the kingdom of love to the kingdom of fear. They think that if they cannot behave as if they were on free and easy terms with Him; if they cannot speak of Him and speak to Him in a familiar way, and just as it comes into their heads; if they cannot talk of His work, His providences, as if He were an active neighbour in an adjoining street, and there was no room for mystery, and they knew all about Him; if they cannot describe themselves as on a footing of such assured intimacy with Him as to exclude all anxiety, and enable them to forecast everything with peremptory confidence, there is no real love between them and Him, no warmth in their religion worth speaking of.

Brethren, do you not see that they make the mistake observable in people who are often to be met with in the world, and who cannot understand how friendship can be sincere if it does not involve familiarity, or how love is genuine which does not permit others to take liberties? In sober earnest, reverence is the salt which preserves the purity of affection, without impairing its intensity. We are so framed that we can only love for long that which we heartily respect. The passion which is lavished for a few hours upon an object which does not deserve respect is unworthy of the sacred name of love. And God, when He asks the best love of our hearts, would preserve it from corruption by requiring also the safeguard of reverence. He will have us remember that He does not cease to be awful because He is unspeakably tender and condescending. Nay; He teaches us awe of Him first: love for Him afterwards. When Daniel was prostrate at the vision, "Behold," he says, "an hand touched me, which set me upon my knees and upon the palms of my hands. . . . Then said He unto me, Fear not, Daniel: for from the first day that thou didst set thine heart to understand, . . . thy words were heard."[a] When the Apostles had sunk to the earth in terror at the voice at the Transfiguration, Jesus came and touched them, saying, "Arise, be not afraid."[b] St. John had fallen at our Lord's feet as dead. But "He laid His right hand upon me, saying unto me, Fear not; I am the First and the Last: I am He that liveth, and was dead; and behold, I am alive for evermore, Amen; and have the keys of hell and of death."[c]

So, brethren, it is always in the kingdom of souls, now and to the end of time. We begin with awe, we end with love; and reverence links our earlier spiritual education with our later and higher privileges. Unless the disciple whom Jesus loved, and to whom He gave the greatest pledge of personal affection, is no model for us; unless we can suppose that those high intelligences, who veil their faces and bend in incessant adoration before the Throne of the Most Holy, do not really love the Divine Object of their worship as strongly and purely as do the sons of men; it is certain that the purest love goes ever hand in hand with the deepest reverence, and that in another sphere of being the one grace will be seen to be nothing less than necessary to the very existence of the other.

[a] Dan. x. 10, 12.    [b] St. Matt. xvii. 7.    [c] Rev. i. 17, 18.

# SERMON XXIX.

## ENDURANCE OF WRONG.

1 ST. PETER II. 19.

*This is thankworthy, if a man for conscience toward God endure grief, suffering wrongfully.*

THE Epistle for to-day,[a] it has been suggested, would have been better suited for one of the Sundays before Easter, if not for Good Friday itself. The subject of this Epistle is patience under undeserved wrong, as illustrated by the example of our Suffering and Sinless Lord. Such a subject does seem, at first sight, out of keeping with the thoughts and joys of the Easter season. But the truth is, in those early days when, with a few exceptions, our present Epistles and Gospels were selected, the Death and Resurrection of Christ were looked upon, as indeed they are treated in Scripture, as events inseparably connected with each other. They are two aspects of a single whole; the self-sacrifice and triumph of the Divine Love manifested towards ruined man are one in purpose from first to last. And thus it is that, even when Easter has come and gone, the lesser lessons of Good Friday are heard echoing down the weeks which

[a] Second Sunday after Easter.

follow the great festival. It seems as though the Church felt that she could not learn at the time all that the Passion of her Lord was meant to teach her: so she returns to the scene of His sorrow, to gather up what had escaped her amid the distractions and bewilderment of the day of His Death. Certainly this applies to to-day's services. The Collect speaks of our Lord Jesus Christ as a Sacrifice for sin; in the Gospel He is the Good Shepherd Who lays down His life for His sheep: in the Epistle He is the Great Sufferer, patient and faultless, Who by His sublime endurance teaches patience and resignation to those who suffer wrongfully throughout all time.

I.

If we look at the context of this passage, we observe first of all, that St. Peter is not writing, as the extract selected for the Epistle might suggest, to Christians in general. He is addressing one class of Christians, namely, household slaves. "Slaves," he begins, "be subject to your masters with all fear; not only to the good and gentle, but also to the froward. For," he adds, "this is thankworthy, if a man for conscience toward God endure grief, suffering wrongfully."[a] Our translation, "servants," was perhaps intended to make the passage practically useful, by suggesting its application to that class among ourselves who so far resemble the ancient slaves, that they have duties to perform in obedience to a human master. But in truth the word "servants," with all its modern associations, misleads us seriously as to the Apostle's meaning. A servant in an English household has very little in common with a slave in that old-world society for which St. Peter wrote. A servant is a

[a] 1 St. Pet. ii. 18, 19.

free man or woman, who undertakes to do a certain kind and amount of work, in return for a certain stipend. This undertaking is a contract. It may be brought to an end, by giving due notice, at any moment. It involves, while it lasts, no forfeiture of the protection which the law extends equally to servant and master. Long before an English servant "suffered wrongfully," in the sense contemplated by St. Peter, the law would step in, and punish any personal assault or cruelty, or withholding of covenanted salary, with impartial justice.

Far otherwise was it with the ancient slave. He had no rights before the law. He was looked upon, so a great writer of antiquity puts it, as "an animated piece of property." He was bought, just like the cattle in the homestead, or the furniture about the room; if indeed he was not born and bred on the estate. He was often taught a profession that he might be useful to his master, or might fetch a high price if sent to a sale. He was a cook, a poet, a jeweller, a cabinet-maker, an architect, a physician, a mechanic, a private attendant, a hairdresser, a field-labourer, an epigrammatist;—just as the case might be. He was lent out to a friend, or sold for a song, or flogged to death, or crucified, or made a pet of,—just as the caprice of his owner might dictate. He, too, had his attachments, like the rest of us. But he might be willed away, from the associations of a lifetime, to a strange owner and a distant home, without a suspicion of his destiny; or he might, quite in his old age, pass at the death of a kind and considerate master to some young heir, selfish and reckless, who viewed him simply as worn-out property, and treated him with indifference or cruelty. Worst of all was his precarious hold on those sacred rights which marriage carries with it. If he was married, his wife and his children were his, only on sufferance; and his family might be broken up, at a moment's notice, to fill the purse or to gratify the passions of the thoughtless owner. And all this while the slave was, not unfrequently, in everything but civil position, his master's superior; a man of wider cultivation, of larger capacities, of finer moral make, of nobler sympathies. He might be an Epictetus; he might have those rarer gifts and graces which are wont to win the homage of the best among mankind. It mattered not. He had no rights before the law: no redress against brutal wrong: no claim which would be recognised by public opinion as entitling him to consideration and justice. Not seldom his very superiority was his ruin: it moved the jealousy or it stimulated the caprice of his owner to some exceptional act of cruelty or oppression.

Certainly, now and then, the natural conscience of Pagan rulers moved them to do something—it was little enough—to improve the condition of the slaves. At one time the old Pagan Roman law restrained the right of the master to kill a slave without some assignable cause; at another it obliged him to get an authorisation from a magistrate; at a later period, when Christianity had now made itself felt, the law only permitted him to inflict bodily punishment short of death. In the same way, custom allowed the slave to have a little property; legally, of course, a man who was himself property could not hold property. In this way a slave would sometimes hoard enough to buy his freedom. But all this came to very little: the cruelty and degradation attendant on slavery were gigantic. And from time to time there were wild attempts at resistance; when tens of thousands of armed slaves sought freedom from their oppressors in death on the field of battle, or in victory. In the age of the Apostles no social question was more pressing throughout the Roman Empire than this question of slavery.

When, then, the Apostles addressed themselves to the conversion of the world, they found at once that they had this matter on their hands. Christianity was especially the religion of the suffering and the ill-used; and the slaves welcomed it as a heaven-sent friend. As St. Peter thinks over the Jewish converts to Christ "throughout Pontus, Galatia, Cappadocia, Asia Minor, and Bithynia,"[a] he remembers that multitudes of them were slaves · Christian slaves in Pagan households. They have, he reflects, a great claim upon his charity. What should help them to bear the hardships of their lot, if the Faith and Church of Jesus did not help them? The Apostle scans them over; smarting, as they were, under a sense of accumulated wrong; crushed down, as they were, beneath an iron system, which looked, no doubt, to themselves and to their masters, as secure as anything human can be. What can he say to them that will lighten their dreary prison-house? How can he suggest the consecration of unmerited sorrow by the Divine Sufferer, and the hope of a brighter life hereafter? "This is thankworthy," he says, "if a man for conscience toward God endure grief, suffering wrongfully."

II.

St. Peter teaches that suffering is thankworthy; that it is a gift from God, and in turn acceptable to Him, if it be accompanied by two conditions.

1. It must be undeserved. A slave, too, might be punished for doing what would merit punishment in a

[a] 1 St. Pet. i. 1.

free man.  A slave, too, might be violent, or abusive, or careless about that which belonged to others, or intemperate, or dishonest, or treacherous.  If punished for offences of this kind, he might not complain.  "What glory is it," asks St. Peter, "if, when ye be buffeted for your faults, ye shall take it patiently?"[a]  The rule that punishment follows wrong-doing is not suspended in the case of a slave.

2. Such suffering must also be "for conscience toward God."  It must be borne for His cause and sake, and with a good hope of His approval.  This it is which makes pain at once bearable and bracing, when the conscience of the sufferer can ask the Perfect Moral Being to take note of it, just as David does in so many of the Psalms.  "Look Thou upon me, and be merciful unto me: Lord, be Thou my Helper."[b]  Mere suffering, which a man dares not offer to God, though it be borne patiently, through natural pluck or courage, has no spiritual value.  "Father, into Thy Hands I commend My Spirit;"[c] this is the consecration prayer of sorrow.  It was uttered on the Cross.  It is uttered, if in other terms, wherever men suffer for conscience toward God.  And by it suffering is already changed into moral victory.

In short, St. Peter says to the Christian slaves: 'If you like, you can turn the hardest circumstances of your lot into very choice blessings.  Suffering is not necessarily an evil; it may be a signal good.  If it is undeserved, so much the better for its religious efficacy: it then is a certificate of honour sent you from God.  Let it be accepted as from Him and for His sake, and it at once becomes a great grace; a token of near likeness to our Lord Jesus Christ.'

[a] 1 St. Pet. ii. 20.   [b] Ps. xxx. 11.   [c] St. Luke xxiii. 46.

St. Paul deals with this question in a similar spirit. He bids the slaves at Ephesus be obedient to their masters, not with eye-service, as men-pleasers, but as the slaves of Christ:[a] and he uses almost the same terms in addressing the slaves at Colosse.[b] He desires Titus, as a Bishop in Crete, to exhort slaves "to be obedient to their own masters, and to please them well in all things: not answering again, not purloining, but showing all good fidelity; that they may adorn the doctrine of God our Saviour in all things."[c] Writing to Timothy, Bishop of Ephesus, he desires generally that slaves should count their masters worthy of all honour; and in particular, that slaves belonging to Christian masters are not to think the worse of them because they are brethren who yet keep slaves, but rather do them service because they are Christian believers and objects of God's love.[d] He advises Christian slaves at Corinth, even if they can be free, not to care to use their opportunity.[e] Everywhere the advice given is substantially this; 'Submit and obey cheerfully; endure patiently; remember that time is short; remember that the accidents of our outward condition here matter little as compared with our state in the unending future.'

III.

Here it may be asked, Why did not the Apostles denounce slavery as an intolerable wrong? Why did

[a] Eph. vi. 5, 6.   [b] Col. iii. 22-24.
[c] Titus ii. 9, 10.   [d] 1 Tim. vi. 1, 2.
[e] 1 Cor. vii. 21. Cf. Meyer *in loc.*, who supplies an object to χρῆσαι thus:—"nämlich als Schlave berufen worden zu sein." The καί and thrice-repeated ἕκαστος μενέτω seem to make this interpretation certain. In the judgment of the Apostle, the Future Life was too near at hand and too unspeakably important to make it worth a man's while to trouble himself greatly about his condition in this.

they thus trifle with it, and allow the Church which succeeded them to trifle with it? Why did they seem, indirectly at least, to sanction it, by advising slaves to honour and obey their owners? Was not this of the nature of a compromise between good and evil; between the high principles of Christian morals on the one hand, and the debased institutions of heathen life on the other? Would it not have been better to break with slavery at once and altogether; better for the honour of the Christian Revelation; better for the best interests of man?

Certainly, my brethren, nothing can well be more antipathetic than the spirit of the Gospel and the spirit of slavery. For slavery postulates an essential distinction between man and man, which is unknown to the Gospel. The Gospel proclaims the unity of the human race, and the equality of all its members before God: the Gospel is based upon and consecrates the laws of God in nature. And slavery is distinctly unnatural; it is a rejection of the fundamental equality of men; it often and consistently professes to reject belief in the unity of the race. In the mind of a slave-owner the deepest of all distinctions between human beings, is that between the man who is his own owner and the man who is owned by another. In Christ Jesus, exclaims the Apostle, "there is neither bond nor free."[a]

But the exact question which the Apostles had to conder was whether slavery necessarily ruined the prospects of the human souL It was not whether slavery was a bad social institution, or theoretically indefensible. The business of the Apostles lay with the other world, rather than with this; with this world so far as it bears upon the other. What a man's condition might be in this world mattered little in an Apostle's judgment, if he could

[a] Gal. iii. 28.

secure the true end of his being in the world to come. And that a slave could do this was not a matter that admitted of doubt. A slave might be a Christian, the best of Christians, easily enough. If he was harshly treated, that was not peculiar to his condition of life: while it might promote his sanctification. If a man is tempted to do wrong, St. James tells him that he should count this all joy, knowing that the trial of his faith worketh endurance.[a] If a slave had to choose between sinful compliance with a master's will and the punishment of death, he would know his part, if his eye was fixed on the Divine Sufferer. The grace of God may make the soul of man independent of outward circumstances; there is no real slavery when the soul is free. And it often happened that a Christian slave would live more entirely in and for a better world than other Christians, because there was so little to win the homage of his heart in this. To the slave-owner, undoubtedly, slavery was more fraught with spiritual danger than to the slave himself; but, however great the temptations of the position, they were, after all, only temptations. Even a master of slaves might be just, generous, chaste, charitable, humble, tender-hearted, true, unselfish; although, beyond doubt, circumstances were against him.

Slavery, then, in Christian eyes, although undoubtedly bad, is not bad in the sense in which murder and adultery are bad; as an enemy with which a Christian can in any circumstances keep no terms. It may tend to multiply temptations, but it cannot compel to actual sin; since sin is only possible when the will consents. At the same time, although the Apostles were working for another world; in the course of doing so, and incidentally, they were destined to be the reformers of this. They could

[a] St. James i. 3.

not but dislike slavery; but how was it to be done away with? Was it to be by a sudden revolutionary effort; supposing the thing to be possible? Or was it to be by the influence of new principles, first upon the opinions, and then upon the structure, of society? The Apostles chose the latter method; but it was a method which took time. The Apostles trusted to the silent operation of the law of Christian love, and not to those violent and tragical catastrophes which, even when they succeed, succeed amidst a scene of sin and ruin. It was not the duty of the Gospel to proclaim a social war. There were sects at that time nearly related to Judaism, the Essenes and Therapeutæ, whose teaching was certainly familiar to St. Paul. They held that the slave should at once refuse all obedience to his master in the name of human rights. But Spartacus with his thousands of slaves, maddened by oppression into rebellion against society, would never have put an end to slavery. The better way was to teach a higher ideal of life, both to the slave and the master, and meanwhile to proclaim: "This is thankworthy, if a man for conscience toward God endure grief, suffering wrongfully."

From the first slavery was so changed, when in Christian hands, as to lose most of its worst features. Christian slave-masters at Ephesus are reminded by St. Paul that they have a "Master also in heaven, neither is there respect of persons with Him."[a] The Church was incessantly, after the Apostolic pattern, pleading with some Philemon for kindness towards an Onesimus.[b] Already, in her eyes, the slave of the civil law was Christ's freeman.[c] In a Christian household the marriage between slaves was respected, as being what Christ's law had made

[a] Eph. vi. 9.  [b] Philemon 8-10, 17.
[c] 1 Cor. vii. 22.

it—sacred and indissoluble.[a] In Christian households a hundred courtesies softened the hardship of the relation between master and slave; the sense of a common brotherhood in Christ had already sapped the idea of any radical inequality between them. Did they not both owe existence to the same Creative Will? Were they not both redeemed by the same Atoning Blood? Had not both been washed in the Sacrament of Regeneration? Did they not kneel side by side to receive the Body of the Lord? Were they not alike striving day by day to deepen faith, hope, charity in their souls? Did they not look forward to a common home in heaven? Thus it happened that Christian slaves occasionally rose even to high places in the ministry of the Church. Callistus, Bishop of Rome at the beginning of the third century, was a slave. Sometimes slaves were martyrs for Christ. Blandina of Lyons, who died for Christ in the year 177, was a Christian slave. And martyrdom, the highest act of moral freedom of which man is capable, more than wiped out the degradation of slavery; within the Church martyrdom was the patent of nobility. Then came the legislation of the Christian Councils; and the Codes of the Christian Emperors.

It is welcome to-day [b] to remember how, in this great field of human improvement, religion and law went for centuries hand in hand; religion seeking ever and anon the assistance of law; law, in such codes as those of Theodosius and Justinian, drawing its best inspirations from the guidance of religion; until at last slavery died utterly away within the precincts of civilisation, although, alas! it has lingered on elsewhere even to our own days, as the disgrace of selfish commercial enterprise pursued at the expense of the feebler races of mankind.

[a] St. Matt. xix. 6.
[b] This Sermon was preached before the Lord Mayor and the Judges.

## IV.

But it may be asked, whether the advice of St. Peter to submit quietly to wrong does not destroy manliness and force of character, if it is acted on.? Does it not tend to create a race of effeminate, spiritless men, who may give little trouble to a bad institution or a bad government, but who have parted with all that can be called "moral strength"?

This question involves another. In what does moral strength consist? It is sometimes taken for granted that moral strength must catch the eye, must strike upon the ear, must inflict itself on the imagination; that it must be something bustling, pushing, demonstrative, aggressive; that it must at least have colour, body, muscle, to recommend it. No, brethren, this is not the case. Moral strength, in its very finest forms, may be the reverse of all this: when it makes no show, and is passive, it is often at its best. Many a man who can act with great courage in moments of great personal danger, in a struggle with a brigand, or in a burning house, cannot go through an illness as bravely and patiently as a little girl. The courage which was shown by the men who, after seeing the safety of the women and children on board, went down in the *Birkenhead*, may have been greater than that of the men who charged at Balaclava. Animal effort, or the excitement of a great crisis, makes courage easy. The hardest thing often is to do nothing; to await the approach of danger or of death, and yet not to lose nerve and self-possession.

No moral strength in the whole history of mankind ever equalled that which was displayed on Calvary; where all that awaited Him was present from the first to the Mind of the Divine Victim, " Who, when He was reviled,

reviled not again; when He suffered, He threatened not; but committed Himself to Him that judgeth righteously."[a]

Nothing that has been said will be so greatly misconstrued as to be taken to imply that cruelty, tyranny, oppression, can be agreeable to the Mind of God. He permits these things among men, from time to time, just as He permits much else that is evil, for His Own wise ends. He brings good out of them; yet He condemns them. By and by He will punish them. Who can read the Jewish Prophets, and not mark how, one after another, they maintain the cause of the helpless, whether against bad Jewish kings, or against heathen conquerors? Who can use the Psalter, especially the Psalms of David himself, without sharing the fire of his moral indignation against oppression and wrong? If St. Peter advises oppressed slaves to " endure grief, suffering wrongfully," for " conscience toward God," because " this is acceptable with God," he does not therefore sanction the caprice or cruelty of the master. Nowhere does the New Testament approve of selfish indifference to wrong inflicted upon others on the part of a bystander: if it is a duty to submit to violence, it is equally a duty to rescue those who suffer, as opportunity may suggest. Nowhere has the Gospel repealed the stern sentence which Prophet and Psalmist alike utter against public or private tyrants: "Why boastest thou thyself, thou tyrant, that thou canst do mischief; whereas the goodness of God endureth yet daily? . . . Therefore shall God destroy thee for ever: He shall take thee, and pluck thee out of thy dwelling, and root thee out of the land of the living."[b] Nowhere is it implied in the Bible that the systems involving the oppression of man by man have vested rights in the moral universe, or that the circumstances which permit it are even tolerable,

[a] 1 St. Pet. ii. 23.   [b] Ps. lii. 1, 2, 6

unless they are perpetuated for very different purposes indeed. The days will come when Englishmen will look back to the Abolition of the Slave Trade by the English Parliament as a greater title to glory than was Trafalgar or Waterloo; as among the very greatest in the course of our history. Wilberforce and Clarkson will rank even before those celebrated commanders, to whose courage and genius, under God, we owe the independence of our country. Great days they were when English gentlemen endured every species of unpopularity and insult in pursuit of one noble and disinterested object; when England, not without long debate and hesitation, but at length deliberately, sacrificed her material interests to the amount of thirty millions sterling, that she might secure freedom and well-being to the enslaved races of Africa. Have there been no symptoms of late that some sections of English society have lost something of this generous impatience of cruel wrong; have learned to listen to the cry of anguish raised by millions of our fellow-creatures, and to listen, if not unmoved, yet without making an effort to help them?

Be this as it may, the truth announced by St. Peter is always widely applicable in every age and country. Among yourselves there are probably some who, for conscience toward God, endure grief, suffering wrongfully. There are no slaves, thank God, on English soil, but there are multitudes of persons in positions of dependence whose lives can easily be made miserable by the cruel ingenuity of their betters, and too often for no worse crime than that of obeying a higher sense of right. Every rank in society has its petty tyrants and its secret confessorships; to suffer wrongfully for conscience toward God is the monopoly of no one class. Here is a cadet of a noble family who will not consent to a transaction which he knows to be unjust; and he is cut off with a shilling.

There is an apprentice or clerk in a large city house who will not abandon the duties or restraints of a Christian life, in deference to pressure, or abuse, or ridicule from his companions; and he has a hard time of it. Yonder is a governess who has learnt a higher estimate of life and duty than her wealthy and ostentatious employer; or a clergyman, who feels too keenly the real character of Divine Revelation, and the tremendous issues of life and death, to acquiesce in some popular but shallow misrepresentation of the Gospel, which makes his people comfortable, without bringing them nearer to God. These, and such as these, must, "for conscience toward God, endure grief, suffering wrongfully." Law can do but little for them; the province of law lies outside the spheres of the heart and the conscience; the whole world of motive is beyond it. But religion can do much, or rather everything, by pointing to the Crucified and Risen Prince of that vast company in all ages, who have cared less to avoid discomfort than to be true to known truth and duty; by pointing to the unapproached bitterness of His sorrow and to the completeness and splendour of His triumph.

# SERMON XXX.

## CHRIST OUR EXAMPLE.

1 ST. PETER II. 21.

*Leaving us an example, that ye should follow His steps.*

THERE is a purpose in the order of the words of the opening sentence of the Collect for to-day:[a] "Almighty God, Who hast given Thine only Son to be unto us both a Sacrifice for sin, and also an Ensample of godly life." The first reason for the gift of the Incarnate Son to a perishing world, is that He might be a Sacrifice for its sin. The second reason is, that He might be an Ensample of godly life to those who believe in Him. We sinners cannot invert the order, and say that He was given, first as our Example, and secondly as our Sin-offering before God. For we cannot imitate Him until He has redeemed us from the power and guilt of sin; the first need of a sinner is pardon and moral freedom, the second, the Ideal of a new life.

Surely it is not without an object that our Lord's example is thus put forward by the Church so soon after Easter. The great anniversary of His Atoning Death and glorious Resurrection fills men's thoughts and hearts with

[a] Second Sunday after Easter.

gratitude for one result of His coming among us; it does this so exclusively, as, for the time being, to put others out of sight. With our hearts thus full of what He has done for us, we may forget too easily what He expects us to do: and the Church, here, as always, practical, does not allow us to forget it. "And also an Ensample of godly life." She does not for a moment deny that the supreme significance of Christ's coming is His sacrificial Death; but she urges that He is also an Example, and that we may not safely lose sight of it.

That there is from time to time a danger of doing this, a glance at our own religious history will show. When a great revival of religion took place at the end of the last and at the beginning of the present century, the point on which it mainly insisted, was the value of Our Lord's Atoning Death. In the cold and dreary eighteenth century, Christianity had been wellnigh resolved into a republication of natural morality; a means of promoting a very moderate standard of good conduct, by appeals to the emotions and the imagination. Against this poor and soulless substitute for the religion of the Crucified a protest was raised, which, so far and so long as it was earnest and positive, achieved a great work for God. Such, however, is the finiteness of our minds, that a vivid apprehension of one truth too often blinds us to others; and, in the fervour with which Christ's Atoning Death was preached, His example, to say nothing of other aspects of His mediatorial work, was too largely lost sight of. It was even said, at the time to which I refer, that to insist on Christ's example was not to preach the Gospel; that it was legal and unevangelical; although, as you know, the four Evangelists are almost entirely devoted to setting it forth. Something of the same kind may at times be also observed in that deeper, and, strictly speaking, more

Evangelical movement which has succeeded the so-termed Evangelicalism. To the rallying-cry of the earlier revival, "Pardon through Christ," this later movement adds, with St. Paul, "Union with Christ." Men had strangely overlooked the vital truth, so constantly insisted on by the great Apostle, especially in such epistles as that to the Ephesians —that Christians in a state of grace are one with Jesus Christ; that He is throned in all living souls as an inward Presence, as the guarantee of their future glory. Some of us may remember how, when once we had caught sight of this, we read the New Testament with new eyes. Of this union with Christ the Christian Sacraments are the appointed instruments. Only thus have they any rightful place in a religion, whence mere shadows of absent or future blessings have departed, and where all is real. Yet here, too, there has been at times a danger of overlooking our Lord's Example. Christ in the soul has seemed so precious, that, like Christ on the Cross, He has been remembered, while men have forgotten the Ensample of godly life in the Gospels. Against this one-sidedness the Church, like the New Testament, is ever on guard. They both remind us that Christ is not only our Righteousness and Sanctification,[a] but also our Model;[b] that He is the perfect Man, to the measure of Whose stature[c] redeemed souls should constantly strive to attain; that He has left us, not merely pardon for the past, and grace and strength for the future, but also an external standard of conduct; that He has left us an Ensample that we should follow His steps.

I.

Here a question which has to be considered is,—why we need such an Example at all.

[a] 1 Cor. i. 30.  [b] 1 Cor. xi. 1.  [c] Eph. iv. 13.

Let us ask ourselves what it is which makes human nature radically different from that of any of the creatures that surround us. The great characteristic of man is the possession of free will. Man's will may control, not merely external circumstances to a considerable extent, but man's self,—his character. It is true of every man, within very large limits, that he is what he makes himself to be. This is not true of the creatures beneath us. They are what they grow to be. A tree is tall or stunted, it is leafy or bare of leaves, in accordance with the law of its growth: the soil, the situation, the climate foster, or check its vital force, as the case may be. But it has no control over its destiny; it becomes what it is without reference to any standard external to it or to any deliberate efforts of its own. And an animal too grows to be what it is in obedience to the law of its species; its growth is retarded or aided by climate, food, rest, and exercise; and it instinctively makes the most of these. Instinct, indeed, leads the young to copy the parent: but this imitation is not reasoned; it is not a matter of choice; it is determined by something which could not but determine it; by unreflecting impulse. The case is otherwise with man. The growth of the human body indeed is as little within man's control as is that of an animal: as our Lord reminds us, "Thou canst not make one hair white or black."[a] But human character, and so much of the bodily life as bears on character, is as much under our control as are the canvas and the colours under that of a painter. Our passions, our inclinations, our thoughts, our sympathies, our antipathies, our habits, are at the disposal of our wills; we are what we have gradually made ourselves. Many influences have co-operated, have been appropriated, or have been overcome in the process. It is a long and

[a] St. Matt. v. 36.

chequered history with many of us, and One Eye only surveys it from first to last in its completeness. But, whatever the elements of thought or of feeling, internal or from without, of nature or of supernatural grace, that have contributed towards it; we are, each of us, in the last resort, what, using the gifts which God has given us, we have made ourselves to be.

Man, then, is an artist. And as an artist he needs not merely the material out of which to mould some expression of thought, but an example, an ideal, to copy. He cannot leave that vast assortment of moral material, which he is himself, to develop itself by hazard. He must mould and shape it in accordance with some pattern external to himself. He will sink, with fatal certainty, if he does not sustain himself by looking beyond himself; if he thinks to grow, as a tree grows, by the free self-assertion of some internal impulse, unchecked by any outward model or rule. The need of an ideal is felt by man in all ages, and everywhere. What school is there in which there are not one or two boys, to whom, for their character or their accomplishments, the rest, by unexpressed consent, look up? What profession, or department of human activity, in which there are not some typical men, whose skill or success has made them models to be imitated, though at a distance, by their fellows? What nation, which does not recognise in some one of its sons, living or dead, an ideal representation of its best temper; so that, as the successive generations pass, they look up and say, Let us copy him! Indeed, the greatest misfortune that can happen to a nation, or a society, or a man, is to be without an ideal, or, as the proverb goes, to admire nothing. That undisturbed satisfaction with what is, is more fatal than a dozen misplaced enthusiasms; it is the certain presage of degradation. Man can only escape imprisonment within whatever is lowest in his nature, by perseveringly looking beyond himself to a Model of ideal excellence, and striving to attain it.

It may indeed be asked whether it will not do as well to obey a precept as to copy an example. Example, it is said, is vague ; Precept is explicit. Precept is active ; it seeks you out and addresses you. Example is passive ; it lets you imitate if you will. Example merely says, 'This may be done because it has been done.' Precept says, 'Do it.'

No, brethren, you especially who, as parents or masters, are responsible for influence on others; assuredly, no. Example goes further than Precept. Precept is a challenge : it rouses in our fallen nature those elements of resistance, which start into life at the approach of authority in any guise. Example is an invitation : it gently stimulates our sense of emulation ; it encourages our hopes ; it allays our apprehensions. Precept leads us to the foot of a precipitous mountain, and it cries, 'Scale that height.' But Example whispers : 'Mark what I do, and then do it ; it cannot be hard for you since it is easy for me. See how I place this foot here ; now copy me : and that just there ; and this hand on that ledge of rock. Look how I step over that crevice, and rest on this projecting foothold, and tread lightly and quickly along that insecure bit of the path. Watch me ; keep close to me. You see how easy it is : all that is needed is a cool head and close attention to what I am doing. Then all will be well in the end.'

This is the silent language of Example : and it is, I say much more persuasive than the spoken language of Precept It is Precept made easy ; Precept, and something more human and sympathetic than Precept ; it is Precept and Obedience all in one. And it is proportionally persuasive.

## II.

We do then need an example, and our Lord has satisfied this need of our nature, and completely. In Him we have before us an Example which is unique. He passed through life in the humblest circumstances: yet He belongs to the human race. Until He was thirty years of age, He was a working carpenter. His associates were the very poor. He was not noticed by any persons of wealth or influence; He spoke the language of the Galilean peasantry. As the Jews said of Him, He "never learned letters;"[a] He certainly never wrote a book. Literature, society, the great traditions of learning, of thought, of administration, which do so much for most of those who sway the world, did nothing for Him. Yet He is a worldwide Example. He belongs to no sect, such as the Pharisees or Sadducees; to no country, for although He is born of a Jewish mother, all races may claim Him as their own; to no historical epoch, for He had no visible part in the great events of His day, and does not bear their impress. He alone in the world is the Universal Man; He is the one Man Who corresponds to that ideal of humanity of which there are traces in the minds of all of us; He is the great Example.

1. That which strikes us, first of all, in the example which He has left us, is its faultlessness. We are startled by His Own sense of this. He nevers utters one word to the Father or to man which implies the consciousness of a defect. Read the lives of the great servants of God in the Old or New Testament. Abraham, Moses, Samuel, David, Elijah, St. Peter, St. Paul: they all confess sin.

[a] St. John vii. 15.

They humble themselves before men, they implore the mercy of God. Think of any good man whom you have ever known, or whose life you have studied. He has feared God, loved God, worked for God during long years. Yet he is full of a sense of inconsistency and imperfection pervading life and conduct; he is profuse in his acknowledgments of weakness and of sin. Nay; if he were not thus eager to confess sin, we should question his goodness. His self-depreciation is, we instinctively feel, only honesty. But Jesus Christ reproaches Himself for nothing, confesses nothing, regrets nothing. He is certain of the perfect faultlessness of all that He says and does. "I do always those things that please the Father."[a] "The prince of this world cometh, and hath nothing in Me."[b] "Which of you convinceth Me of sin?"[c]

Was this an illusion, or did it correspond with the fact? He was surrounded by jealous observers; by men whom not a few motives rendered anxious, if they could, to show that He was, after all, like others around Him, like themselves, a sinner. He could reckon on no forbearance, no generosity, no equity, in his opponents. Yet He passed their criticism unscathed. "Which of you," He could say, "convinceth Me of sin?" And there was silence. Vague charges indeed there were, such as that He was in league with the powers of evil,[d] or that He was a revolutionist.[e] But these soon refuted themselves. And ever since, during eighteen centuries, the curiosity and the passions of mankind have been at work upon the records of His life, and have succeeded no better than did His contemporaries. Now and then the critics think that they have made good a case against His moral per-

[a] St. John viii. 29. [b] Ibid. xiv. 30.
[c] Ibid. viii. 46. [d] St. Matt. ix. 34; xii. 24.
[e] St. Luke xxiii. 1, 2

fection. But presently it is shown that some fundamental circumstance in His position and claims has been overlooked, or that some unwarranted assumption has been imported into the discussion. And again He asks, "Which of you convinceth Me of sin?" And again there is silence.

In this sinlessness He is, although our Model, yet beyond our full reach of imitation. In our broken lives we cannot reproduce the complete image of the Immaculate Lamb. The best of men knows that in his best moments he is beset by motives, or thoughts, or inclinations, from which Christ was utterly free. "If we say that we have no sin, we deceive ourselves, and the truth is not in us."[a] But this does not destroy, it rather enhances, the value of Our Lord's example. In all departments of thought and work, the Ideal is, strictly speaking, unattainable by man; yet man should never lose sight of it. In the Gospels Ideal Human Life appears in a form of flesh and blood; it is the Ideal, and beyond us; yet not the less precious as a stimulus and a guide to our efforts at self-improvement.

2. Secondly, we are struck by the balance and proportion of excellences in our Lord's human character. As a rule, if a man possesses some one excellence in an unusual degree, he will be found to exhibit some fault or shortcoming in an opposite direction. If he is dignified, he is probably proud; if he is kind and communicative, he is not unlikely to be wanting in self-respect. If he is thoughtful and reflective, he is also, it may be, cold and unsympathising; if he is affectionate and warm-hearted, he is liable to gusts of thoughtless impulse. Is he sincere? —he perhaps thinks it necessary to exhibit his honesty in

[a] 1 St. John i. 8.

sulkiness or incivility. Is he civil and considerate?—perchance, he carries his courtesy to the verge of insincerity. The intellectual are often wanting in affection; the affectionate are sometimes unintelligent. Our finite and fallen nature exhausts itself by an effort in a single direction; it would almost seem bound to atone for a temporary success by some compensating failure.

Of this want of balance in excellence, of this exaggeration in particular forms of excellence which entails an accompanying defect, there is no trace in our Lord. Read His Life over and over again, with this point in view; and nothing will strike you more than its faultless proportions. In so vast a field, take one illustration out of many: the balance which He keeps between severity and tenderness.

Certainly there is a severity in His attitude towards evil, especially towards insincerity, which startles us. It flashes from Him only now and then; but with terrible force. He calls the generation in which He lives adulterous,[a] evil,[b] sinful,[c] wicked,[d] perverse.[e] He says that the blood of all the prophets which has been shed from the foundation of the world shall be required of it.[f] He announces that Capernaum, which is exalted unto heaven, shall be cast down to hell.[g] He is unsparing in His denunciations of the Pharisees and Scribes: "Ye love greetings in the market-places;"[h] "Ye bind heavy burdens on men's shoulders, but ye yourselves touch them not with one of your fingers;"[i] "Ye compass sea and land to make one proselyte;"[k] "Ye strain at a gnat, and swallow a camel;"[l] "Ye devour widows' houses, and

[a] St. Matt. xii. 39 : xvi. 4.   [b] *Ibid.* xii. 34.   [c] St. Mark viii. 38.
[d] St. Matt. xii. 45.   [e] *Ibid.* xvii. 17.   [f] St. Luke xi. 50.
[i] St. Matt. xi. 23.   [h] St. Luke xi. 43.   [i] *Ibid.* xi. 46.
[k] St. Matt. xxiii. 15.   [l] *Ibid.* xxiii. 24.

for a pretence make long prayers;"ᵃ "Whited sepulchres, ye appear righteous before men, but within ye are full of hypocrisy and iniquity."ᵇ

We do not know enough of our fellow-men ever to use this language: but at least we may endeavour to follow our Lord in the hatred of evil which He thus expresses. No good man can be indifferent towards evil. "Neither doth he abhor anything that is evil,"ᶜ is the note of the reprobate.

Yet there is a tenderness in our Lord, which is not elsewhere found in combination with such severity. He is not a cold philosopher, who exposes weakness, and has no pity for sorrow. He does not condescend to us as from a superior level: He is, among us, as one of ourselves, "touched with a feeling of our infirmities."ᵈ He is at home at Bethany; "Jesus loved Martha, and her sister, and Lazarus."ᵉ He sheds tears at the grave of Lazarus.ᶠ He weeps over Jerusalem at the thought of its approaching ruin.ᵍ He absolves the sinner, knowing all about her past history; as she seeks Him out in the Pharisee's house, and bathes His feet with her tears.ʰ He takes the part of the convicted adulteress against her accusers: "Neither do I condemn thee."ⁱ All this would be easy if He were indifferent to moral evil. He hates it as man never hated it before, yet He is tenderness itself towards its victims.

3. Consider again a feature which runs through His whole character; its simplicity. In nothing that He says or does can we detect any trace of contrivance or of aiming at effect. We all know how rare in ordinary life is

ᵃ St. Matt. xxiii. 14.   ᵇ *Ibid.* xxiii. 27, 28.   ᶜ Ps. xxxvi. 4.
ᵈ Heb. iv. 15.   ᵉ St. John xi. 5.   ᶠ *Ibid.* xi. 35.
ᵍ St. Luke xix. 41.   ʰ *Ibid.* vii. 37, 38, 48.   ⁱ St. John viii. 11.

an approach to perfect simplicity of character. "Every man," says a cynical maxim, "is, at some time, an actor." The effort to create an impression is the result sometimes of timidity, sometimes of vanity. But it always mars moral beauty, whether in speech or work. Our Lord always says what He has to say in the most natural and unpretending words. His sentences unfold themselves without effort or system, just as persons and occasions demand. He uses the language, not of the schools, but of the people; as, in other circumstances, we may be sure, He would have used the language, not of the people, but of the schools. He is thus at once simple and profound; profound, as was never man before, because so simple. We all of us understand the Sermon on the Mount, or the Last Discourse in the Supper-Room. Yet we are conscious, dimly though it be, of heights and depths behind the well-known words, which reach away into infinitude. He takes the illustrations which come ready to His hand, or which meet His eye: the birds of the air,[a] the rain,[b] the red and lowering sky,[c] the lily,[d] the grain of mustard-seed,[e] the corn,[f] the ruined tower of Siloam.[g] On these He grafts this or that fragment of the Eternal Truth. We cannot enrich His teaching by any additions. Our crude efforts could not but disfigure its incomparable beauty.

As with His words, so is it with His actions. He acts with a view to the glory of God the Father, and with a view to nothing else. Hence a directness and transparency in His conduct, which we feel in every detail of it. He is a poor Man, and He never affects to be independent of His class. He is never eccentric. His dress, His mode

[a] St. Matt. vi. 25, 26.  [b] Ibid. v. 45.  [c] Ibid. xvi. 2, 3.
[d] Ibid. vi. 28-34.  [e] Ibid. xiii. 31.  [f] St. John xii. 24.
[g] St. Luke xiii. 4.

of life, His habits, are without a trace of pretension or singularity. He pursues His great work sitting by a well,[a] or on a mountain,[b] or in a fishing-boat,[c] or on the shore of a lake,[d] or in a synagogue,[e] or in one of the porches of the Temple,[f] or as He walks along the road.[g]

Every situation yields its opportunity ready to His Hand. He attends a wedding,[h] He cures a paralytic,[i] He writes upon the ground,[k] He eats with the Pharisees,[l] He raises the dead to life,[m] He washes His disciples' feet;[n] as each occasion comes, from day to day, from hour to hour. The most important and awful acts follow on with the most trivial and ordinary. There is no effort, no disturbing or pretentious movement. All is simple, as though all were commonplace. This absence of anything like an attempt to produce an unusual impression reveals a Soul possessed with a sense of the majesty and power of Truth. Depend upon it, in the degree in which any man becomes really great he becomes simple also.

4. One further point to be remarked in our Lord's Example is the stress which it lays upon those forms of excellence which make no great show, such as patience, humility, meekness, and the like. As we read the Gospels, we are led to see that the highest type of human excellence consists less in acting well than in suffering well. The ancient world never understood this. With the ancients virtue was active force. Yet the conditions

---

[a] St. John iv. 6-26.  
[b] St. Matt. v. vi. vii.  
[c] St. Matt. xiii. 2-52.  
[d] St. John xxi. 4-22.  
[e] St. Matt. iv. 23 ; xiii. 54.  
[f] St. John x. 23-38.  
[g] St. Luke xxiv. 15-29.  
[h] St. John ii. 1-11.  
[i] St. Mark ii. 3-12.  
[k] St. John viii. 6, 8.  
[l] St. Luke vii. 36.  
[m] St. Matt. ix. 23-25 ; St. Luke vii. 12-15 ; St. John xi. 43, 44.  
[n] St. John xiii. 4, 5.

of our human life are such that, whether we will or not, we are more frequently called upon to endure than to act. Therefore the spirit in which we endure is of capital importance. Our Lord restored passive virtue to its true and forgotten place in human conduct. He revealed the beauty, the majesty of patience, meekness, uncomplaining submission. He Himself achieved more than any of the sons of men. But we may dare to say that He suffered more than He achieved, or rather, that His work was largely achieved by suffering. It is this side of His example of which St. Peter is thinking as being so useful to the Christian slaves to whom for the moment he is writing. "Who, when He was reviled, reviled not again; when He suffered, He threatened not; but committed Himself to Him that judgeth righteously."[a] Christ had before Him a purpose of infinite beneficence; that of recovering man to God and to endless happiness. Yet in carrying it out He met with scorn, resistance, hatred, persecution. He was suspected, denounced, traduced. His Name was cast out as evil. Justice, alike in its form and its spirit, was conspicuously violated in order to crush Him. Religion itself was prostituted to the lowest purposes of private animosity. He was led forth to die, amid a tempest of denunciation, which was from first to last unmerited. Man's ingratitude and hatred pierced His soul. Yet no unkind or impatient word falls from Him. He bears in silence the contradiction of sinners against Himself.[b] He prays, "Father, forgive them."[c] He is obedient unto death.[d]

"Leaving us an example, that ye should follow His steps." 'Yes,' it is said, 'it is a beautiful, a transcen-

[a] 1 St. Pet. ii. 23.
[b] Heb. xii. 3.
[c] St. Luke xxiii. 34.
[d] Phil. ii. 8.

dental picture; and if Christ were merely man, we might perhaps imitate Him! But then the Church and the Bible tell us that He is God as well as Man; and this seems to remove Him from the category of beings whom man can imitate. He has a Higher Nature, distinct capacities, another sphere of action. He is a superhuman Personage. His theological glory in the fourth Gospel is fatal to His moral value as a human Model in the first three.'

My brethren, the difference between Jesus Christ and ourselves is indeed infinite; it is the difference between the Creator and the creature. And yet He is also truly Man; and for the purposes of imitation the truth of His Manhood secures all that we require. For the purposes of imitation, He is practically not more out of our reach than is a father of great genius and goodness out of the reach of his child. There are many actions, many words, many silences which the child can understand; they are quite independent of the father's superiority, and they have the same significance whether the father is their author or the child. Nay more, identity of nature is not necessary to imitation. We may at times imitate even the lower creatures with advantage: in their generosity, their patience, their brightness, their forgivingness. And if we saw the blessed angels who are around us and tend us, we should surely see majestic beings, in many ways utterly above us, yet whose patience and love and industry we might well copy. Our Lord Jesus Christ Himself bids us be perfect even as our Father Which is in heaven is perfect.[a] Certainly we cannot imitate Jesus Christ when He heals the sick, or raises the dead. But we can enter into and cherish the spirit of those high works of mercy. We can do the natural kindnesses which

[a] St. Matt. v. 48.

are akin to them. And there are deeds and words of His which we can copy in the letter as well as the spirit.

Indeed, the objection has been already solved by the experience of eighteen centuries. The Imitation of Christ is the title of that exquisite book of the Flemish recluse, Thomas à Kempis, which approaches more nearly to the perfect spirit of the New Testament than any which has been written since the death of the Apostles. The Imitation of Christ is the perpetual source of saintly effort in the Church of Christ. Generation follows generation, looking unto Jesus.[a] One man says, I will imitate His patience; and another, I will copy His humility; and a third, I would practise, though afar off, His obedience; and a fourth, His love for men; and another, His simplicity; and another, His benevolence; and another, His perpetual communion with the Father; and another, His renunciation of His Own will. When one point is gained, others follow. Thus, little by little, "Christ is formed,"[b] as St. Paul expresses it, in the characters of His servants. Thus, practically speaking, experience has shown that our Lord's Divinity is no bar whatever to our imitation of His life as Man.

This imitation of our Lord is not a duty which we are free to accept or decline. "The elect," says St. Paul, "are predestined to be conformed to the image of the Son of God."[c] If there is no effort at conformity, there is no true note of predestination. We cannot enter into the designs of God in giving us His Son, if we are making no efforts to be like Him. It has been said with truth that every good man with whom we meet in life adds to our responsibility. One day we must account for the use we have made of his example. But what must be our responsibility for the knowledge of that Life Which is described

[a] Heb. xii. 2.  [b] Gal. iv. 19.  [c] Rom. viii. 29.

in the Gospels? "Never but once passed before the imagination of man, and never but once was witnessed on this earth so heavenly a vision." "There alone, in all human history, we meet a Being Who never did an injury, and never resented one; Who never uttered an untruth; never lost an opportunity of doing good; Who was generous among the selfish; upright among the false; pure among the sensual; wiser far than the wisest of the sons of men; loving, gentle, yet withal invincibly resolute; never so meek and patient as when persecuted by a cruel and ungrateful world."[a] A devoted layman of the Church of England[b] said on his deathbed, that, on reviewing his life, the omission which he chiefly deplored was that he had not made a daily effort to study and imitate Jesus Christ as He is described in the Gospels. Is not this a common omission even with serious Christians? Should we not do what we may, while yet we may, thus to follow in the footsteps of the Perfect Man?

And to return to the words of the Collect: if we have any fear lest, in copying our Lord's example, we should forget His Atoning Death, or His indwelling Presence; that too will be best decided by experiment. His Example shows us what we were meant to be; but it also reveals to us, with unsparing frankness, what we are. There is a sense in which Christ's Example is like the Jewish law. Like the old Jewish law, it is a standard of life; only a far higher and more exacting standard. Like the Jewish law, the Life of Christ reveals to us our own sins and shortcomings; like the law, the Life of Christ is a schoolmaster to bring us to the Cross of Christ. We come to Him, out of heart with ourselves, emptied, happily emptied, of self; crushed by a sense of our utter un-

[a] Young, *Christ of History*; quoted from memory.
[b] Mr. John Bowdler.

worthiness to bear His Name and to wear His livery. And once more He extends His pierced Hand to pardon, and He offers His Body and His Blood to strengthen our souls for such work as may be needed to make us more like Himself. Surely those of us will most thankfully receive Christ's inestimable benefit, in becoming the great Sacrifice for sin, and, by His Presence within the soul, the hope of Glory,[a] who have known what it is to try, ever so feebly, " to follow in the blessed steps of His most holy Life."

[a] Col. i. 27.

# SERMON XXXI.

## TRUTH THE BOND OF LOVE.

2 St. John i, 2.

*The Elder unto the elect lady and her children, whom I love in the truth; and not I only, but also all they that have known the truth; for the Truth's sake, Which dwelleth in us, and shall be with us for ever.*

HOW much is implied, very often, by the phrase or style with which a letter is begun or ended! How different is the formal "Sir" from "My dear Sir;" and, again, how much does this differ from the intimacy which addresses by a Christian name! How many shades of feeling are represented by "Your obedient servant," "Your faithful servant," "Yours truly," "Yours very faithfully," "Yours affectionately," "Yours most affectionately"! Those different styles mean a great deal; and as it is now, so it was in the Apostolic age. The opening words of St. John's Second Epistle are full of interest of this kind. They introduce us to a whole department of private or personal feeling, just as truly as any letter we may receive by the post to-morrow morning.

How does the writer describe himself? "John, an Apostle of Jesus Christ," or "John, a servant of Jesus Christ?" No; this is the style of other Apostles: of St. Paul, St. Peter, St. James, St. Jude. St. John calls himself simply "the Elder," both in this and his third letter, to Gaius. Perhaps the word had better be rendered "Presbyter," as indeed it stands in the original. It has led some persons to suppose, both in ancient and modern times, that these two Epistles were not written by the Apostle John at all, but by a Presbyter named John, who lived at Ephesus at the same time as the Apostle. But to say nothing of the prevailing belief of the Church, this opinion is not fairly borne out by the contents of the Epistles themselves. To mention one particular only, it is inconsistent with the tone of Apostolical authority in which the writer refers to the "many deceivers who have come into the world" as "antichrists" in the Second Epistle,[a] and to Diotrephes, with his passion for pre-eminence, in the Third.[b] The truth would appear to be that St. John calls himself by way of endearment "the Presbyter," when writing to a family with which he has been long on terms of intimacy. Nothing is more welcome to persons of simple character who are in high office than an opportunity of laying its formalities aside; they like to address others and to be themselves addressed in their personal capacity, or by a title in which there is more affection than form. Every one knows how largely this might be illustrated from the annals of royalty; and years before St. John wrote, St. Peter had set the example of dropping his Apostolic title when writing to his brethren in Christ's work. "The elders," or presbyters, "which are among you I exhort, who am also a presbyter and a witness of the sufferings of Christ."[c] And so it would seem that, just as we might speak of some one person as "the Vicar," or "the Colonel," as if there was no one else in the world who held these offices, so St. John was known in the family to which he writes by the affectionately familiar title of "the Presbyter." And he introduces

[a] 2 St. John 7.     [b] 3 St. John 9.     [c] 1 St. Pet. v. 1.

himself to them by a description around which so much affection had gathered, and which seemed to have acquired a new appropriateness in his advanced age. Although in the eye of the whole Christian Church he filled the great place of an Apostle of Jesus Christ, and as such had jurisdiction over the whole body of the faithful; although he had been admitted by the Divine Master to an intimacy of affection shared with no other Apostle; although he was now the only surviving representative of the Sacred College; yet he puts out of sight this weight of high station and of untold responsibility; and when he would pour out his heart to the chosen mother and her children, he calls himself by a name which at once puts them at their ease with him. He is simply "the Presbyter."

To whom does he write? "The Presbyter to the elect lady and her children." There is no sufficient reason for supposing, with some writers, that by "elect lady" St. John is personifying a particular Christian Church. He is writing to an actual individual: to a Christian mother and her family. It may be that the word translated "lady" is really a proper name, "Kyria." But this would not affect the idea we must form of her position and character. She was an elderly person, probably a widow, living with her grown-up children. When St. John says that she was loved by "all them that knew the truth," he makes it plain that her name was at least well known in the Asiatic Churches, and that she was a person of real and high excellence. There were many such good women in the Church of the Apostolic age. What Dorcas was to St. Peter;[a] what Lydia of Philippi,[b] and Phœbe of Cenchrea,[c] and Priscilla,[d] and many others, were to St. Paul, such was this Christian lady to St. John. Long before this, as it

[a] Acts ix. 36-39.    [b] Acts xvi. 14, 15.    [c] Rom. xvi. 1.
[d] Acts xviii. 1-3, 18, 26; Rom. xvi. 3, 4.

is probable, the Blessed Virgin Mother, whom our Lord, speaking from His Cross, had committed to the care of the most beloved of His disciples, had been taken to her rest. And the "elect lady and her children, whom he loved in the truth," would have helped to brighten, with human affection, the later years of the aged Saint who had thus outlived all his contemporaries.

Here then, within the sacred canon, is an Apostolic letter; and to whom is it written? Not to Apostolic Christendom, as was St. John's First Epistle; not to some separate Church of more or less importance, as were most of St. Paul's Epistles; not to great bishops, as were the pastoral instructions to Timothy and Titus; not to a fellow-labourer with Apostles, as the letter to Philemon; not to a Christian, whose works of charity were witnessed before the Church, alike by brethren and by strangers, as was St. John's last correspondent, Gaius. St. John writes to a lady and her children, living apparently in retirement, with no public title to a claim on the attention of the Apostle. And thus, in the Bible itself, we are face to face with a relationship of intimate friendship, which might have existed, and the like of which does constantly exist, in our own days not less truly than in those of the Apostles. The Christianity of Ephesus under St. John's eyes was not an ideal and abstract thing, acting upon men and upon life quite differently from anything we witness now. Then as now it was a living practical influence; a domestic friend, multiplying, modifying, colouring, brightening, purifying the daily relations of life. It came home to Christians in the first century as it comes home to them in the nineteenth, as a bond of friendship. In this view, and with an eye to practical guidance, St. John's affectionate address to the Christian mother and her family deserves careful attention.

Let us then consider the moral atmosphere which surrounded, and the motive-power which created and sustained, that strong bond of affection which bound the heart of St. John to the Christian lady and her family.

i.

The atmosphere of this friendship was sincerity. "Whom I love," not in *the* truth (there is no article in the original), but "in truth." Not "truly:" St. John would have used an adverb to say that. What he means is that truth—truth of thought, truth of feeling, truth of speech and intercourse—was the very air in which his affection for this Christian lady had grown up and maintained itself. And the word which he uses to describe this affection points to the same conclusion. It does not mean instinctive personal affection; affection based on feeling and impulse, such as exists between near relations. Still less does it denote that lower form of affection, which has its roots and its energy in passion and sense. It stands for that kind of affection which is based on a reasoned perception of excellence in its object; and thus it is the word which is invariably used to describe the love that man ought to have for God. But such a love as this between man and man grows up and is fostered in an atmosphere of truthfulness. It is grounded, not on feeling or passion, but on a reciprocal conviction of simplicity of purpose; and, being true in its origin, it is true at every stage of its development. It is mortally wounded, this "love in truth," when once it is conscious of distinct insincerity. When once it has reason to doubt the worthiness of its object; when once it falters, in its utterance of simple truth, from a secret fear that there is something which cannot be probed to the quick, or which cannot bear the sunlight, then its life is gone, even though its forms and courtesies should survive. It may even be strengthened by a temporary misunderstanding when each friend is sincere. It dies, when there is on either side a well-grounded suspicion of the taint of insincerity.

That the sense of a common integrity of purpose, a common anxiety to be true, and to recognise truth, is an atmosphere especially favourable to the growth of personal friendships, is observable at this moment in England among students of the natural sciences. Here and there you may note petty jealousies; the desire to anticipate a rival; the envy of a great reputation; the disposition to patent for purposes of selfish gain a discovery which belongs rightly, not to any single genius, but to humanity at large. But these things are the exception: they are not the rule. The rule is that the pursuit of scientific truth, in this respect unlike the practice of a common profession or art, has a tendency to create a sense of fellowship which soon ripens into friendship. The common investigation, prosecuted day by day, into natural facts and laws; the assurance of a common nobility of purpose, of a common liability to failure, of a common anxiety to pursue and proclaim fact—creates a feeling of brotherhood which traverses other differences, and is an enrichment of human life. It is not a common share in ascertained truth which is here in question, because there may be the widest difference as to what truth is ascertained. It is a common determination to be loyal to truth; to assert when assertion is a duty, and at all costs; to retract when retractation is a duty, and at all costs. Thus there is a communion of the truthful in the halls of Science, as there is a communion of the saints on earth and in Paradise: there are signs discerned by the far-sighted penetration of truthful minds in all who bear the same patent of moral nobility, and these signs at once form a title to affection and respect.

It was in a common sense of truthfulness of purpose that St. John's love for the lady and her children grew and strengthened. Differing, as we know they did, in the positions they respectively filled in the Christian Church; differing, as we may presume they did, in other moral and in almost all spiritual endowments, very greatly indeed; they yet had this common bond between them, that they loved truth for its own sake. Truthfulness was the atmosphere in which they both lived, and which made each an object of affection to the other. "The Presbyter to the elect lady and her children, whom I love in truth."

St. John loved this lady and her children "in truth;" and therefore he did not hesitate, when occasion made it a duty, to put a strain on their affection. Those who love in truth, like St. John, can, when it is necessary to do so, carry out St. Paul's precept about speaking the truth in love. There is such a thing as speaking the truth in ill-nature, or in hatred. We may insist on truth, not for the sake of those to whom we speak, but because truth happens to coincide with our own prejudice. We wish to have our fling. We are more anxious to have truth on our side than to be on the side of truth. Many true things are said, not in the interests of truth, but in the interests of passion; not for the benefit of the instructed, but for the gratification of the instructor. This is to speak the truth in selfishness; and it rouses a keener sense of opposition than is roused by the proclamation of simple falsehood. For it is felt, and felt truly, that truth is here made to do work which, if it were possible, would degrade her, by thus harnessing her to the chariot of selfish passion; and the very force and power which is inseparable from truth is the measure of the antagonism which is created by a conviction that it is not for her own sake, but for something very different indeed in nature and purpose, that she is invoked at all.

St. John, as a great master of faith and charity, could be at once tender and uncompromising. It was necessary in these days at Ephesus. There were dangers to which the Apostle could not close his eyes. His love was not a vague sentiment, unregulated by any principle; it was a love of all men, but it was pre-eminently a love of each man's immortal soul. Therefore in proportion to its sincerity and intensity it was outspoken. There were new teachers at Ephesus who confessed not that Jesus Christ had come in the flesh.[a] They denied the very fundamental truth of the Incarnation of the Son of God. St. John rejoices to hear that some of the children of this lady walked in truth.[b] But he also implies that some did not. He entreats the family not to imperil his work among them; they must see to it, "that we lose not the things that we have wrought."[c] He advises them to shun contact with erroneous teachers: what chance, humanly speaking, would this Christian mother have in an intellectual encounter with the trained and subtle apostles of falsehood? "If any come unto you, and bring not this doctrine," namely, that of the Apostles, "receive him not into your house, neither bid him God speed: for he that biddeth him God speed is a partaker of his evil deeds."[d] St. John, the Apostle of love, uses language which the world, with its strange fondness for the charity of indifference, would call uncharitable. Yet it is because St. John loves, not in a sentimental, hazy, fruitless way, but in truth,

[a] 2 St. John 7.   [b] Ibid. 4.   [c] Ibid. 8.   [d] Ibid. 10, 11.

and because he knows that the accents of love will not be misunderstood, that he is thus outspoken.

It would be well, brethren, if there was more of love in truth, as distinct from love by impulse, among us; among those of us, for instance, who are already bound to each other by ties of natural affection. Sincerity does not chill natural love; but it raises a mere passion to the rank of a moral power. How much trouble might parents not save their children in after years by a little plain speaking, dictated, not by the desire to assert authority, but by simple affection! How many a son can and does give as his excuse for doing wrong, "My father never told me that there was any harm in it"! Too often parents love their children, not in truth, but with a purely selfish love. They will not risk a passing misunderstanding, even for the sake of the child's best interests hereafter. And they live to find that in the event such love defeats its object, by forfeiting those solid titles to gratitude and respect which a perfect sincerity can alone secure.

II.

What was the motive-power of St. John's love? St. John replies,'"For the Truth's sake, Which dwelleth in us, and shall be with us for ever." He adds that all who knew the Truth share in this affection. Here we have an article before "Truth": "the Truth" means here, not a habit or temper of mind, but a body of ascertained fact, which is fact, whether acknowledged or not by the mind to be so. What is here called "the Truth" by St. John, we should in modern language speak of as "the True Faith." This was the combining link, as sincerity of purpose was the atmosphere, of the affection which existed between this Christian lady and St. John.

Doubtless there are many other links which produce among men a feeling of brotherhood. A sense of common wrong will do this. It is not to be supposed that the match-makers, who walked through the City last Monday, were all of them on terms of mutual endearment before the Chancellor of the Exchequer announced his budget in Parliament. They were probably many of them rivals in their trade.[a] But you could not meet them without feeling that they were, at least for the time being, on terms of the greatest intimacy; this intimacy was created by their sharing in common the sense of a real or supposed wrong. The same effect is sometimes produced by a common triumph. After a victory or a political success men's hearts are opened towards each other; and travellers tell how, among the warm-hearted and impulsive peoples of Southern Europe, this shows itself in outward demonstrations of affection,—hand-claspings, embraces, tears,—which would be unnatural in us colder Englishmen. But in cases of this kind feeling is transient: it passes with the occasion. By this time, no doubt, the match-makers, having gained their point, have returned to social feelings of an average temperature.

What was wanted for humanity was a bond, strong enough in itself, and in the permanency of its effects, to link heart to heart, wherever it was acknowledged. It has been urged that the consciousness of being a man, of having a share in the great brotherhood of humankind, ought to do this of itself. It ought, no doubt, according to the original design of God. But, does it? As a matter of fact, does man love his brother man? Do the Europeans, as a rule, love the African races, simply

[a] Procession of the match-makers to the Houses of Parliament, to deprecate Mr. Lowe's proposed addition to the budget, on Monday, April 24, 1871.

because they are men? Do Englishmen love foreigners? Did they, two generations ago, love Frenchmen? Do you now love Russians? Nay; does the sense of a common humanity suffice to cancel the differences which political and social causes create among ourselves? And if not, why not? Have we not here one of the many evidences of some disorganising influence in humanity, which makes all expectation of a widespread love of man as man utterly Utopian, unless a new tie shall bind together human hearts, with a more than human power?

Yes; another link was needed to bind men together; and St. John recognised this link in that body of Divinely revealed facts which he calls "the Truth." By the Truth St. John here means a something the very existence of which appears improbable or impossible to some minds in our own day. He means a body of ascertained facts about God, about the soul, about the means of reaching God, and being blessed by Him, about the Eternal Future, about the true rule of man's conduct, and the true secret of his happiness and wellbeing. Other knowledge which human beings possess is no doubt true; such, for instance, as that which enables us to make the most of the visible world in which God has placed us. But St. John calls this higher knowledge *the* Truth; as being incomparably more important; as interesting man, not merely in his capacity of a creature of time, but in his capacity of a being destined for eternity. And this truth, as St. John conceived it, was not merely a set of propositions resting upon evidence. It was that: but it was more. It centred in a Person, Whom St. John had seen, heard, touched, handled; Who had lived as man never lived before, had spoken as man never spake before, had died in agony, and had risen in triumph from death, and had left the world with an assurance that He would return to judge it. That

Teacher, Whom St. John had known, did not merely say, "I teach the truth;" other teachers have said that. He said in so many words, "I am the Truth."[a] He meant that what He said and did was final and absolute; that man would never get beyond Him to a higher knowledge of God; that all truth centred in or radiated from Him. St. John believed this. While others, early Gnostics for instance, maintained that every religious creed, Christianity included, is but the product of an effort of the human mind to hold communion with the Infinite; that every creed therefore is only relatively true, combining a certain proportion of truth with a certain proportion of error; that to ascribe absolute truth to any one creed is an intellectual impertinence; St. John proclaimed, simply, fearlessly: "We know that the Son of God is come, and hath given us an understanding, that we may know Him that is true, and we are in Him that is true, even in His Son Jesus Christ."[b]

To share this faith was to share a bond of common affection. To have the same Ideal of conduct before the soul; the same view of the meaning of life; the same hopes and fears about that which will follow it; above all, the same devotion to a Person,—the Incomparable Person of Jesus Christ—was to have a vast fund of common sympathy. Students who have worked side by side; soldiers who have fought side by side; children who have been brought up in one household, know something of this sympathy which is the full inheritance of Christians. It traverses differences of age, differences of station, differences of culture. It unites St. John, soaring with his eagle eye to the highest heavens, and the sincere but probably commonplace mother of a family in Ephesus. It had created this friendship. St. John was Christ's

[a] St. John xiv. 6.   [b] 1 St. John v. 20.

Apostle because of his faith in Christ; and this faith was the binding link between himself and the Christian mother. To us it might have seemed that, with the Church expanding around him, St. John's mind would have been wholly occupied with the larger interests of administration; and that he would have had no leisure to attend to the wants of individuals. And if St. John had been only a statesman, endeavouring to carry out a great policy, or only a philosopher intent upon diffusing his ideas, he would have contented himself, to use the modern phrase, with "acting upon the masses." But as an Apostle of Christ he had a very different work to do: he had to save souls. And souls are to be saved, not gregariously, but one by one. Each soul is the fruit, generally speaking, of much patient and loving toil on the part of some one Christian worker. This work is too great, too awful, to be done compendiously; there is nothing in the spiritual world which really corresponds to those inventions in machinery which supersede the need of individual hand-labour. Souls are saved in all ages through the earnest efforts of other souls, themselves illumined by Christian truth, and warmed by Christian love. They who are brought out of darkness and error into a knowledge and love of God and His Blessed Son, generally are brought, as were Timothy of Derbe, Lydia of Philippi, Philemon of Colosse, Kyria of Ephesus, and Phœbe of Corinth, by the loving interest and care of some servant of Christ. No philosophy can thus create and combine. The philosophers of all ages, even if good friends among themselves, can only set up a fancied aristocracy of intellect for themselves, and are very jealous about admitting the people into the Olympus of their sympathies. No political scheme can do this: history is there to answer. But love, with sincerity for its sphere, and with Jesus Christ for its object, can do it. Love did it of old, love does it now.

But already I hear the retort which this assertion provokes. 'Do you venture,' some one says, 'to say that love still binds Christian to Christian, when our society is itself divided by the divisions of Christians, when the very world is deafened by the noise of Christian controversy? Do you suppose that your rhetorical pictures will for one moment stand the test of our actual experience? And if they will not, is it not imprudent to challenge a comparison between the ideal and the reality; between that which is before our eyes, and that which ought to be?'

My brethren, I admit that within Christendom, within the Church, there are divisions, many and regrettable. But were there none, think you, at Ephesus in the days of St. John? Only read what he writes to Gaius, in his Third Epistle, about Diotrephes.[a] But, you reply, are not our divisions more serious? Do they not at times deepen into a severance on fundamental points? So it was in St. John's day, at least in the case of Cerinthus and his sympathisers; for such there were still within the Church.[b] Yet love, the love of the Apostle for all the faithful, the love of the faithful for each other, remained. True, we hear much and unavoidably of Christian differences to-day: and the world anxiously chronicles our misunderstandings, if it does not exaggerate them. It says nothing of that which underlies them; the deep, loving, praying, working life of the Church of Christ. It photographs the spots on the sun's surface, but it says

---

[a] 3 St. John 9, 10.
[b] The teachers alluded to in 1 St. John iv. 1-3 must not be confounded with those in 1 St. John ii. 19. The former were still in communion with the Church: the latter had passed out of her.

nothing of the sun. It studies the life of Christendom as a certain student is said to have studied the history of England: he confined himself upon principle to the great rebellion of the seventeenth century. It forgets that men do not quarrel about that which does not interest them, and that it is easy to be charitable when you are profoundly indifferent. But anything is better than the torpor of a materialised people, to whom God and eternity are as if they did not exist. If unity is better far than the misunderstandings of brethren, any misunderstandings are preferable to stolid unconcern about matters of the first importance. And as I have said, the relative importance of differences may be easily exaggerated. The surface of the Atlantic may be swept by a hurricane till its waves run thirty feet high. But a few fathoms below this agitation there are tranquil depths in which the storm is as unfelt as if all was calm, and which will be as they are when the tempest has abated.

And, among the counteracting and restorative influences which carry the Church of Christ unharmed through the animated and sometimes passionate discussion of public questions, private friendships, formed and strengthened in the atmosphere of a fearless sincerity, and knit and banded together by a common share in the Faith of ages, are, humanly speaking, among the strongest. One and all, we may, at some time, realise to the letter the language of St. John to this Christian mother. Many who are here must realise it now. They have learnt to love in truth, not by impulse. They have learnt to bind and rivet their love by the strong bond of the common and unchanging Faith. All who know anything of Jesus Christ know something of this affection for some of His servants: some of us, it may be, know much, much more than we can feel that we deserve. May He of His grace nevertheless strengthen it; may He strengthen all love that is nurtured in an atmosphere of truth, and secured by faith in His Adorable Person and His Redemptive Work. For such love is not like a human passion, which dies gradually away with the enfeeblement and the death of the nerves and of the brain. It is created and fed by the truth which "dwelleth" in the Christian soul, and which, as St. John adds, "shall be with us for ever." It is guaranteed to last, even as its Eternal Object lasts. It is born and is matured amid the things of time. But from the first it belongs to, and in the event it is incorporated with, the life of Eternity.

# SERMON XXXII.

## FREEDOM AND LAW

1 St. Peter ii. 16.

*As free, and not using your liberty for a cloke of maliciousness, but as the servants of God.*

ST. PETER here touches a note which appeals to the human heart in all ages and everywhere. Freedom is one of those words which need no recommendation: it belongs to the same category as light, order, progress, law. It is one of the ideas which, in some sense or other, mankind accepts as an axiom; as a landmark or principle of healthful life which is beyond discussion. What do we mean by freedom? We mean the power of a living being to act without hindrance according to the true law of its life. A mineral, therefore, is in no sense capable of freedom; it neither grows nor moves; it does not live. A tree, in a very attenuated or in a metaphorical sense, is capable of freedom: a tree does contain within itself the mystery of a vital principle, which requires certain conditions for its necessary development: and thus we may speak of its having freedom to grow. The lower animals, in very various degrees, are capable of something which may with much better reason be called freedom; their capacity for it varies proportionately to their approach to the frontier of self-conscious, self-determining life as manifested in human beings. The brute does not merely grow, he moves from place to place. He does not move by any fatal necessity, but can take this direction or that as his instinct prompts him. To interfere with his movement is to limit his freedom. Still it is only instinct which he obeys. He does not reflect; he does not choose, while comprehending his power of choice; he is really, from moment to moment, governed by that which is for the time being the strongest impulse or passion upon him. If he is free to run about, to eat what he likes, to sleep and rest when he likes, he has all that he wants. His instinct will probably guide him to sleep, eat, and take exercise in such proportions and at such times as the law of his life requires.

With man it is otherwise. For man is a moral being: he reflects, and knows what he is doing when he reflects; he chooses, and knows what he is doing in this exercise of choice. Much of man's life, no doubt, is vegetative, like that of a tree. More of it is sentient and under the government of instinct, like that of an animal. We men go through thousands of movements and acts, every day of our lives, without, as we say, thinking about them. We obey instinct, or habit, or some governing inclination, without throwing any conscious and deliberate energy into the act of obedience. But our true life is higher than this. Man lives and acts as man; he asserts that which is properly his human freedom, when he obeys some law which he knows he can disobey. For man is a moral being, and in this his greatness consists. We may often hear or read fine platitudes about the insignificance of man as compared with the planets; with the stars and suns that shine above our heads. Certainly, if the greatness of created beings is to be determined by their material bulk, man is insignificant enough. He ranks far below many other animals around him on his own planet. But man can do that which no planet can do: he can obey or refuse to obey the highest law of his life. The planet cannot leave its appointed orbit. It circles on, age after age, in obedience to the law which governs it: God has "given it a law which shall not be broken."[a] Man can disobey the highest law of his life: this liberty is at once his prerogative and his danger. The highest law of man's life is to know, to love, and to serve the Being Who gave it him; the Being Whose very existence has not dawned upon the most intelligent of the creatures below man. God wills that man should obey Him freely: that is, that he should be able to refuse obedience, and yet should obey. Thus man's consummate prerogative is necessarily linked to a fearful capacity for declining to exercise it. If man obeyed God only as a planet revolves, or only as a brute eats, he would not be man.

Now man's freedom is exercised in three main departments of his life: in his life as a social being, or his political life; in his life as a thinking being, or his intellectual life; and in his life as a moral being, or his spiritual life. In each of these departments of human activity Christ has made men free.

### I.

Christ has given to us men, first of all, political or social freedom. He has not indeed drawn out a scheme of government, and stamped it with His Divine authority, as guaranteeing freedom. We Englishmen rightly prize a Constitutional Monarchy as the best form of government, especially when it is recommended by the character of

[a] Ps. cxlviii. 6.

such a sovereign as our Queen. But while we cannot even entertain the idea of abandoning our own constitution for any other, we may admit that a citizen of the United States ought to feel himself as much at home amid the political doctrines of the New Testament as a subject of Her Majesty. The New Testament only notices two necessary elements of man's life as a political or social being. One is the existence of some government which it is a duty to obey; be it assembly, president, king, or emperor. Each of these may be a higher power to which every soul is to be subject; "because there is no power but of God: the powers that be are ordained of God."[a] The other element is the freedom of the individual Christian under any form of government whatever.

There had been something like freedom in the ancient heathen world: freedom for particular classes; freedom for particular races; freedom for the masters of conquered provinces; freedom for the owners of thousands of slaves. The ruling race, or the ruling class, spoke, acted, much as it liked; and jealously noted any attempt on the part of a more aspiring tyrant to destroy its liberty. This was an external rather than an inward, a political rather than a moral, liberty. It was the liberty of the few, the enslavement of the many. As it had no moral and internal basis, it was an accident rather than the spirit of the ancient world. And as political constitutions grew old, it died away into a tyranny. When our Lord came, all that could be called civilisation was under the sway of the Roman Cæsars. Yet with our Lord there came also the germs of political liberty. When individual men had learnt to feel the greatness and the interest of life; the real horizon which stretches out before the soul's eye beyond the grave; the depths of being within the soul; its unex-

[a] Rom. xiii. 1.

hausted capacities for happiness and for suffering; the reality and nearness of God, of His Divine Son, of our fellow-citizens the blessed angels; the awful, inexpressible distinction of being redeemed from death by the Blood of the Most Holy, and sanctified by the Eternal Spirit;—it was impossible not to feel also that each man had, in the highest sense, rights to assert and a bearing to maintain. Thus a Christian was a free man, simply because he was a Christian. The political or social accidents of his position could not touch that unimpeded movement of his highest life in which his true freedom consisted.

It has often been alleged, and will have occurred to you, that, as a matter of fact, our Lord left the great despotisms of the world for a while untouched. Jesus Christ taught, He was crucified, He rose, He ascended. But the Cæsar Tiberius still sat upon the throne of the Roman world. There never was a more odious system of personal government than that of the Roman Emperors; the surviving forms of the extinct republic did but make the actual tyranny which had succeeded it more hard to bear. Yet it was of such an Emperor as Nero that St. Paul wrote, "Let every soul be subject to the higher powers; for there is no power but of God;"[a] and St. Peter, "Submit yourself to every ordinance of man for the Lord's sake, whether it be to the emperor as supreme, or unto governors," that is, proconsuls and prætors, as they were termed, "who are sent by him" into the provinces of the empire "for the punishment of evil-doers, and for the praise of them that do well."[b] And in the same way Apostles advise Christian slaves to give obedience to their masters as unto the Lord; to obey, not with eye-service, as if they had only to do as much as might be insisted on by a jealous owner, but with

[a] Rom. xiii. 1.   [b] 1 St. Pet. ii. 13, 14.

singleness of heart, as men who throw every energy into their work.[a] It may be asked, How are such precepts, such advice as this, compatible with the assertion that Christ gave us political freedom? The answer is that He gave us a moral force which did two things. First, it made every Christian independent of outward political circumstances, and secondly, it made the creation of new civil institutions only a question of time. The slave who could not speak to a fellow-slave except when he was spoken to; who could not move as he would even once throughout the day; whose every look and gesture was regulated by an implacable etiquette; whose life was, at least during long periods of Roman history, entirely at the disposal of his owner, was yet, if a Christian, inwardly free. He had a sense of freedom, of power, of living according to the higher law of his being, which the Cæsar on his throne knew not of. That was enough for him, at least for the present, if he knew his own happiness and the will of his Lord. By and by the moral seed which had been sown would bear fruit in his emancipation; in new public institutions; in a changed face of the world. For it was not our Lord's part, like that of some agitators of the time, to promote a rising among the slaves, to rouse a province into resistance against the Roman power, to issue programmes for a political and social revolution. That would have been at issue with the blessed lessons of submission, tenderness, long-suffering, charity, which He came to teach. But His doctrine of the worth and dignity of redeemed men was like leaven deposited in the corrupt mass of human society; and in time the whole would be leavened politically, as in other ways.

The process has been advancing for centuries; it is

[a] Eph. vi. 5-8: Col. iii. 22-24.

still going on. We English owe much to it; more, perhaps, than any nation in the world. It has, indeed, been said that "if despotism in England ceased with the Stuarts, liberty is still confronted by the Statute-book." Of course it is. How could it be otherwise? The objection assumes that between law and liberty there is some sort of necessary antagonism. We know unhappily that abroad this opposition is sometimes taken for granted. There are some countries in which order and liberty are treated as implacable enemies; in which order is only secured by the confiscation of every personal liberty; in which liberty only raises its head, if it does raise its head, amid the ruins of order and of law. We may well thank God that He has spared us these trials. When your Lordships worship in this temple of Christ,[a] you represent two great causes; the sacred interests of liberty no less than the sacred interests of law. Law is the guarantee of liberty, not its enemy; liberty is the enthusiastic ally of law. Each rests upon a fact which is Divine in its origin; liberty on the moral majesty of individual human life; law on our Divinely-implanted social instincts, and, as a consequence, on the Divine origin of society, and on the necessity of upholding and protecting society, by rule or law, against selfish passion. To crush true liberty in the name of law is to sow the seed, sooner or later, of social insurrection. To depreciate or insult law in the name of liberty is to make of liberty a cloke of maliciousness, and to insure its ruin. Nothing can be more deplorable than any conflict between these sacred principles. An old psalmist, reviewing the tyrannical administration of law by the judges of Israel, exclaims that "all the foundations of the earth are out of

[a] Preached on occasion of the visit of the Judges to St. Paul's, April 21, 1872.

course."[a] The whole social fabric totters to its base when there is a conflict between human law advocating order, and Divine law enthroned in conscience; when law and the highest liberty are foes. To avoid such a misfortune must be the aim of all wise legislators: to deprecate it the heart-felt prayer of all good citizens.

## II.

Christ gave men also intellectual freedom. He enfranchised them by the gift of truth. He gave truth in its fulness; truth not merely relative and provisional, but absolute and final. Until He came the human intellect was enslaved. It was enslaved either to degrading superstition, or to false and one-sided philosophies. Man must think about himself, his place in the Universe, his destiny, his relation to a higher Being. And if he has not truth at hand, he makes the best he can of error. He may change "the glory of the incorruptible God into an image made like unto corruptible man."[b] Still that is better than nothing. He may listen to a teacher, who, " promising him liberty, is all the while himself a servant of corruption."[c] Yet that is more endurable than utter silence. Man's interest in the great problems around him betrays him to his intellectual foes; unless he have embraced the Truth; unless the Truth, in its greatness, has made him free.

It is undeniable that the religion of Christ gave an immense impulse to human thought. It made men think as they had never thought before. It made them feel what it is to have within this puny body a spirit which takes the measure of the spheres. When Christ, in all the glory of His Godhead and His Manhood, had enthroned Himself in the soul, He taught men to think

[a] Ps. lxxxii. 5.  [b] Rom. i. 23.  [c] 2 St. Pet. ii. 19.

worthily of the greatness of God and of the greatness of man, notwithstanding man's weakness and corruption. He freed men from all the narrow, cramping influences of local philosophies, of local teachers, of petty schemes and theories for classes and races. He led men out into the great highways of thought, where, if they would, they might know the Universal Father, manifested in His Blessed Son, as the Author of all existence, as its Object, and as its End.

Here we are asked whether, as a matter of fact, Christianity does not cramp intellectual liberty by insisting upon the necessity of believing Christian doctrine; whether dogmatic Creeds, for instance, are not hostile to mental liberty.

Certainly our Lord has given us a body of Truth, which we can, if we like, reject, but which it is our happiness to believe. What He did for men in this way is embodied in His Own teaching, in the writings of His Apostles, and in the Creeds of the Universal Church. These are to intellectual liberty what law is to social liberty. They protect, they do not cramp it. They furnish a fixed point, from which thought may take wing. They do not enchain thought. If man would think steadily, fruitfully, he must begin with some solid, ascertained truth. You cannot survey the surface of the ocean while you are tossing upon its waves. You must plant your foot upon a rock in order to command, from a basis which is fixed, the scene which is perpetually shifting around you. To plunge off the rock into the waves is to surrender this vantage-ground. It is with the Creeds as with law. If you repudiate law, you may become the slaves of any individual will. If you repudiate the Creeds, you may become the slaves of any petty intellectual dogmatiser. In rejecting the Creeds you leave the broad, public highways of Christian Faith, the many-sided and comprehensive thought of the Universal Church, for the cramped and morbid speculations of individual thinkers. You abandon yourselves to all the petty tyrannies, to all the insolent usurpations, of private thought; to all the formulas of individual and human masters, from which Christ our Lord has willed to make us free.

If it would be a mistake to tear up Magna Charta in the supposed interests of freedom, because it recognises the obligation of law, it is also a mistake to mutilate or to disuse any Creed of the Universal Church, under the idea that you are securing mental liberty. The Creed does but state what every well-informed and faithful Christian wishes to believe. Christian doctrine, I repeat, is to man's highest life of thought what law is to his social life: to reject the one in the interests of the other is to turn mental liberty into a cloke of maliciousness.

### III.

Lastly, Christ has made men morally free. He has broken the chains which fettered the human will, and has restored to it its buoyancy and its power. Man was morally free in Paradise: he became enslaved, in consequence of that act of disobedience which we name the Fall. Man then forfeited the robe of grace which had secured the beauty and perfection of his nature in its earlier and happier stage; he could not transmit to his descendants that which he had lost himself. Man's will lost its spring, its superiority to circumstance, its independence of passion, its lofty unlikeness to mere instinct. Man fell more and more fatally under the dominion of nature; under the dominion of his senses enslaved by nature. He became by degrees what St. Paul, in the

Epistle to the Romans,[a] describes him as having become. He was a slave; because the sovereign power within him, his will, had lost the secret of its freedom, and was itself enslaved.

How was he to be enfranchised? There came to him One Who said, "If the Son shall make you free, ye shall be free indeed."[b] What had been lost was to be more than regained in Christ.[c] Not merely was the penalty of old transgressions to be paid so, that man was redeemed from a real captivity: but the will was to be reinvigorated by a Heaven-sent force or grace, once more placing it in true harmony with the law of man's life. Of this St. Paul speaks in saying that when Christians were made free from sin they became the servants or slaves of righteousness.[d] There is no "Oregon territory" in the moral world; no tract of unoccupied neutral ground which runs between the frontiers of the empire of Christ and of the realm of Evil. They are conterminous to each other: and to have been rescued from the one is to become at once a subject of its antagonist.

Here it is objected that moral freedom is not worth having if it be only a service after all. 'You talk of freedom,' men say, 'but you mean rule. You mean restrictions upon action; restrictions upon inclination; restrictions upon speech. You mean obligations: obligations to work; obligations to self-discipline; obligations to sacrifice self to others; obligations to all the details of Christian duty.'

My brethren, you are right: certainly we do. A Christian lives under a system of restrictions and obligations; and yet he is free. Those obligations and restrictions only prescribe for him what his own new Heaven-sent

[a] Rom. i. 21-32.　　[b] St. John viii. 36.
[c] Rom. v. 16, 17.　　[d] Rom. vi. 18.

nature would wish to be and to do. They would be very annoying, no doubt, to the old nature which he has put off. They would exasperate what St. Paul calls "the old Adam, which is corrupt, according to the deceitful lusts."[a] But they are acceptable to, they are demanded by, the "new man, which, after God, is created in righteousness and true holiness."[b]

Whatever a Christian may be outwardly, he is inwardly a free man. In obeying Christ's law he acts as he desires to act: he acts according to this, the highest law of his life, because he rejoices to do so. He obeys law; the Law of God. But then he has no inclination to disobey it. To him, obedience is not a yoke. Disobedience would be a torture. His inclinations are in accordance with his highest duty: that which emancipates him is itself a law. "The law of the Spirit of life in Christ Jesus hath made me free from the law of sin and death."[c] He is, as St. Peter says to us to-day, a servant of God;[d] but then, as he would not for all the world be anything else, his service is perfect freedom.

The Antinomian plea that the rules and laws of a Christian life are an infringement upon Christian liberty is only a way of making Christian liberty a cloke of maliciousness. The care of conscience, regular habits of devotion, system in doing good to others, and in the disposal of time, caution as to what passes in conversation, avoidance of bad company, precautions against temptation; —these things are represented as inconsistent with freedom. Inconsistent they are with mere natural impetuosity, with a purely animal impatience of restraint, with that notion of human liberty which places it in the indulgence of the lower instincts and desires at the cost of the higher. True

[a] Eph. iv. 22.  [b] Ibid. 24.
[c] Rom. viii. 2.  [d] 1 St. Pet. ii. 16.

freedom, let us be sure, consists in the power of acting without hindrance according to the highest law of our being. To do wrong does not assert our liberty. It degrades, it enslaves us. It may have been necessary that we should have the power of doing wrong, in order to do right freely. But none the less we forfeit freedom, if we do aught but right. A man is not really more free because he steals, because he swears, because he murders. This false notion of liberty is its worst enemy. Our highest liberty is secured by our free and complete obedience to every detail of God's eternal law.

Brethren, let us look up to our Great Emancipator. Our freedom is after all His gift: but He has left us the power, the perilous power, of forfeiting it, that we may, if we will, retain it for His glory. Let us see that we do not forfeit it by cloking under it the "maliciousness" which repudiates law. The laws of the land protect our social liberty. The Laws of the Church, the laws of natural and revealed Truth, protect our mental liberty. The Moral Laws of God protect our spiritual liberty. All true law meets in, radiates from, the Divine Person of Christ, the Everlasting Legislator, our Deliverer from political, intellectual, moral slavery.

If we repudiate law we turn His gift of freedom against Himself. If, through our willing obedience, we find in law the very countersign of our freedom, we are—and in this way only can we be—free indeed.

# SERMON XXXIII.

### JESUS THE ONLY SAVIOUR OF MEN.[a]

1 COR. I. 13.

*Was Paul crucified for you?*

CERTAINLY this question was intended to startle St. Paul's readers at Corinth; and, no doubt, it did startle them. He is writing them a letter by way of answer to their inquiries; and he suddenly stops to ask them whether he, the writer, had been crucified for them. What was it that provoked him to use language so strange and paradoxical?

St. Paul had been told on good authority that after his leaving Corinth the Church in that place had been split up into separate groups; and that these groups named themselves, one after himself, another after the Alexandrian teacher Apollos, another after the great Apostle St. Peter, and a fourth even after Christ our Lord. These names would have represented ideas which ought never to be separated, and which in the present day we should call respectively Christian freedom, Christian philosophy, Church authority and organisation, and personal devotion

[a] Preached at St. Paul's for the Bishop of London's Fund, April 25, 1880.

to Christ. But the Corinthians were Greeks, and they had carried some of their old mental habits with them out of heathenism into the Church of God. For ages the Greeks had identified each shade of opinion in philosophy with the name of an individual teacher. It was natural for them to look at Christianity itself mainly as an addition to the existing stock of thought in the world, which admitted of being treated as other systems which had preceded it had been treated. Moreover, it was true in the Apostolic age—as now, and always,—that Religion is differently apprehended and presented by different minds. But to dwell on different aspects of the one Truth is one thing, and to hold contradictory beliefs is another. To-day, on the festival of an Evangelist,[a] we are naturally reminded how differently our Blessed Lord's life presented itself to His four biographers: as the fulfilment of prophecy, as the life of the Ideal or Perfect Man, as the cure for human sin, and as the manifestation in the flesh of the Eternal Son of God. And in like manner to St. Peter the Christian Religion and Church appeared chiefly as a continuation of the Jewish, with some vitally important differences; to St. Paul, as the absolute reconciliation between God and man, intended to embrace all the nations of the world; to Apollos, as the solution of those many serious questions about human life and destiny which had been asked by human philosophy. The Life which the four Evangelists described was one. The Doctrine which Peter and Paul and Apollos preached was one. But different aspects of the Life and of the Doctrine recommended themselves to different minds. Thus in the teaching of the Apostles, as in the Gospel Narratives, there was an apparent diversity grouped around a substantial harmony; a harmony inspired by the Truth so variously appre-

[a] St. Mark.

hended and described. The history of England is not less a single history, because one writer mainly addresses himself to the story of the Monarchy, and another to the social and material condition and development of the people, and another to our relations in different ages with foreign countries, and a fourth to the successive phases of art or of literature.

The fault then of the Corinthians lay in their treating a difference in the way of presenting religious truth as if it were a difference in religious truth itself. To them Paul, Peter, and Apollos were the teachers of distinct religions. Nay more, the holiest Name of all was bandied about among the names of these His servants and messengers; just as if all truth did not centre in Him as its Source and Object; just as if He too could be appropriated by a little clique, who prided themselves, no doubt, on not being party men, while they thus used the saving Name to cover the narrowest of the forms of Corinthian partisanship. Surely to St. Paul this degradation of our Divine Master's Name must have been unspeakably distressing; only less distressing, perhaps, than the position of virtual equality with Christ assigned to himself; as though he, an Apostle, were the centre and author of a distinct religion! Hence the pain which he feels, and which finds vent in the question, "Was Paul crucified for you?"

I.

St. Paul's question suggests first of all the difference between the debt which Christians owe to our Lord Jesus Christ and that which they owe to any, even the most favoured and illuminated, of His servants. And certainly it was no slight debt which the Corinthians owed to the Apostle. He had preached the Faith and had planted the Church of Christ among them. Some of them had been Jews before their conversion, and to these he had taught the true end of their law, the true meaning of their prophecies, the true scope of their sacrificial worship. He had taught them how in Christ they could assuredly find all that they had sought in vain in the religion of Moses. But the Corinthian Christians generally were converts from heathenism. As such they owed St. Paul a much larger debt of obligation than did the converts from Judaism. He had taught them, not only the truths which Christians believe and which Jews reject, but also the truths which Jews and Christians hold in common, and which heathens reject. These once heathen Corinthians had learnt from St. Paul, not merely that Christ, the true Messiah, and the Lord from heaven, had come in our flesh to save mankind from spiritual ruin, by His Death upon the Cross, and His gift of the Holy Spirit, but also that God is One, that He is Almighty, All-wise, and All-good, that He is the Creator of heaven and earth, and that the heathen religions contained, at the very best, small detached fragments of truth about Him, buried beneath a mass of error and folly. In short, the Corinthian Christians as a body owed to St. Paul the truth they knew about subjects of the highest interest to man; about man's nature, about God's Nature, about God's relations with man, about the Eternal Future. It was, to say the least, a vast obligation; it was a debt which could never be repaid. But the Apostle suggests its utter relative insignificance by his question, " Was Paul crucified for you?"

Not that St. Paul had taught the Corinthians the Faith of Christ without suffering. At Corinth, as elsewhere, he preached " with much contention,"[a] nay, not seldom

[a] 1 Thess. ii. 2.

with his life in his hand. With the arrival of Timothy and Silas from Macedonia, the first efforts in the house of Aquila and the synagogue, the quiet days of the Corinthian mission came to an end. St. Paul felt it a duty to put our Lord's claims more distinctly forward in the synagogue than he had done at first. He "was pressed in the spirit, and testified to the Jews that Jesus was Christ."[a] The result was an outbreak of violent fanaticism; St. Luke calls it "blasphemy."[b] The Apostle left the synagogue with the exclamation that the blood of his opponents was on their own heads, and that henceforth he turned to the heathen. This was followed by a great Jewish riot, after which he was brought before the tribunal of Gallio.[c] The preaching of the Gospel then had involved sacrifice and suffering; the suffering and sacrifice which in some shape or other is inseparable from any serious effort on behalf of Truth in a world which openly rejects or secretly dislikes it. But all such sufferings had differed in kind from that which was glanced at by the question, "Was Paul crucified for you?"

Yes! let me repeat it, in that question St. Paul implies that his work differed from that of his Redeemer, not merely in degree, but in kind. The relation of the Apostle to Christ our Lord was altogether unlike that which ever existed or could exist between the pupils of a great human teacher and their master. One fine day a man like Socrates appears on the stage of history. He teaches some truths which are new to his generation, or he teaches some old truths in a striking and original way. He sets everybody thinking. He founds a school. His work, or some part of it, is taken up by his pupils according to their ability. This or that pupil adds a touch of subdued originality which saves his own performance from being

[a] Acts xviii. 5.   [b] *Ibid.* xviii. 6.   [c] *Ibid.* xviii. 12-17.

merely a repetition. But, in the main, it is the master's teaching which is continued until a new system takes its place. Here from first to last the master and his successors are on a virtual level. They are all alike teachers. If they teach any truth, they teach something which is independent of all of them. It might have been taught just as well by some one else. And if in the end the master drinks a cup of hemlock, it may show his belief in the value of some of his speculations, or the fickleness or injustice of his fellow-citizens. In no other sense could it be of any importance either to his pupils or to mankind.

When St. Paul asks, "Was Paul crucified for you?" he implies how utterly different was his own relation to Jesus Christ from that of his great pupils to Socrates. For St. Paul did not think of Christ our Lord only or chiefly as a great Teacher whose work he had continued, after the fashion of a second Plato, in a way peculiarly his own. To St. Paul Christ was not merely the Author of Christianity, but its Subject and its Substance. Christianity is not, as Lessing maintained, only what Christ Himself taught. It is also the Apostles' teaching about Christ; it is the true account of the work and the Person of Christ. Not merely what He said while He was on earth, but what He did and suffered, and Who He is, that His sufferings and acts should be invested with a transcendent interest;—all this is of the essence and heart of the Christian Faith. And hence the immense significance of the Apostle's question. St. Paul was not indeed crucified; he was beheaded some years later, as a martyr for Christ. But excepting the testimony which he thus bore to the truth which he preached, his death was without results to the Roman Christians, and to the world. He was beheaded for no one. And had he been crucified at Corinth, the sin of no single Corinthian would have been washed away by his blood; no one soul would have been placed in a new relation with God by his sufferings. Do, teach, or suffer what he might, he was but a disciple. Such was the difference between the Master of Christians and His greatest disciples, that it made their work differ, not in degree, but in kind.

## II.

And St. Paul's question suggests, further, what it was in the work of Christ our Lord which, in the Apostle's judgment, had the first claim on the gratitude of Christians.

It was not His miracles. They were designed, no doubt, to make faith in His Divine mission natural and easy. They were more frequently works of mercy than works of conspicuous power. They were acted parables. Each of them revealed something respecting the nature of Christ's work and His kingdom. But others also have worked miracles. And the miracles of Christ our Lord have not touched the heart of the world more than His words.

Was it then His teaching? Certainly when He was on earth men wondered at the gracious words which proceeded out of His mouth. Even in our own day some who reject His miracles profess to be devoted to His teaching. Nor will human speech ever say more to the conscience of man than did the Sermon on the Mount, or more to the heart of man than did the Discourse in the Supper-Room. Yet He Himself implies that what He did would have greater claims on man than what He said. And the history of Christendom certainly confirms this.

Was it then His triumph over death at His Resurrection? Certainly the Resurrection was the supreme certificate of His Divine Mission: it was the warrant of faith to which the Apostles appealed. But the claim of the

Resurrection upon our gratitude is so great, because it is intimately bound up with the tragedy which had preceded it, and of which it is at once the reversal and the interpretation.

"I determined," says the Apostle, "not to know anything among you save Jesus Christ, and Him crucified."[a] "God forbid that I should glory, save in the Cross of our Lord Jesus Christ."[b] "We preach Christ crucified, unto the Jews a stumbling-block, and unto the Greeks foolishness; but to them that are called, both Jews and Greeks, Christ the Power of God, and the Wisdom of God."[c] We see now what is meant by the question, Was Paul crucified for you?

Yes! on the Cross Jesus our Lord speaks to the heart of man, more persuasively than when working His miracles, or when teaching multitudes or His disciples, or when rising from His tomb. On the Cross He reminds us of our utter misery and helplessness until we are aided by His redeeming Might. On the Cross He reveals the astonishing love for each single soul, which drew Him from His Throne of glory to a life of humiliation, and a death of pain and shame. On the Cross He is still preaching as on the Mount and in the Supper-Room; but it is in the more cogent language of action. "Greater love hath no man than this, that a man lay down his life for his friends."[d] On the Cross He bears our sins in His Own body:[e] He is made sin for us Who knew no sin:[f] He is washing us from our sins in His Own Blood.[g] As He hangs on the Cross before the eye of faith, St. Paul points to a Propitiation for sin,[h] a Redemption from sin,[i] and a Reconciliation with the Father.[k] To expand, connect, explain,

---

[a] 1 Cor. ii. 2.   [b] Gal. vi. 14.   [c] 1 Cor. i. 23, 24.
[d] St. John xv. 13.   [e] 1 St. Pet. ii. 24.   [f] 2 Cor. v. 21.
[g] Rev. i. 5.   [h] Rom. iii. 25.   [i] Eph. i. 7.
[k] 2 Cor. v. 18-20; Heb. ii. 17.

justify, these aspects of His Atoning Death is no doubt a labour of vast proportions. But in their simple form they meet every child who reads the New Testament, and they explain the hold of Christ Crucified on the Christian heart. The Crucifixion means more for the Christian believer than any other event in the whole history of the world, or even in the Life of Jesus Christ our Lord. And we understand the pathos and the strength of the appeal, "Was Paul crucified for you?"

### III.

And thus at the present day St. Paul's question enables us to measure the true worth of efforts for improving the condition of mankind.

In our age, it has been said, a larger proportion of human beings than ever before are engaged in doing good of some kind for their fellow-creatures. Certainly philanthropists of all types are hard at work, sometimes more earnestly than wisely, but always, or almost always, so as to command respect. Charity is organised; drainage is carried out; suffering of all sorts is alleviated; nearly every leading disease has its separate hospital, or at least its special students and remedies. The blind, the deaf, the dumb, the consumptive, the victims of cancer or of dropsy, the convalescent, the incurable, the orphans, the foundlings, the idiots, are each provided for, and sometimes on a scale of splendid generosity. We may well thank God that He has put it into the hearts of so many of our countrymen to found and to support institutions and enterprises so rich in their practical benevolence. But when it is hinted that efforts of this kind satisfy all the needs of man, we are obliged to hesitate. The needs of the soul are at least as real as those of the body. The pain of the conscience is at least as torturing as that of the nerves. The Invisible World is not less to be provided for than the world of sense and time. We are sometimes almost pressed, in view of the exaggerated claims of a secular philanthropy, to ask whether this or that benevolent person was crucified for the poor or the suffering, who are relieved by his money, or by his skill.

In like manner, when somebody[a] comes forward to tell us, in a more refined, if less forcible, tongue than our own, that we should all be much better if we would give increased time and thought to the Emperor Marcus Aurelius, we naturally listen.

That Marcus Aurelius was, for a Pagan emperor, more than respectable; that there are many fine and true things in his book of *Thoughts;* that his life was marked by excellences which were, in his day, and especially in his position, eminent, must be frankly granted. But when we are told that his book is an everlasting gospel, and when he is spoken of in terms which suggest a comparison only less absurd than it is irreverent, we look around us. Surely, we say, literary infidelity has done this man a wrong by the very excesses of its panegyric. For we cannot but ask whether the characteristic virtue of himself and of his sect was more than the social luxury of a very select and fastidious clique; whether it had the slightest effect upon the indescribable degradations of the multitudes who lived close to the gates of his palace; whether it prevented the imperial philosopher from associating with himself in the government of the Empire a worthless trifler, or from deliberately bequeathing his responsibilities to a profligate buffoon, who inflicted great miseries on mankind; whether it even suggested a scruple respecting his cruel persecutions of the one Religion that

[a] M. Renan.

could make mankind at large love, if they did not practise, disinterested virtue. These are questions which history may be left to answer. And her judgment would make another question only more grotesque than profane—"Was Marcus Aurelius crucified for you?"

Yes; only One ever was crucified out of love to sinners, and with a will and power to save them. And it is in order to bring hundreds of thousands in this great city within the reach of His Redemption that I am hoping to interest you to-day on behalf of the Bishop of London's Fund. Perhaps the Bishop of London's Fund labours under a certain disadvantage on the score of its name, which at first suggests a financial rather than a religious enterprise. Yet it would be difficult to propose a substitute. The descriptions of religious work which it furthers are very various; and no one of these could be employed to describe it without giving the impression that its field of operations is much narrower than it really is. Thus it supports missionary clergy and lay agents; it builds houses for clergymen, schools, mission buildings, of various descriptions; it lends a helping hand to the erection and endowment of permanent churches, and to any special objects which may appear to our Bishop to be likely to promote religion in his diocese. What are these agencies but the material and outward aspect of that preaching of Christ Crucified, which now, as in St. Paul's days, is the one great remedy for human misery and sin?

To say that all the undertakings which this Fund supports are equally efficient, that all the workmen in its employ are equally masters of their heavenly craft, would be to overstate the case. No doubt, here and there we should find less activity, less perfect teaching of Christian truth, than elsewhere. But it would be unworthy of a generous and Christian temper to refuse support to what is in its conception, and on the whole, a very noble undertaking, on the ground of any such incidental shortcoming or failure. As a whole the agencies supported by this Fund do actively promote the knowledge of Christ Crucified. They bring the Christian Faith and Church within the reach of thousands who else would be ignorant of them. They thus reduce the area of accumulated ungodliness which covers so large a portion of this great capital.

Those who wish to see in detail what the Fund has done during the past year should obtain a copy of the Report. A study of this will show how extensive and how various are its operations, and yet how far short it falls of meeting the ever-increasing needs of London.

The yearly increase of population in this metropolis, accelerated as it has been during the last thirty years by the centralising influence of the railway system, keeps constantly in advance of the Church's efforts to overtake it. Nay, rather, it outruns the labours of all the Christian bodies put together. During the year 1879 twenty thousand new houses have been built in the suburbs of London; the largest number that has ever been returned. This represents a possible increase of 120,000 inhabitants, that is to say, of a population nearly rivalling that of Bristol, and more than three times as large as that of Oxford. What, think you, will happen, in this world, and in the next, if this new city—for such it is—be left to fester in the mental and moral misery which is inseparable from such an accumulation of human lives?

Within the last fortnight a great deal has been said and written about the social dangers which attend on the advance of Democracy. Without at all indorsing much of this language, we may recall the saying of a shrewd observer of human nature,[a] to the effect that where civil liberty exists in anything like perfection, order can only be secured by one of two agencies; by principle or by force. If there is no principle enshrined in the hearts of men, then selfishness, rapacity, excesses of every description, will break out in private and public conduct, until at last, in order to defend society against the perils which threaten it, government has to be strengthened by being furnished with the means of repressing disorder and crime. In the hands of any unscrupulous government this increase of strength may easily be turned against the existence of liberty itself. There is but a short step from social anarchy to the appearance of a so-called "saviour of society;" an adventurer who confiscates personal liberty, nominally in the interests of order, but really in the interests of some kind of selfish despotism. In a free community, therefore, the aim of a wise foresight will always be to secure order by the means of generally recognised principle; since, in such proportion as principle is diminished, you increase the need of force. But, if you set aside the Faith of Christ, what influence is to supply principle on such a scale as to secure society against the solvents which are ever latent in human selfishness? What do you seriously suppose will happen to the social life of vast communities, such as those which are added year by year to London, if it should come to be generally believed that the solemn truths which religion holds up before the eyes of every class in the community may be dispensed with?

"Once let it be supposed," says an American who cannot be suspected of tenderness towards Christian orthodoxy, "once let men thoroughly believe that they are the work and sport of chance, that no superior intelligence concerns

[a] Montesquieu.

itself with human affairs, that all human improvements perish for ever at death, that the weak have no guardian and the injured no avenger, that there is no recompence for sacrifices to uprightness and the public good, that an oath is unheard in heaven, that secret crimes have no witness but the perpetrator, that human existence has no purpose, and human virtue no unfailing friend, that this brief life is everything to us, and death is total, everlasting extinction,—once let men thoroughly abandon religion, and who can conceive or describe the extent of the social desolation that would follow? We hope perhaps," he adds, "that human laws and natural sympathy would hold society together. As reasonably might we believe that were the sun quenched in the heavens our torches could illuminate and our fires quicken and fertilise the earth." [a]

The faith which St. Paul preached, the faith in Jesus Christ, the Eternal Son of God manifest in our flesh and crucified for the sins of man, does, when sincerely received, protect society against those dangers which are inseparable from human progress at certain stages of its development. For this faith in Christ Crucified addresses itself to each of those poles of society, which, when left to the ordinary selfish impulses of human nature, tend to become separate and antagonistic. To the wealthy, to the noble, to the fastidious, the figure of the Crucified Saviour is a perpetual preacher of self-sacrifice for the sake of the poor and needy; He enjoins the surrender of income, and prejudices, and time, and tastes, for a cause which is His Own. And to the poor, the desolate, the unbefriended, the figure of the Crucified is no less a perpetual lesson of patience under wrong, specially under undeserved wrong; on the Cross Christ teaches men more persuasively than any

[a] Channing, *Theol. Works*, p. 332.

other the beauty, the majesty of entire resignation. Thus does the truth which is at the very heart of the Christian Creed contribute most powerfully to the coherence and wellbeing of society; and we live in days when society is not able to dispense with its assistance. Not that the preservation of society will be a Christian's strongest motive for helping forward a work like this. For us Eternity is of more account than time; and the Day of Judgment than any possible event that can precede it; and the endless existence of souls, in this or that condition, beyond the grave, than any established order of society here and now.

As we walk down the new streets which are being raised in every suburb of London, without any spiritual provision to meet their needs, let us ask ourselves, what will be the condition of their present inhabitants fifty or a hundred years hence? If we have any true Christian feeling, the answer to that question must bid us assist, as we may, this effort to spread the knowledge and love of Jesus Christ in this diocese. And there are three ways in which, in whatever degree, every one here present can lend a hand to this great work. The first is to give of what God has given us, such a portion as we can dare to offer before Him, towards a work for the promotion of which all London Christians are surely responsible; since God has appointed them, more than other men, to do it. Give something that you will really miss; give it for the sake of Jesus Christ our Lord, if you would have your gift accepted on high. The second is to take and show an interest in the work, and to get others to do so; to give the help of prayer and sympathy when you can do no more: to welcome any opportunity of making it known to those who can effectively promote it. And the third is to remember that all efforts to advance Christ's kingdom impose a serious responsibility upon those who make them; the responsibility of being consistent. Our first labour for any religious truth, as we know, should be within ourselves. When this has been carried out quietly, unostentatiously, thoroughly, as at the foot of the Cross of Jesus our Lord, we shall be more than ever anxious to do what we may, in our day and generation, to enable others to share the blessings which we here enjoy, that they may partake in these joys, to which, as we trust, the Eternal Mercy will admit us, hereafter.

# SERMON XXXIV.

## THE APOSTOLIC COMMISSION.

ST. MATT. XXVIII. 18-20.

*And Jesus came and spake unto them, saying, All power is given unto Me in heaven and in earth. Go ye therefore, and teach all nations, baptizing them in the Name of the Father, and of the Son, and of the Holy Ghost: teaching them to observe all things whatsoever I have commanded you: and lo, I am with you alway, even unto the end of the world. Amen.*

THESE sublime words, with which St. Matthew closes his Gospel, have for us to-day a twofold attraction. On the one hand, they are among the most significant of those sayings, which, uttered by our Lord in the course of the forty days after His rising from the dead, invite particular consideration during the Easter season. On the other hand, as the Collect which was used in this evening service will have reminded us, to-morrow is the festival of the Apostles St. Philip and St. James: and these are the words in which our Lord completed the endowments with which He invested His Apostles before He left the earth. As, when instituting the Holy Sacrament of His Body and Blood, before He suffered, He bade them "Do this as a Memorial of Me;"[a] as after His rising from

[a] St. Luke xxii. 19.

the dead, in the Upper Chamber, He breathed on them, saying, " Receive ye the Holy Ghost; whosesoever sins ye forgive, they are forgiven unto them;"[a] so now, before He leaves the world, He gives them a world-wide commission, to make disciples and to baptize: 'Go, make Christians of all the nations, baptizing them into the Name of the Father, and of the Son, and of the Holy Ghost: teaching them to observe all things whatsoever I commanded you: and lo, I am with you all the days, even unto the end of the world.'

And before giving this last commission, our Lord makes an announcement: "All authority has been given to Me in heaven and on the earth." To His Human Nature this authority was a gift. It had been given at His Incarnation; and at His Resurrection He had as Man entered fully upon its practical possession. But the point of what He is saying lies not in the source or transfer of this authority, but in its character and range. As Man, so we Christians believe, He has authority in heaven; authority to place Himself at the right hand of the Father; to send down the Holy Spirit upon the earth; and to draw upwards to Himself His living members, and bid them reign with Him. Henceforth no principalities or powers in the world of spirits may defy or disown His all-pervading sway. And as Man He has authority on the earth, to complete the foundation of His Church as a kingdom of souls; to protect, to cleanse, to extend, to perpetuate it; to bring the nations, one by one, into its fold; to convert sinners, to sanctify souls, to prepare men for that solemn moment when He will come again to judge the living and the dead, and to render to every man according to his works. "All authority has been given to Me in heaven and on the earth."

[a] St. John xx. 22, 23.

Such is the announcement. And then follows the practical consequence. It has been doubted, I do not say with any great reason, whether our Lord used the one word translated by "therefore." But there is no room for question as to the connection of the thought. Because He wields all authority on the earth and in heaven, He bids the Apostles convert, baptize, instruct, all the nations of the world; relying on His presence with them to the end of time. In every word of this commission we feel the authority of the Speaker; and with this aspect of the words in view we will go on to consider them in detail.

I.

Let us notice first of all the substance of this commission. What was it that the Apostles had to do?

They were to make disciples of all the nations, and they were to do this by baptizing them into the Name of the Father, the Son, and the Holy Ghost, and by teaching them to observe all the commands of our Lord Jesus Christ. The Name into which the nations were to be baptized was itself a revelation of the Inner Being of God. The rite of Baptism, as our Lord had instructed Nicodemus,[a] was much more than a ceremony by which admission was to be given into a new religious society: it was the instrument by which the Holy Spirit would deposit in the soul the germ of a new life. And the baptized nations were to be taught to observe or to guard all that Christ had commanded His first followers to believe and do. All that He had taught directly Himself, all that He would teach indirectly by the Apostles, when the Spirit had come to guide them into all truth, was to be enjoined on the new disciples to the end of time. As He said of

[a] St. John iii. 3-13.

Himself, "He that followeth Me shall not walk in darkness,"[a] so He said to His Apostles, "He that heareth you heareth Me."[b]

"Teaching them to observe all things whatsoever I have commanded you." We cannot fail to note here the consciousness of a plenary authority. The Speaker does not propose; He commands. He does not argue. He has decided.

It has not been uncommon to compare the Utterer of these words with Socrates. Socrates, as we know, was a celebrated Athenian, who employed his time in endeavouring to make his countrymen think. Looking at the torpid, stagnant condition of the minds of the majority of men, and at their way of mistaking prejudice for wisdom, or a command of phrases for an acquaintance with things, Socrates set himself to cross-question them in a manner which was possible in such a society as that of Athens then was. And he certainly produced some great results. He made men think; and out of their thoughts arose, in another generation, philosophies, which have never since ceased to interest the world. Socrates made men think; but he could not do more. He could not discover any such truth to them as would satisfy the yearnings of aroused thought. And, after all, thinking is not an end in itself, any more than walking or eating is an end in itself. We walk in order to promote health, or to reach a particular spot; we eat that we may support bodily strength; and we think, if we do think, that we may by thinking arrive, if we can, at truth, or at something that leads to it. Socrates could set men thinking. But he could not satisfy thought: he was perfectly alive to his failure to do so. The authority of Socrates was, in its way, great: he towered far above any of his contem-

[a] St. John viii. 12  [b] St. Luke x. 16.

poraries. But it was a relative authority; it was bound up with the state of things in Athens at that time. For Socrates his fellow-citizens alone were, practically, his fellow-men: his notion of virtue was that it consisted in the public conduct of a good citizen. All moral obligations were discharged, as he thought, if the laws of Athens were obeyed. He saw no harm in conquering an enemy by injuring him; or in advising a courtesan, like Theodota, how to display herself to the best advantage. However he might make men think, he was himself an ordinary man, and he had nothing to say that could permanently satisfy conscience. He did not, in the gravest matters, rise above the standard of his day and country. In perpetually cross-questioning men, he was like a farmer who should break up his fallow ground, yet have nothing to sow in it; so labouring for a harvest which would not in the event reward his pains.

Here then we see the difference between Socrates and our Lord: it is the difference between earth and heaven. Certainly our Lord did also rouse the minds and consciences of men, by forcing them to think steadily on familiar but uncomprehended truths, on obvious but neglected duties. Witness His conversations with Nicodemus,[a] with the woman of Samaria,[b] with Simon the Pharisee.[c] But then He did not arouse thought and conscience only to let them die back presently into disappointment, or despair, or even into forgetfulness and stagnation. He aroused them, and forthwith presented them with an adequate object; with His Own clear instructions; with Himself. Never, for one moment, is His moral and religious horizon bounded by the narrow requirements of public law, or by the conventional opinions of the men of His day: He rises above these petty and

[a] St. John iii. 1-21.    [b] Ibid. iv. 6-26.    [c] St. Luke vii. 36-47.

# XXXIV] *The Apostolic Commission.* 245

perishing standards with a majestic decision into an atmosphere where criticism is too impossible, to await rebuke: He exhibits an ideal of life which will awe the human conscience to the end of time, since in His case it is at once taught and lived. "I am the Light of the world."[a] "Come unto Me, ye that labour and are heavy laden, and I will refresh you."[b] "For no man knoweth the Son but the Father, neither knoweth any man the Father save the Son, and He to whomsoever the Son will reveal Him."[c] And therefore the Apostles were not to cross-question the nations, but to tell them a higher truth than any thinking that could be stimulated by cross-questioning could possibly lead them to. They were to teach everything in the sphere of thought, or in the sphere of practice, which Jesus had commanded in terms or by implication. "Teaching them to observe all things whatsoever I commanded you."

This is not the least noteworthy feature of our Lord's words, that He does not foresee a time or circumstances when any part of His teaching will become antiquated or untrue, inappropriate or needless. Some of us may know what it is to be reminded of a conversation in bygone days; to stumble upon an old letter, or upon a diary, which we wrote years ago. We have almost lost the clue to the state of mind which led us so to express ourselves then; we find this remark trivial, that a platitude, another of questionable accuracy, a fourth wanting in what now seems to us to be good feeling or good taste. The document is perhaps pervaded by an impulsiveness which we think absurd, or by a want of heart which shames us. It even appears to us that we have so changed, it may or may not be for the better, that we can with difficulty believe ourselves to have uttered

[a] St. John viii. 12.   [b] St. Matt. xi. 28.   [c] *Ibid.* xi. 27.

the reported words, or to have written the lines before us.
And one or two such experiences as this makes us distrust what we say or write now, and to reflect that a time may come, whether in this life or in another state of existence, when we shall regard what we now put forward with unhesitating confidence, as entitled to very scant attention. For in truth, brethren, we men are, at our best, always learning, always revising, correcting, supplementing what we have learnt heretofore; never able to express ourselves positively on subjects which deeply interest us, without feeling that hereafter we, or others, will trace shortcomings, or exaggerations, or elements of paradox or falsehood, in what we say. Our Lord is haunted by no such apprehension as this. He is confident that what He has taught His disciples will hold good for all time; for all races and classes of men; for characters, moods of thought, moral and intellectual atmospheres the most diverse. As He said, "My word shall not pass away,"[a] so now He fearlessly bids His Apostles teach the nations "whatsoever I have commanded you." He reigns, alike in the moral and the intellectual world; and He is certain of the authority of the commission which He gives to teach.

## II.

Secondly, let us observe the range of this commission. It was to embrace all the nations of the world. "Go ye, make disciples of all the nations." This command must appear, when we consider it, to be simply astonishing. Here is, as it seems, a Jewish peasant, surrounded by a small company of uneducated followers, bidding them address themselves in His Name to races, ancient, powerful, refined; to win their intellectual and moral submission to

[a] St. Matt. xxiv. 35.

doctrines and precepts propounded by Himself. "Go make disciples of all nations." The only idea of empire of which the world knew was the empire of material force. Wherever the legions of Rome had penetrated, there followed the judge and the tax-collector: and the nations submitted to what they could not resist, until at length their masters became too weak to control or to protect them. As for an empire of souls, the notion was unheard of. No philosopher could found it, since a philosopher's usual occupation consisted mainly in making intellectual war upon his predecessors or contemporaries. No existing religion could aim at it, since the existing religions were believed to be merely the products of national instincts and aspirations; each religion was part of the furniture of a nation, or at most of a race. Celsus, looking out on Christianity in the second century of our era, with the feelings of Gibbon or of Voltaire, said that a man must be out of his mind to think that Greeks and Barbarians, Romans and Scythians, bondmen and freemen, could ever have one religion. Nevertheless this was the purpose of our Lord. The Apostles were bidden to go and make disciples of all the nations. Yes; all the nations. There was no nation in such religious circumstances, none so cultivated, none so degraded, as to be able to dispense with the teaching and healing power of Jesus Christ, or to be beyond the reach of His salvation.

*a.* Take the Jewish people; the race to which our Lord Himself and His Apostles belonged. The Jewish nation, not less than others, was to be taught by Christ's Apostles; nay, it had a first claim upon their time and labour. This claim our Lord Himself had already, in fact, acknowledged and satisfied. Yet the Jewish nation and religion stood upon a very different footing from all others in the world. The Jewish religion had come from heaven; and the Jewish nation was a Church. The Jewish Church was an imperfectly organised Church, and the Jewish revelation was but a guide to a higher Revelation that was to follow it. But still they were both of God, in a sense which is not true of any other nation or religion in the world. We may sometimes read of attempts made by able men in foreign countries or at home to obliterate this distinction; to represent the worship of Jehovah and the religious institutes of Israel as not very different from those of the deities and nations around. But such negative critics may themselves remind us of a story which is not inopportune, when everybody is still thinking of the late Mr. Darwin. One day two gentlemen visited the site of the old Roman city of Silchester. The accomplished antiquarian, who until lately used to show strangers over the ground, to their great advantage and enjoyment, observed that on this occasion his visitors paid but scant attention to what he had to tell them. He discoursed about the streets, the public buildings, the private houses, the general physiognomy, and the special points of interest in the place; but they were, he said, entirely absorbed in examining the proceedings of earthworms. Earthworms are of course to be found elsewhere than on the site of Silchester; they are to be found where there is nothing of great human and historic interest in the immediate neighbourhood: but these visitors, who were working for the great naturalist, were engaged in discovering what earthworms could do in a long course of centuries to bury out of sight the remains of an ancient city. Now the modern negative critics might seem not seldom to visit the Old Testament in a similar spirit; they have some one subject of secular interest in view to the exclusion of all others; they discuss the chronology, or the age of documents said to be cited or used by the sacred writers, or the successive phases of the Hebrew language, or the traces of historical events which have been lost sight of or unrecognised. Of what they say, some things may be true, and some things false. But rarely or never have they an eye for the real interest of the literature which they attempt to discuss; for its true heights and depths in the world of conscience and of spiritual things; for its moral and religious, as distinct from its external, secular, or literary interest. In these matters we men find, generally speaking, just what we seek. If we are in quest of heavenly things, the veil is lifted, and they are disclosed to us; if only for what belongs to this world, it is ready to our hand, and we get what we look for. These negative critics are on the site of a diviner Silchester, yet looking only for earthworms; and it is not surprising if they should leave with an impression that the field which they explore is like any other field in the world. We need not be alarmed if they tell us that the Old Testament history only resembles other ancient histories; their report on the subject can hardly be deemed decisive.

No! Israel would never have been what it has been to the human race, unless its religious annals had been altogether unique; unless it had been flooded with a light which was not given elsewhere. For Israel was especially the people of religion, the people of Revelation: although its Revelation was only partial, and in our Lord's day its practical religion had wellnigh shrunk to the proportions of an outward form. And therefore, if the command had run, " Go, teach the Jewish people," it would have been a very bold command. For all the conditions of success were wanting, apparently, to the Apostles; social distinction, learning, political weight, familiarity with the methods by which influence is won and held; while these things belonged to the classes which were decisively opposed to Jesus of Nazareth. Yet no exception is made. Or rather, Israel is to have a first claim [a] upon the missionaries who are sent forth with the commission, " Go, make disciples of all the nations."

β. It may indeed be said that the Apostles and the mass of the Jewish people would find a common ground, in the Mosaic Law, in the theocratic sense of all Jews, in the instinct of race; an instinct of extraordinary power in the instance before us. All this the Apostles had to fall back upon, so long as they confined their labours to their own countrymen. And they might have reflected that, in past days, some men, of no social weight or consideration whatever, of no learning, of no standing in the State, or in the priestly or prophetic order, had yet exercised the greatest influence upon the destinies of Israel. The peasants of Galilee might at least be to their generation what Amos had been to his: and if the task was difficult and dangerous, it was not, at least, utterly paradoxical.

But the command runs, "Go, make disciples of all the nations." The great peoples of the world knew nothing of the historical and religious past of Israel, or knew only enough to feel for them an unconcealed aversion and contempt. Think how our Lord's instructions to the Apostles would have been regarded by an educated Greek of the time. Greece was the home of scientific and artistic culture. She lost her political freedom when she came into conflict with the legions of Rome; but in everything that touches thought and taste, and art and imagination, she gave laws to her conquerors. Yet for all that, she needed the teaching which the poor Galileans had to give. What

[a] St. Luke xxiv. 47.

was the religion of Greece? It was mainly a worship of corrupt human nature under various forms; a worship of human strength, human cleverness, human waywardness, human wickedness. Nothing is more remarkable than the failure of the Greek theology to attain in Zeus a supreme absolute divinity. And in the religion of the Greek people we find nothing like an Almighty, much less a Holy God, while a God of Love is utterly undreamt of. All the fiercest and most debasing passions of men were freely attributed by the Greek people to their deities, without a suspicion that they were thereby degrading the divinity; until at last an effort was made by some leading minds, such as Plato, to raise the conception of God to something more pure and, as we should say, spiritual. But this experiment cannot be said to have succeeded. The old popular religion was too brittle and baseless a thing to be tampered with. To discuss its origin, to assign a higher meaning to its usages and ideas, was, in fact, to subject it to a process of dissolution. It decayed, slowly but inevitably, as a religion, while philosophy tried to rehabilitate it; and when this process was complete, philosophy could not take its place. For, say what men will, philosophy is one thing and religion is another. Philosophy, at any rate, deals exclusively with thought, religion largely with conscience. Philosophy can never be for the many; while religion is evidently false to its essential character if it exists only for the few.

Thus it was that, while in Greek life, as it met the eye, everything seemed so proud and fair, there was an undertone of disquiet and pain, which more than justified the merciful words of our Lord Jesus Christ. If in all that relates to the outward grace of human existence, or to the higher culture of man's mental faculties, Greece had everything to teach, it is most certain that, so far as man's heart and conscience were concerned, she had everything to learn. A few years hence, and there would be plenty of work for St. Paul to do, not only in Philippi and in Thessalonica, but in Corinth, and in Athens. Greece, if any country, would dispute the claims of a Jewish Peasant to teach her what was true. And yet Greece had deep need of the eternal Gospel; and the scorn which might have been provoked by the words of Christ would assuredly die away, when the time came, into the gratitude of worship and of love.

'Ah!' it will be said, 'this is an old story. You are talking as if we knew only of the ancient world as our fathers conceived it a hundred years ago; the world of classical antiquity, of Greece and Rome. But since then men have learnt to entertain a much wider and juster idea of the religions of antiquity, particularly of the religions of the ancient East. First on the Continent, and then in this country, the sacred books of these religions have been rendered into the languages of modern Europe, and we read, in our own tongues, the ancient words which were to Persia, to India, to China, what our Bible is to us. We find ourselves in intimate contact with religions, compared with which Christianity is a modern innovation; and it is too late to parade pretensions which were only tolerable when knowledge was limited, and thought on these subjects was not yet free.'

This is what may be said; but we shall, I think, find that our larger knowledge, while enhancing our sense of the boldness of our Lord's claim to teach all the nations, does not diminish our sense of its justice. Undoubtedly of late years we have learned to see more clearly that in the ancient religions there were primary elements of truth imbedded in blocks of surrounding error, and often even gigantic errors which were but distortions of hidden truths. Had it not been so, these religions would long since have broken up altogether. They have lasted so long only in consequence of the incorporated elements of truth which have made their reception possible. But their course was and is, upon the whole, a downward course; the truth in them becoming less and fainter, the error greater and darker. This might be illustrated from the case of the Indian religions. The earliest religious notions are far purer than the later ones; the early Vedas than the later commentaries on the Vedas. The modern idea that the religious history of mankind is a progressive and ascending movement from fetichism to Theism, is at issue with St. Paul's account, at the beginning of his Epistle to the Romans, of the progressive perversion and degradation of the idea of God, through man's disloyalty to the light of nature and conscience.[a] And St. Paul's account is really in accordance with the facts. The falsehood which was in all the old heathen religions constantly dragged them down to a lower and lower point of degradation. As men lost sight of God, they fell more and more entirely under the power of the natural world. Thus, while as in the two forms of Indian religion the higher minds saw the end of man in the absorption of the individual in the universal life of nature, or in an universal annihilation, the mass of the people, as in all Pantheistic Nature-religions, worshipped the several powers of Nature, as so many separate divinities. And how deeply degraded the worship of Nature's productive powers might become, we see in the Moloch and Baal worships that meet us in Holy Scripture, where sensuality and cruelty were direct results of the very idea of the worship. The more we know of the heathen religions of the ancient East, the more striking is the contrast between the impotence of

[a] Rom. i. 18-32.

the germ of truth which they severally embody, and the power of the falsehood and degradation with which it is associated, and which made our Lord's commission to His Apostles so needful as an errand of mercy.

True indeed it is, that, in respect of these ancient religions, Jesus Christ is still on the threshold of His work. But those who know most about India and Japan, tell us that in these populations there has already begun a fermentation of thought, not unlike that which preceded the conversion of the Roman Empire fifteen centuries ago. And, whatever for a time may be the discouragement of the Christian army, while laying siege to these fortresses of ancient error, despair is impossible, if only for the reason, that whether in Palestine or Greece, or India or China, or Japan or Persia or Africa, the Christian commanders know that they have friends within the walls. They have a friend in man's inextinguishable thirst for truth, which nothing but God's one revelation of Himself in Christ can satisfy; they have a friend in man's conscience, never utterly beyond the reach of an appeal to the sense of sin, and never to find perfect rest, save in the atoning work of Jesus Christ Crucified; above all, they have a friend in the latent capacity of every human being for the Divine Life, which, nevertheless, can only be lived in union with Him Who is both God and Man. Sooner, or later, these allies within the walls will open the gates of each city of error, and bid the Christian hosts take possession of it in their Master's Name.

## III.

Thirdly, observe the encouragement which is to persuade the Apostles to undertake this commission: "Lo, I am with you alway, even unto the end of the world." Here, it well might seem, the consciousness of authority reaches its climax. No mere man, being in possession of his reason and judgment, would have dared to utter these words. You and I are looking forward to that great change which we name Death. Do we know enough to say to any friend, or child, or pupil: "When I am gone from sight, I will still be with you." These great words of Jesus Christ are not satisfied by saying that Christ's character, or teaching, or atoning Death, would be the perpetual possession of His Church. "I am with you all days" means, if anything, a personal Presence; and such a promise, most assuredly, He alone could make, Who, as being truly God, knew Himself to be Master of both worlds. "I am with you all days." He promises us, not the gift of a good memory, but His Presence.

Let us reflect how different the case would be if He had only said, 'The memory of My life and work shall be with you alway.' What a difference there is between a mere memory and a presence! At first, indeed, when we have just lost a relation or friend, memory, in its importunity and anguish, seems to be and to do all that a presence could do—perhaps even more. It gathers up the past and heaps it on the present; it crowds into the thoughts of a few minutes the incidents of a lifetime; it has about it an eagerness and a vividness which was wanting, while its object was still with us! But then a memory decays. That it should do so seems impossible at first: we protest to ourselves and to the world that it will be as fresh as ever to the last day of our existence. But memory is only an effort of the human mind, while a presence is independent of it. And the human mind has limited powers, which are easily exhausted; it cannot always continue on the strain. So a time comes when memory's first freshness passes. Then other thoughts and interests and occupations crowd in upon us, and claim their share of the little all that we have to give; and thus that which seemed to be so fresh and imperishable is already becoming faded and indistinct. Think of some personal friend, or of any of the celebrated men whose names were on every one's lips, and who have died within the last few years. At first it seems as if you might predict with confidence that the world would go on thinking and talking of them for at least a generation. But already the sure and fatal action of time upon a memory, however great and striking, is making itself felt. Even in our thoughts about them, the departed are passing into that land of shadows, where shadows soon die away into the undistinguishable haze and gloom beyond.

It is otherwise with a presence, whether we see it or not. We know that it is here. If our friend is in the next room, busily occupied, and unable to give us his time just now, still the knowledge that he is close at hand, and can be applied to, if necessary, is itself a comfort to us. We can go to him if we like. His being here places us in a very different position from that which we should occupy if he had left us, and we could only think of him as having been with us heretofore, though really absent now. A presence is a fact, independent of our moods of mind: it is a fact, whether we recognise it or not; and in our Lord's Presence there is a fulness of joy[a] which means hope, work, power, eventual victory.

This is a factor in the life and work of the Church of Christ with which persons do not reckon who look at her only from the outside, and judge of her strength and prospects as they would judge those of any human society. They say that she will die out, because this or that force

[a] Ps. xvi. 11.

which has undoubted weight in the affairs of men is for the time being telling heavily against her. If large sections of popular feeling or literature, or the public policy of some great country, or the influence of a new and enterprising philosophy, or the bias of a group of powerful minds, are against her, forthwith we hear the cry, 'The mission of the Apostles is now coming to an end; the Church will fail.' Do not be in too great a haste, my good friends, about this; you have yet to reckon with a force invisible, and perhaps, so far as you are concerned, unsuspected, but never more real and operative than at this moment; you have forgotten the Presence of Christ. He did not retreat to heaven when His first Apostles died; He promised to be with them to the end of the world; He spoke not merely to the eleven before Him, but to the vast multitude of successors, who defiled before His Eye down to the utmost limits of time. "Lo, I am with you all the days, even to the end of the world." With us by His Spirit; with us in the great Sacrament of His love; with us amid weaknesses, divisions, failures, disappointments: He is with us still. And it is His Presence alone which sustains His envoys, and gives to their work whatever it has had, or has, or has to have, of vigour and permanence.

With that work every Christian should associate himself. Every Christian should have in him, together with the love of Christ, something of the heart of an Apostle. Each of us should feel that his creed is, and must be, in the best sense of the word, aggressive: it must assail the forms of sin and error which prevail around it. Every worshipper of Christ must in his measure make disciples, and proclaim the undying commands and truths of Christ. And then with him too there shall tarry the Presence of the Most Holy, as the sanction and warrant of his work.

You are not asked to-day to assist any one missionary object; and therefore it is the more allowable to say that not to be doing something by word, or act, or self-sacrifice, for the extension of Christ's kingdom among men, is to be already losing a true hold on Christianity. If you should desire a practical suggestion, there is the collection for the Bishop of London's Fund throughout the diocese next Sunday; an effort to bring the hundreds of thousands in this great city who live, it may be feared, without any religion at all, within the hearing of the Gospel and Church of Christ. Or there is that noble man—a man of truly Apostolic proportions,—Bishop Steere, on a short visit to England, asking help for his work among the races, for whom he has already done so much, on the eastern coast of Africa; and you might send for him what you can afford to the Office of the Society for the Propagation of the Gospel. Anyhow, do something to associate yourselves with Christ's Apostles; something that, in another life, you may look back upon as having contributed, however little, to carrying on the great enterprise that began when Our Lord bade these simple Galileans make disciples of all the nations, and that will only end with the last hour of time.

# SERMON XXXV.

## WITNESSES FOR JESUS CHRIST.

ACTS I. 8.

*Ye shall be witnesses unto Me.*

AT this Easter season we naturally turn to the consideration of those precious words which fell from our Blessed Lord during the interval that elapsed between His Resurrection and His Ascension into heaven. And among these sayings, the text has the distinction of being the last; it is the parting utterance of our ascending Saviour. "Ye shall be witnesses unto Me both in Jerusalem, and in all Judæa, and in Samaria, and unto the uttermost part of the earth." And then we are told that "when He had spoken these things, while they beheld, He was taken up; and a cloud received Him out of their sight."

Undoubtedly these words of Jesus must have had a meaning for the Apostles which they could have for no other men. The Apostles had been told that they were to "bear witness," because they "had been with" Jesus "from the beginning."[a] And when afterwards St. Matthias was elected unto the place of Judas, the electors were

[a] St. John xv. 27.

reminded that their choice was limited to "those men who had companied with" themselves "all the time that the Lord Jesus went in and out among them," since they needed a "witness to the Resurrection."[a] Thus the text is in fact an anticipation of the history which is afterwards unfolded in the Acts of the Apostles. Parting from the holy city, the circles of missionary effort widen perpetually; they reach beyond Judæa, beyond Samaria, beyond the bounds of civilised heathendom, towards the full measure of their predestined range, "the uttermost part of the earth."

Still, although for the Apostles personally, and for the Apostles as representing their successors in the Episcopate, our Lord's words had this distinguished and unrivalled significance, they also contain a wider range of meaning, which leads me to invite your attention to them this evening. For the Apostles standing before their departing Lord impersonate not merely the Ministry, but the Church; and Jesus, in His last words on earth, speaks not merely to the clerical order; He bequeaths a legacy of glory and of suffering to the millions of Christendom. "Ye shall be witnesses unto Me."

I.

"Witnesses unto Me." Our Lord Himself, in His sacred Person, is the solemn truth, the glorious reality, to which His servants are to bear their witness. Certainly in a parallel passage in St. Luke's Gospel our Lord, when referring to His Passion and His Resurrection,[b] is represented as saying, "Ye are witnesses of these things." But there are some grounds for believing that the words in St. Luke may have been uttered at a slightly

[a] Acts i. 21, 22.   [b] St. Luke xxiv. 46-48.

earlier date than that of the actual Ascension. And although, as a matter of fact, the "witness to the Resurrection" was, from the necessity of their case, the leading feature of the recorded preaching of the Apostles, and witness to His redemptive work was clearly involved in any true witness to the Person of Jesus, still we may not overlook the precise form of expression which our Lord adopts in the text. 'Witnesses unto Me! Others might witness to My miracles, they were wrought in the face of day; others might repeat My discourses, "spoken in the temple, whither the Jews always resort;" and you, in witnessing to Me, will witness likewise to My works and to My teaching. But My works and My teaching are but the rays which proceed from My inmost life, My personality, Myself; and it is to this, to nothing less than this, to all that this implies, that I bid you witness.'

Contrast our Lord's words with what we should expect from a great man at the present day. We should expect him to tell us that his endowments or his achievements were after all the gift of Heaven; that in himself he was nothing, and unworthy of the greatness which had been forced upon him. If he should forget his native poverty, and claim honour for himself, as distinct from the gift or influence with which he had been endowed, then our good opinion would be outraged. We should, in our deep disappointment, proclaim him unworthy of his greatness, as being incapable of that modesty which is so winning in human conduct, because it is so true to the facts of human life. Jesus Christ our Lord defies this rule of human judgments, and the conscience of mankind justifies Him in defying it. He Who could say to the men of His generation, "Which of you convinceth Me of sin?"[a]; He Who could dare to utter the tremendous words, "I and the

[a] St. John viii. 46.

Father are One,"ª could truly feel that it was impossible for Him to eclipse any higher greatness by drawing attention to Himself. His words were His Own. His works were His Own. As God He was the author and giver of the gifts which He received as Man. And therefore He thought it not robbery to draw the eyes of men away from the miracles and words which flashed forth from Him, away from the sights and sounds which heralded a mighty presence, to Himself, the Worker, the Speaker, Who gave their greatness to the words which He spake, and to the works which He wrought. My brethren, the words of Jesus, which challenge " witness," attention, homage, reverence, love, for His personal Self, are only not intolerable because nothing less would have been adequate or true.

II.

But you ask, How can we bear witness to a person? We can describe a fact like a miracle, or we can repeat an instruction like the Sermon on the Mount. We can witness to that which we know; but how can we know, how can we seize, feel, see, possess, so subtle, so impalpable a thing as a person? especially how can we witness to a superhuman person, to One Whom His Apostle describes as " over all, God blessed for ever;"ᵇ to One Whom we name in the Creed, " God of God, Light of Light, Very God of Very God"?

Let me, by way of reply, suggest to you in turn another question. Can we be witnesses to each other? Unquestionably we can; for we can know each other. And by this knowledge we mean not knowledge of the form and colour of the body or features, but knowledge of that which gives to features and to form their interest

ª St. John x. 30.      ᵇ Rom. ix. 5.

—knowledge of the invisible spirit which underlies them. That which interests man lastingly in his brother man, as being the seat and the object of human interest, is the soul. We cannot, indeed, see the soul with the eye of the body. But with the eye of the mind we can see it, and form a very clear conception of it, which we call "character." For in this life the soul is linked to the body on such terms, that it can come forth from the shadow of the invisible world, and assert its presence. It cannot be seen in its essence; but it can be seen in its effects. The body is but its home, and its instrument, which it moulds, bends, subdues, weakens or invigorates, overshadows or illuminates, by its presence. By the organs of the body the soul moves forth from its recesses, and enters into communion with other souls. Learned men have recently been discussing afresh that most interesting problem—the origin of language. But the Church of God has from the first seen in human language a special gift of God, complete when it was first given, and a counterpart of the gift of an immortal soul; an expression of its life; a medium of giving currency to its feeling and its thought. When a man speaks, we read in his language, in its form, in its tone, in its very accent, the movement of an undying spirit. We read the strength or weakness of an understanding, the warmth of a heart, the vigour or feebleness of a will; we read thought, resolve, feeling, character. Language is the living expression of the soul's life; it flows forth from the soul, as the spring of water from the fountain: "out of the abundance of the heart the mouth speaketh."[a] Man cannot really disguise for long periods the true features of the soul, even though, like the ancient hypocrites of the days of David, he should give fair words with the mouth, but curse with the heart.[b]

[a] St. Matt. xii. 34.    [b] Ps. lxii. 4.

For language is too true an instrument to be lastingly tampered with; it is a revelation of soul to soul; it is a relentless witness, which drags the human spirit forth from its hiding-place to be judged publicly, and before its time, at the bar of humanity; it is an artist, who traces, without much real exaggeration or disguise, the lines of beauty which grace the inmost features of an invisible spirit. And as through language the soul speaks to the ear of man, so by action the soul addresses itself to the eye of man. Action is a more perfect unveiling of the soul than language; for it implies more deliberation. When a man acts, specially under circumstances of responsibility or of difficulty, which invest action with emphasis, and make it the product of the whole force of his being, then his true passions, instincts, lines of thought, capacities, all his littlenesses, and all his greatness, come to the surface, and you read his inmost nature in the text of his action. Once more, the soul is too active and imperious a tenant not to leave its mark upon the texture of the body, which it has inhabited for a term of years. We read something of the soul in the human countenance; it speaks through the human eye. This is why when those whom we love or honour have passed away, we love to detain on canvas or in photograph a memorial, which recalls to us something more than an accustomed form, since it is the symbol of a spiritual nature. The eye can rest on nothing beneath the sun so deeply interesting as the face of any child of Adam. Every human face is a point at which we obtain an insight into an unseen world; since every human face, not less by its reserves than by its disclosures, records the play of thought and passion within a subtle immaterial spirit. Fear, joy, pride, lust, rage, sadness, shame, love, patience, —each by reiterated throbs leaves its mark upon the flesh, till at length the soul has moulded the ductile matter, so that it shall truly portray its tale of baseness or of beauty; till at length we have produced a picture which we involuntarily exhibit before the eyes of our fellow-men as a speaking revelation of our inmost life. The bright eye and the lofty forehead proclaim to all thought and genius; while there are lines and features at the disposal of the moral forces of the soul, which can express such scorn, contempt, and hatred as might be natural to devils, and others that can portray the tenderness of benevolence, or the refinement of high sanctity. Thus, through a man's language, his actions, and his countenance, his soul speaks to the soul of his brother man; and while the essence of the soul is still necessarily hidden, the outward effects of its action convey a living and accurate impression of its secret life.

### III.

Now in Jesus Christ, God made use of this provision of His creative wisdom to enter into communion with His creatures. Reason may discover God's existence and His attributes; reason may even attain under favourable conditions to a cold and partial appreciation of His glory. But to reason, unaided by Revelation outside the soul, and by grace within it, God must ever seem abstract, remote, inaccessible; too certain and necessary a Fact to be refused a place in thought, yet too wholly disconnected from human interests to be regarded with anything approaching to that passionate affection, which is a characteristic of the Christian life. Therefore, that He might embrace His fallen creatures with a Revelation of His beauty, so intelligible and so captivating, that rejection, or even resistance, should seem wellnigh impossible; therefore, that in characters, which from long practice man would read at sight, God might reveal to man His inmost Life; the Most High robed Himself in a human body and a human soul. This was the Incarnation. The thoughtful Gentile might have learnt something concerning Him in the natural world; the devout Jew might have read more of His true character in the Mosaic law; but a living personal revelation of what He is was reserved for the faith of Christendom.

There are strangers, alas! to our faith, who yet confess that in the Gospels they encounter a Form of unapproached grace and power. In the last age not merely the insulted and suffering Church of France, but infidel writers like Diderot and Rousseau challenged the sceptics of the time, in language which has since become classical, to match, if they could, the moral beauty of the Gospel. For in the Gospel we meet with One Who in His pre-eminent humanity is perfectly one with us, yet also most mysteriously distinct. So rare and refined is His type of manhood, that He escapes the peculiarities of either sex, since He combines the tender sympathies of woman with the strength and decision of man. He is a carpenter, but no trade or calling has dwarfed or narrowed the lofty stature of His life: He is pure benevolence, tied to no one form of human existence, yet adapting Himself to all. He is born in extreme poverty, yet He has no grudge against wealth; the wealthy classes are in the Gospel "the unfortunates." He is born of the race of Israel, on whom there has ever been stamped a national spirit of fierce and unrivalled intensity, yet His Jewish blood carries with it no trace of Jewish prejudice. He rises in His mighty charity above the barriers of race and character which divide the nations. He is claimed as their representative, by Greek and Roman, and African and Teuton, no less truly than by the children of His people; yet the closest scrutiny can discover in Him as little of the formalism and fanaticism of the Jew as of the cynical intellectualism of the Greek, or of the ambition and statecraft of the Roman. No class prejudice, no professional prejudice, no national prejudice, has left its taint upon that Ideal Form, so as to make it less than representative of pure humanity. Yet, so far is He from being a cold, passionless statue, divested of all interests, strictly human, that there is a warmth and vividness in His character which none who have truly loved or wept can fail to understand and to embrace. Thus He loves with the passionate tenderness that shed tears over the grave of Lazarus, yet His affections contract not the faintest trace of an earthly blemish. He hates evil, and He denounces it in stern and unsparing words, but He is never, in the heat of opposition or condemnation, betrayed for one moment into an unbalanced statement; Herod does not make Him a revolutionist, the Pharisees do not force Him to be an Antinomian. His triumphs cannot disturb, and His humiliations do but enhance, the serene, the incomparable grandeur and self-possession of His soul. Earnest and yet calm, full of tenderness yet full of resolution, living in contemplation yet ever ready for action, He combines as none other, that which compels our reverence with that which provokes our ecstatic affection. The nobleness and the loveliness of the human spirit, which ever elsewhere are found apart or joined in unequal proportions, are in Him fused and blended so perfectly, that —I quote the noble words of a layman of our own day —"though the mental eye be strained to aching, it cannot discover whether That on Which it gazes in the Gospel be more an Object of reverence or an Object of love."[a]

Well might we surmise that such a character as this

[a] Goldwin Smith.

was more than human. We know ourselves too well, my brethren, to suppose that human nature would conceive the full idea, much less that it could create the reality. Even to the Roman officer, who stood beneath the Cross on the evening of Good Friday, the Truth revealed itself; the flash of moral beauty lightening up the darkness which then might seem to have closed in upon the world. "Truly this was the Son of God."[a] Nay, more, Jesus Himself had used language which no intimacy of union between God and holy souls would warrant if it were not literally true. He speaks to the Father of the "glory which I had with Thee before the world was."[b] He says solemnly, "Before Abraham was, I am."[c] Again, "No man hath ascended up to heaven but He Which came down from heaven, even the Son of Man Which is in heaven."[d] These and such-like sayings, which the Jews understood and condemned as blasphemy, which the Apostles understood and accepted as statements of the literal truth, force us to a dilemma. Either we must resign that vision of beauty which we meet in the character of Jesus as an untrustworthy phantom, since it is dashed with a pretension involving at once falsehood and blasphemy, or we must confess that Jesus is Divine; Divine, not in the sense in which men in a vague way ascribe divinity to the highest human excellence without meaning to assert literal Godhead; but Divine in that absolute and incommunicable sense, in which we ascribe Godhead to the Universal Father, Whose Power, Wisdom, and Goodness know no bounds. Jesus is God; and in the acts, the words, the very physiognomy of Jesus, the Apostles came face to face with the Supreme, Infinite, Perfect Being of beings. Although dwelling in light

[a] St. Matt. xxvii. 54.  
[b] St. John xvii. 5.  
[c] St. John viii. 58.  
[d] *Ibid.* iii. 13.

which no man could approach unto,[a] He had passed forth from His inaccessible home; He had taken our nature as an instrument through which to act upon us, but also as an interpreter who should translate His Own matchless perfections into audible words and visible actions; so that He might be felt, studied, surveyed, known, ay, even handled, and then witnessed to with all the devotion that is due to a revelation of the highest truth and of the highest beauty. "That which was from the beginning, which we have heard, which we have seen with our eyes, which we have looked upon, and our hands have handled, of the Word of Life; (for the Life was manifested, and we have seen It, and bear witness, and show unto you that Eternal Life Which was with the Father, and was manifested unto us;) That which we have seen and heard declare we unto you."[b]

Surely this very week we have witnessed, or rather we have experienced, in this metropolis the power which a strong character can wield over the thoughts and feelings of men.[c] London has just offered to a stranger of European reputation a welcome so spontaneous, and wellnigh so universal, that at this very moment the unaccustomed spectacle of your enthusiasm rivets the eyes of astonished Europe. Yet they who study the subtle laws and currents which affect opinion, have told us that, in this remarkable demonstration, it would be an error to recognise sympathy with any political or religious opinion: since the enthusiasm has been shared by men of all classes and creeds. You have been paying homage to courage, dis-

[a] 1 Tim. vi. 16.  [b] 1 St. John i. 1-3.
[c] General Garibaldi entered London on Monday, April 11, 1864. Since these words were uttered, the preacher has learned facts respecting Garibaldi's attitude towards Christianity, which would now oblige him to suppress the allusion in the text, or to express himself differently.

interestedness, and simplicity; to a man who, having power and wealth within his grasp, cared not to clutch them; to personal qualities, which always and everywhere exact a tribute of admiration and respect, whether we detect them in the past or in the present, whether in a countryman or in a foreigner, whether in the service of a cause which forfeits or of a cause which commands our sympathies. But permit me to remind you that an enthusiasm, of which the object is merely human, must pass away, since its object is necessarily transient and imperfect. As you, my countrymen, sit before me, with the ashes of Wellington beneath your feet, you little dream of the warmth with which Englishmen named their great general on the morrow of Waterloo. One only has succeeded in creating an impression, which is as fresh in the hearts and thoughts of His true disciples at this moment as it was eighteen centuries ago; and as we listen to His words, and watch His actions, and almost seem to gaze on His face, irradiated with superhuman beauty in the pages of the Gospels, we feel that He, as none other, had a right to command distant and unborn generations to echo the enthusiasm of His first followers, and to say to us Englishmen of the nineteenth century, "Ye shall be witnesses unto Me."

### IV.

Witnesses unto Me! Brethren, it is a most solemn question; is there anything in our conduct, or our words, anything that we do, or that we endure, that really bears witness, before the eyes of our fellow-men, to the life and work of our ascended and invisible Saviour? Or are we living, speaking, feeling, acting, thinking, much as we might have thought, acted, felt, spoken, and lived, if He had never brightened our existence; if we had been born of Pagan parents, and had never heard of Bethlehem and Calvary? Or are we bearing Him what our conscience tells us is a partial witness; a witness of language but not of conduct; a witness which attests those features of His work and doctrine which we prefer, rather than all that we know or might know about Him, and about that heritage of grace and truth which He has brought from heaven? For, if we believe in our hearts that Jesus is God, we must see how from this glorious and lofty faith there results a derived faith in all the words and works of Jesus; just as when we stand upon a central mountain height we command a panoramic view, we overlook all lesser elevations, and we understand how all the diverging valleys at our feet are fertilised by the streams which flow from the rock we have climbed, and which towers so conspicuously above them. If we have the happiness sincerely to believe the fact that Jesus is God, it cannot be a difficulty to us that His Death is a world-redeeming sacrifice for sin, that His Scriptures are inspired and infallible, that His Sacraments are channels of His quickening life. And as we witness to His Person, we must witness, according to our measure, to all that He has attested or authorised or wrought; because He in Whose truth and wisdom we place absolute reliance has authorised and attested and worked it. Rising from an analysis of His character to a belief in His Godhead, descending from a faith in His Godhead to a perfect acceptance of all which He teaches us; we meet the clear, unequivocal, inalienable duty, of witnessing to Him, His Person, His Work, His Words, as the distinctive law of the Christian life.

This witness is the debt which all Christians owe to Jesus Christ our Lord. No class, or sex, or disposition, or age, or race, can claim exemption. We cannot delegate our profession of belief in Jesus, and of love for Jesus, to our clergy. It is not merely that we are bound to witness to Him. If we are living Christian lives, we cannot help doing so. The power and beauty of the Christian life does not depend upon the accidents which part men from each other in this world; it has nothing to do with station, education, income, or blood. In Christ Jesus neither the presence nor the absence of these things availeth anything, but the new creation. There is a ray of heavenly light which plays almost visibly upon the soul that enjoys real communion with Jesus; a beauty of spirit and temper, which tells its own tale, and which is an eloquent missionary. The soul that believes and prays cannot close up the doors of feeling and of thought; cannot prevent the escape of that heavenly virtue, of those powers of the eternal world, which have renewed its own deepest life. Such a soul recommends prayer, and sacraments, and all that brings men close to God by the mere fact of its own felt unearthliness.

Be Christians indeed, and you will forthwith witness for Jesus. You who are at the summits of society, and you who are at its base; you who teach, and you who learn; you who command, and you who obey; masters and servants, old and young, unlettered and scholars, each of you may bear his witness to our Almighty Saviour. In the lower and feeble sense they who practise the natural virtues, witness to Him, Who is the Source of all goodness. And thus courage under difficulties, and temperance amid self-indulgent livers, and justice truly observed between man and man, are forms of witness. They bear this witness who are in power, and who, renouncing selfish purposes, aim at the good of others. They too bear it, who have wealth, and who spend it not in perishing baubles, but in relieving the mass of bodily or spiritual suffering, which in this metropolis presents such a ghastly contrast to the luxury that might seem to forget its existence. The friendless young man in London, who leads a pure life amidst strong temptations; the maid-of-all-work, who serves a hard master faithfully and affectionately; the delicately-bred lady, who renounces the empty attractions of society, to nurse the fever-stricken sufferer in the ward of a hospital, or to teach a fallen sister, from whom her own pure nature shrinks, that it is possible to be pure,—these, turning their eye on Calvary, witness to Jesus. To sacrifice self for others, to sacrifice self for truth, is to bear the witness. Each one whom I see before me, if he loves Jesus Christ, may witness to Him. Yes, my hearers, though you are in weak health, or in narrow circumstances, or elderly and unmarried, or have a sensitive respect for public opinion, and such a dread of putting yourselves forward, that anything like a public profession seems to you to imply insincerity, you too may forget your prejudices and your sensitiveness in forgetting self at the feet of your Lord. And you, who have a strong nature, a hard head, or overmastering impulses; you, who fancy that your self-development into a healthy animal, or into a vigorous thinker, is your highest mark of destiny; you who cultivate originality, and who proudly disdain the lessons or precepts which would force you, as you deem, into the type and mould of common men; you, too, after a while, may learn that you were in the Heart of Jesus, when He said to the representatives of His Church, "Ye shall be witnesses unto Me." For nature is the raw material which grace moulds for God; and a strong nature does not lose its strength because it has been made holy and pure. Such is the range and power of grace, that we can despair of no man. Out of the very stones of pride and of unbelief it can raise up children to the Father of the faithful.[a]

But they, especially, who know our Lord in His pardoning mercy, and who have looked up from the depths of spiritual agony to the Great Sufferer, from Whose open Wounds there streams a tide of atoning virtue, to find in Him rest and peace—they will hardly be content with a silent witness. They will speak for Him, as from a full heart, whenever they can do so. For the disease which He heals is universal, and the efficacy of His cure is undoubted. It is a real distress to them, not merely that He should be wronged or misrepresented, but that He should be forgotten. All of you, believe it, may bear this witness also. The redemptive Love of Jesus, like the sun in the heavens, is the inheritance of all who will come to have a share in it : and, as with the heart that Love is believed in unto righteousness, so with the mouth confession of it is made unto salvation.[b] They who have natural opportunities for influence, who teach the young, who write for the press, who come into contact with many friends or many dependants, can bear this witness for the Lord Who bought them. They need not shrink back from the sense of their own unworthiness, since they are witnesses not merely to His Person but to His grace. It is indeed easy thus to witness for Christ, in a state of society where there is perfect freedom of opinion. It is hardly difficult to witness for Him, in the face of social pressure and against established but disarmed ungodliness. But to witness for Christ, as did the first Christians, when torture and death were the penalty of loyalty; to refuse to scatter the incense to Cæsar when refusal was to embrace an agony ; to speak for Jesus from the rack or rom the scaffold, when the broken accents of the sufferer were

[a] St. Matt. iii. 9.     [b] Rom. x. 10.

raised by the force of his death-struggle to the sublimest height of impassioned and burning eloquence;—this is a witness which Christians have borne, and which is recorded to rebuke our feeble Christianity. Not merely grey-haired Apostles, like James and Peter and Paul; not merely saints of high learning and station, and force of character, like Polycarp, or Justin Martyr, or Cyprian; but rough soldiers and poor working men, and mothers of families, and young lads and maidens; those in whom the pulse of life was strong, and those in whom it was feeble, have thus carried forward again and again their witness for Christ to a point of heroic endurance. If their courage provokes our wonder, it surely might strengthen our weakness or forbid our fears.

In this witness of suffering, and of silent persevering obedience, we see the central element of the growth and victory of the Church. Argument may have done something; but the masses of men have no time for argument, and are inaccessible to its force. Miracles actually witnessed may have done more; although the Gospel-history itself may convince us that the evidence of miracle cannot alone carry conviction to a stubborn unbeliever; he has many resources for evading it. But the Christian life, in which the love of Jesus Christ has dethroned and crushed out the natural selfishness of the human soul, exerts a silent but resistless fascination over at least a large number of those who are brought into close contact with it. It is not the influence of high education, or of vigorous intellect, or of disciplined will. It is moral beauty which is seen, as you gaze at it, to be true and to be strong, and which compels first admiration and love, and afterwards reverence and submission.

Again and again in the early days of Christianity the ordinary current of social influences was reversed, and the aristocracy of birth or wealth learnt how to believe and to obey from the plebeian neighbour or the poor slave who was yet the true nobleman of the Church,—a very peer in the aristocracy of sanctity. Again and again the little maid spoke to Naaman of the healing virtue of the waters of Israel. Again and again Daniel prophesied and suffered in the palaces of the second Babylon. St. Paul tells the Philippians that there were worshippers of Christ shedding forth light and truth among the slaves of the Cæsar Nero.[a] And many a Roman lady must have learnt the preciousness of her undying soul, and the power of the Atoning Blood, from the poor Syrian slave-girl who arranged her toilet or who waited at her table. Thus the Church expanded in the midst of a hostile society in virtue of the power of its secret life. And that which we admire in the glorious past must be our hope in the anxious future; not merely because Christianity maintains its ascendency, by its hold upon the lives of individual Christians, but because society itself would perish if it were not reinforced by an unselfish witness to the Life of Jesus. There are vast reservoirs in which all the ambitions, and lusts, and brutalities of men are confined, as it were, within artificial embankments; and no embankment can permanently resist the pressure, and prevent the overwhelming ruin of a social catastrophe, if the materials of resistance be not welded together by some higher principle than the self-interest of classes; if it do not rest more or less upon the foundation of a charity which witnesses by word and deed to the transcendent moral majesty, ay, to the glorious Godhead, of the Lord Jesus.

Read yonder inscription which commemorates the great architect who built St. Paul's. It bids you look around

[a] Phil. i. 13; iv. 22.

this Cathedral, since this Cathedral itself is his memorial: "Si quæris monumentum, circumspice." And the scattered company of His faithful witnesses are the true monument of the Lord Jesus; they represent to other men something of the glory of their invisible Lord. They may be met with less frequently on the highways of power, or fame, or wealth than elsewhere. But at this moment our Lord is represented in all classes of society by devoted Christians, who hand on from this to another generation the lustre of a life, which is the best evidence of the Gospel. "Si quæris monumentum, circumspice." Look around, watch, and you will see them. Nay, rather, resolve this night by the grace of Christ to join that company of His witnesses. What a power might go forth from beneath this dome into the great city which lies around us, if each Christian who hears me would resolve, God helping him, to bear a true, unflinching witness to the Lord Jesus! What glory to Him Who shed His Blood! what strength to His Church! what blessings to countless souls! what unspeakable gain to those who witness! Every hard effort generously faced, every sacrifice cheerfully submitted to, every word spoken under difficulties, raises those who speak or act or suffer to a higher level; endows them with a clearer sight of God; braces them with a will of more strength and freedom; warms them with a more generous and large and tender heart. Blessed they who here in the days of their trial lose something, or suffer something, for Jesus. For beyond there is a vision which no merely human words may dare to paint; a vision which shall one day be true to all who have witnessed for our Lord; a vision of a world, where all has faded from sight, save only the redeemed souls, and the everlasting Object of their love.

"And one of the elders answered, saying unto me,

What are these which are arrayed in white robes? and whence came they? And I said unto him, Sir, thou knowest. And he said to me, These are they which came out of great tribulation, and have washed their robes, and made them white in the blood of the Lamb. Therefore are they before the throne of God, and serve Him day and night in His Temple: and He that sitteth on the throne shall dwell among them. They shall hunger no more, neither thirst any more; neither shall the sun light on them, nor any heat. For the Lamb Which is in the midst of the throne shall feed them, and shall lead them unto living fountains of waters: and God shall wipe away all tears from their eyes."\*

\* Rev. vii. 13-17.

# SERMON XXXVI.

## DIVINE TEACHING GRADUAL.

ST. JOHN XVI. 12, 13.

*I have many things to say unto you, but ye cannot bear them now. Howbeit when He, the Spirit of Truth, is come, He will guide you into all truth.*

ALL the Gospels appointed for the five Sundays after Easter are taken from that according to St. John. One only, that for the first Sunday, belongs to the period which we are at present commemorating; the forty days which passed between the Resurrection and the Ascension of Jesus Christ. The other four are from discourses of Jesus Christ, pronounced before His Crucifixion; and of these the last three from the one discourse pronounced in the Supper-Room. Historically speaking, these Gospels seem to be, at first sight, out of place; in reading them we go back from Eastertide to a time from which we are separated by the Crucifixion and the Resurrection. But looking to the contents of these Gospels, they are, we must see, strictly appropriate. They are, one and all, preparations for a great departure, and for that which will follow it. They might have been spoken, so far as the contents go—I am, of course, saying nothing of their immediate purpose—they might have been spoken, at least in the main, during the great forty days, just as well as on the eve of the Passion.

Our Lord has referred to His approaching departure, and, as a consequence, " sorrow had filled the hearts of His disciples."[a] In order to relieve this, He proceeds to explain to them that His departure was to be, not merely glorious for Himself, but expedient for them. It He remained upon the earth, the Holy Spirit, or Comforter, would not come to them. He Himself, if He remained among them continuously, could not be an object of a purely spiritual apprehension. Where sight is satisfied, there is no sufficient room for faith, and, so far, no need of that Divine and Invisible Friend, Who is the Author of faith in the soul of man. But if Christ departed, then faith would become necessary as well as possible; and our Lord promised to send the Author and Giver of this grace. " If 1 depart, I will send Him unto you."[b] When He is come, what will He do? First of all, He will achieve a moral victory over the world: "He will reprove the world of sin:" He will convince it gradually of the sin of rejecting Jesus. Next, He will reprove the world "of righteousness:" He will teach it the existence of a new standard of goodness. The righteousness of Christ will be seen to be higher than the righteousness of the Pharisees, when the Ascension shall have demonstrated the righteousness of the ascending Christ. Lastly, He will reprove the world " of judgment:"[c] He will teach it that the Crucifixion, which seemed to be the victory of the evil one, was really the day of his judgment and humiliation. "The prince of this world is judged."[d] But what will He teach to the Church, to those Apostles who had believed in and followed our Lord, and who in losing Him appeared to be losing their all? This is the question before us.

[a] St. John xvi. 6.  [b] Ibid. 7.  [c] Ibid. 8.  [d] Ibid. 11.

This question is partly answered by our Lord's words in the text: "I have many things to say unto you, but ye cannot bear them now. Howbeit when He, the Spirit of Truth, is come, He will guide you into all truth."

Now these words have a doctrinal and a moral significance. They teach us a great truth about Christian doctrine, and a serious duty in the Christian life.

I.

Here we see, first of all, that our Lord's Own oral teaching, during His sojourn upon the earth, did not embrace all necessary Christian doctrine. This is a point of great importance. It is not unusual to hear people say in the present day: 'I am a Christian in this sense, that I accept, I believe, I obey, only the very words of Christ. They are enough for me: I want no more. The Apostles, St. Paul especially, taught some doctrines which Christ Himself did not teach: I do not wish to be bound by these superadded doctrines. The Church has, in her creeds and elsewhere, used language which I do not find in the words of Christ: I may reject that language. It is enough for me to read, to admire, to feel the beauty of the Sermon on the Mount, and of Christ's other discourses. This is genuine, essential, imperishable Christianity. The rest is superfluous. It may be very well in its way, but it stands on a totally different footing, and there can be no great harm in rejecting it.'

This language has been in substance used at least by one recent writer of some reputation; and it recommends itself because it sounds at first hearing so loyal to our Lord. It seems to give implicit credit to His words all the better from refusing such credit to all others: just as politeness towards a single individual is more remarked and remarkable, when the person who shows it is habitually uncivil to the rest of the world. By a confession of faith such as this, men flatter themselves that they can do two things at once; that they can cut down the Christian creed to very narrow dimensions, and at the same time be all the better Christians, for keeping themselves exclusively to the teaching of Christ. It is a raid upon the claims of faith, conducted in the name of an extraordinary reverence professed for its Object. And yet here to-day, as we listen to our Lord, in His last discourse, we find Him saying as plainly as He can, that He Himself did not undertake to teach in person all that it was necessary for His disciples as Christians to know and believe to their soul's health. For He had many things to tell His disciples which they could not bear at the time; and which He meant to tell them, not in person, but by the agency of Another, the Unseen Comforter, or Holy Spirit, hereafter. After He had left the world, so far as His visible Presence was concerned, He would still speak to men from His invisible home. By His Spirit, He would speak in and through His Apostles. What the Apostles taught would be still His teaching, even although it should go beyond the measure of truth which He had taught Himself. For He had not said all that He meant to say: His work of teaching was to be finished by others. To the Apostles He said, " He that heareth you heareth Me;"[a] and " He that receiveth you receiveth Me: and he that receiveth Me receiveth Him that sent Me."[b] A man, then, who should think himself a good Christian for keeping only to the words of Christ, would deceive himself. He could not keep only to the words of Christ, if he really keeps to all of them. For among these words is the saying in the text, which states, as clearly as possible, that over and above Christ's actual teaching there were

[a] St. Luke x. 16.      [b] St. Matt. x. 40.

truths to be taught, in His Name and by His authority; truths which, as coming from Christ, although through others, Christians ought to receive and believe.

There are, indeed, other words of our Lord in this discourse which at first sight appear to be at variance with His saying that He had many things to tell His disciples which they could not now bear. " Henceforth," He said, "I call you not servants; for the servant knoweth not what his lord doeth: but I have called you friends; for all things that I have heard of My Father I have made known unto you."[a] Here there seems to be a contradiction to our Lord's statement that He still had many things to say to His disciples. But there is no contradiction in reality. So far as confidence on His side went, our Lord trusted His disciples unreservedly: they were admitted to His intimate counsels. But there was a want of spiritual comprehension on their side; they were not yet able to receive all that He had to tell them; and He therefore reserved it for a later time. We understand this difference in everyday life. Many a man has a wife, or a sister, with whom he has literally no secrets whatever, although she is not on that account able to share all his intellectual interests. He may be willing to confide everything; but he may know that to enter into an account of all his thoughts at once would be a sheer waste of time; so he defers this fuller disclosure in the hope that it will some day be appreciated. He has already made it in spirit, and intention. He does not trust the less because he does not communicate unintelligible secrets; the time will come, perhaps, when whatever is now unintelligible will be understood.

Our Lord's teaching, then, was completed by that of the Holy Spirit. To see how this was done we need not

[a] St. John xv. 15.

go beyond the limits of the New Testament. "He shall take of Mine," said our Lord, "and shall show it unto you."[a] Our Lord gave the germs which, by the ministry of the Apostles, the Holy Spirit unfolded into momentous doctrines.

Our Lord had spoken, for instance, of the necessity that the Messiah should die, in order to correspond to the words of prophecy, "The Son of Man goeth, as it is written of Him."[b] He had spoken of His Blood as the Blood of the New Testament which was shed for His disciples.[c] In the Apostolic writings this is expanded into the doctrine of the Atonement: by Christ's death man is bought back[d] from captivity to sin and death; a propitiation for our sins and for the sins of the whole world is offered in the free Self-sacrifice of the Perfect Man;[e] and thus between God and man a peace or reconciliation[f] is effected: we are "accepted in the Beloved."[g]

Our Lord had hinted at a new ground of acceptance with God in His parable of the Labourers in the Vineyard;[h] in His eulogy upon the Publican who went down to his house justified rather than the Pharisee;[i] in His precept, "When ye have done all that is required of you, say, We are unprofitable servants."[k] But in St. Paul's writings we find a fully elaborated doctrine of salvation through the grace of Christ, as contrasted with that of obedience to the Jewish law. "By the works of the law shall no flesh be justified."[l] "By grace are ye saved, through faith; and that not of yourselves: it is the gift of God."[m]

Again, in the visit of the Eastern sages to the manger

[a] St. John xvi. 15. [b] St. Matt. xxvi. 24. [c] Ibid. 28.
[d] Rom. iii. 24; 1 Cor. i. 30; Eph. i. 7; Col. i. 14.
[e] 1 St. John ii. 2; iv. 10; Rom. iii. 25.
[f] Rom. v. 10, 11; 2 Cor. v. 18, 19. [g] Eph. i. 6.
[h] St. Matt. xx. 1-16. [i] St. Luke xviii. 14. [k] Ibid. xvii. 10.
[l] Gal. ii. 16; Rom. iii. 19-26. [m] Eph. ii. 8.

of Bethlehem;[a] in the acceptance of the Syrophenician woman;[b] in the interview with the Greeks at the Passover;[c] in the statement that the Good Shepherd had other sheep who were not of the fold of Israel, whom also He must bring, and make one fold under one Shepherd,[d] we have hints that the Pagan nations were in some way to have their part in the Divine Saviour. In St. Paul we find the express assertion that a special revelation had been made to him, to the effect "that the Gentiles should be fellow-heirs and of the same body, and partakers of his promise in Christ by the Gospel."[e] The entire equality of Pagan and Jewish converts within the Church was thus based upon hints in our Lord's Own language and practice, but was only drawn out into a sharply defined doctrine by the Apostle.

Once more, our Lord spoke about Himself, His sinlessness, His claims upon human thought and human affection, His power of enlightening and saving human beings, His future coming to judge all human beings, in a way which we should now-a-days think very extraordinary in any good man; and indeed fatal to his claim to goodness, because inconsistent with sober fact. Yet there is no denying this self-assertion of Christ our Lord; so varied, so persistent, so unflinching. He does not present Himself, as the prophets had done, only to teach men truths about God and duty, and then to withdraw Himself from hearing and sight as quietly as might be. He comes to proclaim Himself, to exhibit Himself, to draw all eyes, all hearts, towards Himself, as the Way, the Truth, the Life of men;[f] as the Light of the world,[g] as the King[h] and Judge[i] of all.[k]

[a] St Matt. ii. 1-12.  [b] St. Mark vii. 24-30.  [c] St. John xii. 20-36.
[d] Ibid. x. 16.  [e] Eph. iii. 6.  [f] St. John xiv. 6.
[g] Ibid. viii. 12.  [h] Ibid. xviii. 37.  [i] Ibid. v. 27-30.
[k] St. Matt. xxv. 31-46.

He teaches, but He Himself is, in the last resort, the subject of His doctrine. He reveals, but He is Himself His revelation. "All men," He says, "are to honour the Son, even as they honour the Father;"[a] "He who hath seen Me," He says, "hath seen the Father."[b] "Before Abraham was, I am."[c] "I and the Father are one thing."[d]

What did this language mean? How was it to be explained? If it was unjustifiable, what claims of any kind would the Speaker have upon the love and trust of men? If it was justifiable, what did it imply as to the Person of Christ? Clearly that He was more than man. And if more than man, what was He? Were such claims as His to be admitted on the part of any created being, angel or archangel, seraph or cherub? Or was He indeed of that Uncreated Eternal Essence, Which we adore as the Source and End of all other existences? Here the Holy Spirit took of the words of Christ, and showed the truth unto the Apostles. Those words only admitted of one explanation. The Speaker was indeed Divine. And accordingly the Colossians were taught that all things were created by Him and for Him, and that He was before all things, and that by Him all things consist;[e] the Romans, that He is over all, God blessed for ever;[f] the Philippians, that even at His human Name men and angels and those beneath should bow in reverence;[g] the Hebrews, that He is the Brightness of the Father's glory, and the Express Image of His Person.[h] And St. John in the Spirit on the Lord's day beholds Him enthroned as the Lamb, slain and glorified, while all the highest intelligences of heaven prostrate themselves before Him and join in the new song of adoration around His throne.[i] And, in harmony with

[a] St. John v. 23.  [b] Ibid. xiv. 9.  [c] Ibid. viii. 58.
[d] Ibid. x. 30.  [e] Col. i. 16, 17.  [f] Rom. ix. 5.
[g] Phil. ii 10.  [h] Heb. i. 3.  [i] Rev. v. 6-14

all this we say in the Creed that He is "very God of very God, begotten, not made, of one substance with the Father." The disciples could not have borne the full splendour of the truth of Christ's Godhead when they listened to the Sermon on the Mount. Yet the truth was the only justification of the Sermon. To revise the law given from Sinai,[a] or indeed to approve and ratify it,[b] implied that the Speaker claimed to be one with Him Who was the Lord of Moses. " These things understood not His disciples at the first; but after Jesus was glorified,"[c] and the Spirit had been given, it became clear what had been really meant. In the deepest sense of the words, "no man could say that Jesus was the Lord but by the Holy Ghost."[d] When the Spirit of Truth had come, He guided men into all truth as to the Divine Person of Jesus Christ.

These illustrations might be extended. But enough has been said to show that, if the New Testament is to be believed as a whole, our Lord's Own teaching was incomplete; and further, that He knew and meant it to be so. This brings us to the second part of our subject.

II.

Why was our Lord's Own teaching thus incomplete; incomplete, according to His Own will and announcement? Why did not He Himself teach all that could properly be called Christian doctrine ? Why did He content Himself with laying the foundations of His religion, while He left the building to be finished, according to His Own express appointment and design, by other hands?

The answer is, that the same motive which led Him to teach men at all led Him to impose these limits and

[a] St. Matt. v. 33-45.
[c] St. John xii. 16.
[b] Ibid. 17, 18.
[d] 1 Cor. xii. 3.

restraints upon His teaching. He taught men in their ignorance, because He loved men too well to leave them in darkness. He taught men gradually, and as they were able to bear the strong light of His doctrine, because He loved men too well to shock or blind them by a sudden blaze of truth, for which they were as yet unprepared. He did not judge that if the Christian Creed was placed before men at once in its completeness they would at once receive it. He knew what was in man.[a] He knew what the prejudices of education, the power of mental habits, the associations of youth, the traditions of a great history, could do to destroy the receptive powers, the moral flexibility of the soul. He was too Wise and considerate to expect too much. As the sun does not flash forth in a moment out of the darkness of night, but gives warning of his approach, and then rises gradually, and diffuses a vast body of light before we see him in his full glory above the line of the horizon, so it was with our Lord. The full understanding of Who He was, and what He came to do, was preceded by a twilight; itself His Own work, which brightened more and more, moment by moment, towards the day. He rose amid the mists of imperfect apprehensions and misapprehensions as to Who and What He was; and not until He was high in the heavens did He permit the full truth to break upon the intelligence of the world.

In this He was true to God's providential action in human history. All along God has taught men gradually. The heathen nations have been taught what little truth, amid their errors, they know, by a succession of minds. Each of these was raised up in the Providence of God, to advance a single step towards the light; as men who had long lived in darkness could bear. The old Jewish Scrip-

[a] St. John ii. 25.

XXXVI]  *Divine Teaching gradual.*  289

tures are a long series of revelations; the Patriarchal, the Mosaic, the Prophetical. Each is an advance upon its predecessors; and all lead up to the final and complete Revelation of God in Christ. "God, Who at sundry times and in divers manners spake in time past unto the fathers by the prophets, hath in these last days spoken unto us by His Son."[a] This unfolding of the Mind of God, gradually throughout the ages, and fully in the last Revelation of Himself which He has made, is based throughout upon God's tender consideration for human weakness. "I have many things to say unto you, but ye cannot bear them now," is inscribed upon every earlier and imperfect revelation; not to depreciate its value, but to explain why it is not fuller than it is; why He Who has spoken is silent a while ere He speaks again.

### III.

This leads us to consider, by way of conclusion, two practical lessons.

1. Observe, first, the true principle of a religious education of children or of the uninstructed. To be solid, it should be gradual; it should be given only as the learner's mind becomes acclimatised to the atmosphere of religious truth. Our Lord's tenderness in teaching religious truth was copied by His Apostles. We find in the Epistles[b] the distinction between "babes in Christ," those who were just beginning to learn Christian truth and duty, and "strong" or perfect men, or adults, who had completed, or ought to have completed, their Christian education. To the first was given that elementary form of instruction in Christian doctrine, which, from its easiness of reception, the Apostle

[a] Heb. i. 1, 2.     [b] 1 Cor. iii. 1, 2; Heb. v. 12-14.

terms "milk."[a] To the second, a much more comprehensive instruction in the mysteries of the Christian creed, and in the range of Christian duty, was imparted, and this the Apostle terms "strong meat."[b] This double order of teaching passed into the primitive Church. The catechumens, that is, converts to Christianity who were in the earlier stage of instruction, were treated quite differently from the faithful, who, after Baptism and Communion, were in full fellowship with the whole life and thought of the Church. The catechumens, it was thought, could only bear one kind of spiritual nutriment; the faithful would be satisfied with nothing less than another.

The principle holds good of secular education, and is too much lost sight of in some modern methods. In these days, the old and deeper idea of education as a means of training and exercising the faculties of the mind, so as to enable the educated man to deal with any subject that might come before him in the path of duty, has been abandoned only too largely for the idea of an education which overloads the mind with huge packages of unmastered and unmanageable knowledge, and not seldom leads to frightful cases of intellectual indigestion. Boys are expected to know something about everything; they too often know nothing about anything thoroughly. The consequence is, that while they can talk with striking but unnatural facility on a great many more subjects than boys did forty or fifty years ago, their mental faculties are really less braced and sharpened, and their actual capacity for meeting the requirements of life is less considerable than that of their predecessors.

And, in teaching religious truth, parents are sometimes apt to fall into the same mistake. They want to teach everything at once, and they end by really teaching

[a] 1 Cor. iii. 2.   [b] Heb. v. 14.

nothing. They forget that most necessary duty of every teacher; the duty of placing himself, by an effort of sympathy and imagination, as nearly as possible in the mental position of his pupil or child. They think chiefly or only of what interests themselves in religion ; not of what might be interesting or intelligible to minds just opening upon life, and catching with difficulty the horizons of truth and duty which meet the gaze. They are interested in these or those controversies of the day; they expect their children to be so. They are accustomed to express themselves on religious subjects in such and such abstract phraseology; they expect their children to understand it. They have arrived at this or that impression as to the heinousness of sin, the preciousness of our Lord's work, the difference between grace and nature, the intimate sense of God's favour which is sometimes bestowed upon holy souls ; they cannot treat their children as other than unregenerate and carnal unless they do so too. What is the consequence? Either the children are alienated from all religion in later life, owing to the thoughtless but well-meant eagerness with which, without anything to make it living and concrete, without any adequate interpretation, it was thrust on them in youth. Or, they learn that most fatal of all lessons in religion, to talk about it easily, without thinking of what they say ; to allow phrases to outrun meaning and purpose; and so, in dealing with the most serious of all subjects, to foster a habit of insincerity, which in the event is only too certain to sap the springs of real faith and life.

2. A second lesson is to remember that until our last day God is teaching us, through the action of other minds, through the events of life; and to be listening for His voice. Each stage of life, up to the very last, leaves some truth

untaught. We are daily adding to our experience. We never complete it. As, in the first flush of youth, a young man or woman exults in the sense of animal vitality and of mental buoyancy, Christ, from His throne of mercy and consideration, looks down and says: 'I have many things to say unto thee, young man or young woman, but thou canst not bear them now.' If He were to teach us all at once; compressing into one awful and overwhelming lesson all the stern and varied experiences of the future, it would be too much to bear; too much for our weakness, too much for our proneness to despair. What life is and means as the threshold of eternity; what is the high and sacred use of disappointment and pain; why it is better to suffer for doing what is right than to succeed by doing what is wrong; what the events, the persons, the things of time are worth when compared to the eternal realities: these lessons are only learnt gradually and painfully. Friends die; health becomes weak; life forfeits its early promise; a brilliant spring-tide has issued in an arid summer and a prosaic and darkening autumn. And thus, at each step, the soul is thrown back from the outward and the transient upon the inward and the eternal. Gradually, imperceptibly, one truth leads the way to another; one difficulty, by being surmounted or interpreted, shows the way to explain and master another. It would have seemed impossible beforehand; but as a fact God teaches all the more surely, because He is so tender, so deliberate, so hesitating, as it seems, in giving His successive lessons. In our early day-dreams we think of the Right Hand and of the Left. But He waits for us by the way to tender the cup of which He drank Himself, and to administer the baptism with which He was baptized.[a]

[a] St. Mark x. 37-40.

What can the soul do but breathe the prayer—

"Lead, kindly Light, amid the encircling gloom,
    Lead Thou me on;
    .    .    .    .    .
Keep Thou my feet; I do not ask to see
The distant scene; one step enough for me"?[a]

He has many things to say to us, which we cannot bear as yet. He knows when life's deepest lessons will be most needed by us. We have to listen for His voice, and to take heed that, when we hear, we obey it.

[a] J. H. Newman, *Lyra Apostolica*, No. xxv.

# SERMON XXXVII.

## DIVINE TEACHING GRADUAL.

St. John xvi. 12.

*I have many things to say unto you, but ye cannot bear them now.*

THE question is sometimes asked why three out of the five Gospels for the Sundays after Easter should be taken from our Lord's last discourse, just before His Passion. Words uttered on the eve of the Agony seem to be out of place on the eve of the Ascension. But the two periods have this in common, that the Divine Speaker is in each case on the eve of a departure. In the discourse in the Supper-Room, the elevation above all that is passing at the moment is so complete, the coming Passion is so lost sight of in the vast survey of an all-embracing purpose, that the language of one period is not unsuited to the circumstances of the other. To exhibit the tranquil superiority to human circumstances which belongs to the Infinite Mind tabernacling in a Human Form was one part of the purpose of St. John's Gospel. In this Evangelist the Crucifixion itself is noticed as a triumph; it is an enthronement of the Incarnate Word, though beneath the canopy of heaven.[a] And the Church

[a] St. John xii. 32.

follows in the footsteps of St. John when she thus makes selections from his report of our Lord's words in accordance with the Evangelist's distinctive principle.

I.

When our Lord tells His Apostles that He had many things to say to them which they could not as yet bear to hear, He may well have taken them by surprise. They may have thought that a discourse like that in the Supper-Room, on the eve of what they felt to be an approaching crisis, would contain the final instructions, exhortations, consolations of their Divine Master. He warns them that there is much still to be told them in a coming time. It would be told them partly during the forty days after His Resurrection; but, much more, as He proceeds to explain, after the descent of the Holy Spirit, Who was to guide them into all truth.

The subjects on which our Lord did speak with the Apostles during the forty days between His Resurrection and Ascension are hinted at in general terms by St. Luke at the beginning of the Acts. He was "speaking of the things pertaining to the kingdom of God."[a] What His kingdom or Church was to be; what it was not to be; what laws and rules were to govern it; how it was to be organised and officered; what were to be the sources of its life and vigour; above all, how it was to assist and expand and perfect the spiritual life of single souls. Such-like topics we may dare to infer were handled by our Divine Lord during these solemn days. And the result may be seen in the Apostolic Epistles, especially in those of St. Paul, who would have been told in after years what had passed by some who were present. When

[a] Acts i. 3.

in the Epistle to the Corinthians he compares the Church to the human body, we learn that its members were to be many, but its life one.[a] When in the Epistle to the Ephesians he calls it the Body of Christ, the fulness of Him that filleth all in all,[b] we see that it was to be no mere voluntary and human association. When he instructs Timothy and Titus how it was to be governed, and ministered to, and provided for,[c] we learn how great a place it was to have in the practical life as well as in the thought of Christians. These features of the Apostolic teaching, passed on by word of mouth from the Eleven to St. Paul, may well have dated from the forty days between the Resurrection and the Ascension.

But it was especially after the descent of the Holy Ghost, and through Him, that our Lord was to say "many things" to His Apostles. "When He, the Spirit of Truth, is come, He will guide you into all truth: for He shall not speak of Himself; but whatsoever He shall hear, that shall He speak: and He will show you things to come. He shall glorify Me: for He shall receive of Mine, and shall show it unto you. All things that the Father hath are Mine: therefore said I, that He shall take of Mine, and shall show it unto you."[d]

This was to be the illuminating work of the Holy Ghost after the Day of Pentecost. He was to enable the Apostles to understand the real meaning of what they had heard from and observed in their Master while He was on earth. "He shall glorify Me: . . . He shall receive, or take, of Mine, and shall show it unto you." He would make it clear to the Apostles that Jesus Christ, Whom they had followed, and Who was now speaking to them in the Supper-Room, and Who within a few hours

[a] 1 Cor. xii. 12, 13.  
[b] Eph. i. 23.  
[c] 1 Tim. iii. 1-15; Titus i. 5-9, etc.  
[d] St. John xvi. 13, 14.

would be crucified, was not merely a righteous Man, a Friend of God, the promised Messiah, the Deliverer of Israel, but that He was and is the Eternal Son of God; that He "is over all, God blessed for ever;"[a] that when He condescended to be made man, and emptied Himself of His glory, and took on Him a servant's form, and became obedient unto death,[b] neither the weakness of His robe of flesh, nor the sufferings and the shame which He voluntarily bore, nor the ignominious death which seemed for the moment to close his career in failure and in darkness, detracted aught from the dignity of His Eternal Person, from the Majesty of His Divine and unchanging Being. "I have many things to say unto you." It was Jesus Himself Who would speak about Himself, through the teaching of the Spirit. The Spirit "shall not speak of Himself: but whatsoever He shall hear, that shall He speak." All that Christ had done and suffered and said, in the days of His flesh, would be suffused with a light from heaven, which would bring out with startling distinctness its real meaning. The world-wide invitations to trust and obey and love; the great sayings, but half understood when they were uttered, about His Oneness with the Father,[c] His Eternal Existence when Abraham as yet was not,[d] His passing the knowledge of all save the Father, Whom He alone also could really know;[e] the claim to judge the whole human race from the throne of heaven;[f] the absolute unhesitating assertion of Self,—so unpardonable if the Speaker was merely human, so inevitable if He was indeed Divine,—all this would be brought to a focus by the teaching, unveiling, systematising Spirit, till the great central truth of Christian Faith, the Absolute Deity of Jesus Christ, as the Everlast-

[a] Rom. ix. 5.  [b] Phil. ii. 7, 8.  [c] St. John x. 30.
[d] Ibid. viii. 58.  [e] St. Matt. xi. 27.  [f] St. John v. 22.

ing Son of the Father, had stood forth in all its awe and all its beauty in the faith and teaching of the Apostles. And from this central truth how much else would radiate : the infinite value of His death, incalculable by any merely human estimate; the virtue of those appointed instruments of contact of His Human Nature with mankind, the Sacraments; the infallibility of all language that can fairly claim His sanction; the power to save to the uttermost all who need and claim His help.

And here we see what is to be thought and said about a representation of Christianity which is not seldom to be met with in our day.

True, genuine, original Christianity, as we are sometimes told, is only what was taught by Jesus Christ Himself. All that can be shown to have been uttered by Him deserves the prestige of that great Name. The very words of Christ, but no words of a follower of Christ, no merely Apostolic words, deserve it. In particular, men have gone on to say, the teaching of St. Paul is something beyond and distinct from the teaching of his Master. It may be Paulinism, and as such, in its degree, interesting. But it is something distinct from, it is an amplification and outgrowth of, pure and original Christianity.

This has a plausible sound; but we see from the text that it proceeds on an assumption which our Lord Himself would have repudiated, and does condemn. It assumes that He meant to teach the world as of primary and absolute authority, only such truth as fell from His Own blessed lips. Whereas He says that He has something else to teach it, which He would teach it by His Spirit speaking through others; that He has "many things" in reserve, which those who heard Him in the days of His flesh could not as yet bear to receive. He has thus made an express provision, it seems, against this particular misapprehension. And we are bound to receive the teaching of His Apostles as His Own teaching; as the teaching of the Divine Spirit Who was to continue His work after He had left the earth at His Ascension; as having no less claim upon the faith and consciences of Christians than the Last Discourse or the Sermon on the Mount.

And why did not our Lord teach everything Himself? Why did He leave many things to be proclaimed in His Name by those who came after Him? The answer is, because the Apostles "could not bear" this added burden of truth in their earlier days. The reception and assimilation of religious truth is necessarily a very gradual process. In the New Testament it is compared to the erection of a building: St. Paul calls it edification,[a] or housebuilding. Of the temple of Christian truth in a human soul, Jesus Christ must be the foundation: "other foundation can no man lay."[b] And on this is raised by a wise master-builder, gradually and surely, wall and column, buttress and roof and pinnacle, the fair fabric of doctrine, and moral precepts, till the whole edifice stands out in its ordered beauty. Now as yet the Apostles were not sufficiently prepared for this: "Ye cannot bear these truths now." They were under the strain of great excitement, bordering upon great distress, and this is not a frame of mind in which high and exacting truths can be easily received and have justice done to them. And they were still left to their natural resources: so that the Holy Spirit was needed not only to reveal "many things" to them hereafter, but to enable them to accept the Revelation, and to distinguish it from any products of human fancy or speculation. If truth is to be received, it must be by a state of mind which is to a certain extent in sympathy

[a] Rom. xiv. 19; xv. 2, 20; 1 Cor. x. 23; xiv. 3, 4, 5, 17; 2 Cor. xii. 19; xiii. 10; Eph. iv. 12, 16.   [b] 1 Cor. iii. 11.

with it. When this sympathy does not exist, truth will be rejected as foreign to the mind; as fanciful, unintelligible, even inconceivable. But the work of the Spirit, creating this sympathy, had not yet begun. And therefore, although our Lord had many things to say to the Apostles, He withheld them: " Ye cannot," He said, " bear them now."

II.

Our Lord's words apply, again, to the Christian Church. In the Apostles He saw its first representatives; but His eye also rested on all the centuries of its coming history; on our own age not less than on those which have preceded or which will follow it. To the Church He had many things to say, which she could not bear to receive in the days of her infancy.

This does not mean that during all the coming centuries, He would go on adding from time to time new truths to the Christian Creed, by a process of continuous revelation. The faith for which Christians are to contend earnestly was, St. Jude says, once for all delivered to the saints in the age of the Apostles.[a] Later ages might explain what the Apostles had taught. They might unfold and state at length and in explicit terms what already lay within the Apostles' teaching. This, for instance, is what was done by the great Council which authoritatively adopted the Nicene Creed in order to defend the truth of our Lord's Divinity. But when in that Creed we confess that Jesus Christ our Lord is of one substance with the Father, we do not say more than St. John says in the introduction to his Gospel: "The Word was with God, and the Word was God,"[b] or St. Paul in the first chapter of the Epistle to the Colossians, "All things

[a] St. Jude 3.      [b] St. John i. 1.

were created by Him, and for Him: and He is before all things, and by Him all things consist."[a] In the same way the word "Trinity," expressing the threefold subsistence of the Divine Nature, is not itself found in Scripture. But the Baptismal formula,[b] and many passages in the Apostolic writings, especially in the Epistle to the Ephesians,[c] obviously imply it. If therefore doctrines, having no ground in the teaching of the Apostles, have been added to the faith, in whatever quarter of Christendom, these do not rest on the same basis as explanations or re-statements of truths which the Apostles had already taught. They are newly imported and foreign matter, and as such would have been rejected by the early Christian Church. We cannot, therefore, include additional doctrines proposed after the Apostolic age under the head of the "many things" which our Lord had to say to His Church. It is not likely, to say the least, that the holiest and wisest of later divines should know more of His will than did St. John or St. Paul.

But the Church is a society, and the life of a society, like that of a man, is a history of experience. In the field of experience God is constantly saying new things to the Church as the years roll on. This language of God is uttered in the sequence of events which is ordered by His Providence.

Consider the history of our own country. What lessons has God been teaching it during its fifteen centuries! Lessons of order to the England of the Heptarchy; lessons of patience and hope to the England of the Norman kings; lessons of the value of freedom to the England of the Tudors and the Stuarts; lessons of the need of seriousness in life and conviction to the England of the Georges.

[a] Col. i. 16, 17.  [b] St. Matt. xxviii. 19.
[c] Eph. i. 3, 6, 13; ii. 18; iii. 14, 16, etc.

And surely in our time He is saying many things, stern and tender, to those who have ears to hear, in the events amidst which, day by day, we are living now. He is teaching us that morality should never be divorced from politics; that the duties of property rank higher than its undoubted rights; that races which trifle with the laws of purity are on the road to ruin; that "righteousness exalteth a nation"[a] much more truly than any financial, or diplomatic, or military success. And much that God teaches us of to-day would have been unintelligible to our ancestors. As we look out on the surface of our national life, on its hopes and fears, on its unsolved, to us apparently insoluble, problems, on its incessant movement, whether of unrest or aspiration, we hear from behind the clouds the more or less distinct announcement of a future which will be at any rate as unlike our present as our past. "I have many things to say unto thee, but thou canst not bear them now."

Look at the history of Israel. Israel was at once a nation and a Church. And its annals are chronicled so fully for this reason, among others: it was to teach us how to look at what is commonly called profane history. Although God gave special privileges to Israel,[b] He is present in the history of all nations. But nations differ from each other, as they do or do not expect to find Him. Each stage in Israel's history had its peculiar lessons: the Exodus, the Wilderness, the Conquest of Canaan, the Anarchy under the Judges, the splendid Monarchy of David and Solomon, the Schism of the Ten Tribes, the Decline and Fall of the royal family of David, the Captivity, the Return, the Persian, the Macedonian, the Herodian periods, the appearance of the Divine Messiah. Nothing could have been antedated with advantage. No

[a] Prov. xiv. 34.     [b] Rom. ix. 4, 5.

prophet could have prophesied before his day, and have been useful, or intelligible. And as each inspired writer passed away, and as each generation was gathered to its fathers, the accents of a Divine voice might have been heard still whispering over the people of Revelation: "I have many things to say unto thee, but thou canst not bear them now."

So with the Church of Christ. In each century of its history God has spoken to it, whether to warn, or encourage, or stimulate, or rebuke. The earlier centuries would not have understood—could not have borne—what He said to the later. The ante-Nicene Church, the Church of the great Councils, the Church of the days of the barbarian conquests, the Church of the schoolmen, the Church of the Reformation period, the Church of the revival of letters, the Church of the nineteenth century,—each has heard, or might have heard, what Christ our Lord, speaking from His throne in heaven, through the urgency of events, has had to tell it. The great teachers of each later age would have been out of place in an earlier day; while they were indispensable to their own. The second Christian century would not have understood St. Athanasius. The third would have been puzzled with St. Augustine; the fourth with St. Gregory. The men of the Reformation period would not have entered into either the object or the method of Butler; and Butler would have felt himself a stranger in much of the Christian thought which is placed before us by some great teachers of our own time.

Will there not be other voices hereafter, for whom we of to-day are as yet unprepared?

Can we suppose that Christ has said His last word to Christendom? Are there not features of our religious faith, and of our religious practice, which may prepare us to hear His announcement, "I have many things to say unto you, but ye cannot bear them now"?

### III.

Once more, our Lord's words apply to the life of each individual man; and especially of each Christian.

The human mind, we all know, has its stages of growth. There is the stage of wonder, in which imagination is the ruling faculty, and in which all that feeds it is welcome. Then comes the stage of awakening reason, when imagination is bidden retire into the background, and everything is scrutinised with an incredulous gaze; and a young man argues in a rigid technical way, without a ray of doubt as to the perfect trustworthiness of his method. Then perhaps reason, especially if ungoverned by conscience, is tempted to give ear to guilty passion, and to take pleasure, rather than truth or duty, as its teacher and mistress. Finally, if the mental growth be healthy, comes a riper stage, when reason is at once stronger and less imperative. Moral arguments are allowed to weigh against mere dialectics, and a subject is looked at, as we say, all round, and not only or chiefly on its logical side. In short, the mind has acquired all that we mean by balance, whether of the faculties generally, or of the judgment in particular. Now it is plain that the truths and considerations which could be received and appreciated at the last of these stages would be quite unintelligible in the first or second, and that to attempt to enforce them prematurely would lead to serious consequences. One reason why faith in Christianity has been forfeited by many minds in our day, is that this obvious but serious consideration has been neglected. The minds of boys have been oppressed by problems and questions which as men they would have relegated to their true place in the world of thought, and without damage to the claims of faith or to the sense of intellectual truthfulness.

In the same way, the purely spiritual life of the soul has its stages of experience; and truths, which are welcome at a later stage, are unintelligible in an earlier one. In the case of those who begin to look at these subjects seriously in adult life, the first stage is almost always that of repentance for past sin. Then the soul understands something of the meaning of moral evil, of the severe and necessary Holiness of God, of the Atoning Work of Jesus, from Whom the penitent claims a new robe of righteousness, and Whose absolving words open a new era in his existence. Then comes the stage of spiritual illumination, when the wider horizons of revealed truth are gradually opened out to the soul's delighted gaze. First one and then another district of the Divine Mind is explored, and the Christian is as glad of the Word of God as one that findeth great spoils.[a] And then a higher stage beyond is that of union with God, in and through union with our Lord Jesus Christ; a union claimed by faith, riveted by Sacraments, but deepened, realised, rejoiced in by a new sense granted to the penitent and illuminated soul, which at these heights learns to say, as very few of us ever can dare to say it, "My Beloved is mine, and I am His."[b] Now, here again the truths which are appropriate to the higher stages would be unintelligible to those below. The second stage might term the language of the highest strained and mystical; and the first stage would account the second speculative or imaginative; while those who had yet to enter on the first,—the stage of penitence,—would probably say that it implied a morbid view of life and conduct, with which they could not

[a] Ps. cxix. 162.  [b] Song of Solomon ii. 16.

sympathise. Yet He Who made and has redeemed us, and Who knows our needs and shortcomings before we tell Him, would whisper to each of these critics—" I have many things to say unto thee, but thou canst not bear them now."

And this may enable us to understand a feature of the system of the early Christian Church, which has often been commented on unfavourably, from lack of due knowledge or consideration. I refer to the gradual way in which converts to Christianity were instructed in the truths of the Christian faith. Before a man was received into full discipleship, and made the vows and received the grace of Baptism, a period of preparation was insisted on, which lasted from two to three years. This delay was intended partly to test the sincerity of his obedience; but, still more, to instruct him gradually, and so thoroughly, in the revealed truths of Christianity. In the whole of this preparatory stage a man was called a Catechumen, and the teaching which he received Catechetical. For he was constantly examined, in order to find out how far he was grounded in the faith of Christ, or in the lines of thought which lead up to its sincere reception. The instruction generally began with those truths which we may learn from natural reason, such as the Being of God, or the law of conscience, or the immortality of the soul; and then it went on gradually to the distinctive doctrines and Mysteries of the Gospel. Thus at first the convert to Christianity was called a *hearer*. He was allowed to attend instructions and the reading of Holy Scripture. Then, at a second stage, he was permitted to remain during public prayers, and was termed a *worshipper*. Afterwards, as the time of his baptism drew near, he was taught the Lord's Prayer and the Creed,—the peculiar treasures, as they were thought

## XXXVII] *Divine Teaching gradual.*

in the early Church, of the regenerate,—and then he was described as *elect*, or *competent*. After baptism he was fully instructed in the deeper aspects of the doctrines of the Holy Trinity and Incarnation of our Lord, and of the One Sacrifice which was made by Christ upon the Cross, and which is presented to God the Father in the Holy Eucharist. But these great and overwhelming truths were withheld until he had been grounded in the lessons which led up to them and made their sincere and intelligent reception possible.

Now this system of graduated teaching had its roots and sanction in Holy Scripture, and was at least begun under the eyes of the Apostles. In the First Epistle to the Corinthians St. Paul distinguishes between the natural or imperfect and the established or perfect Christian. Christianity, he contends, contains that true and profound philosophy after which the sages of the heathen world, with their fragmentary and tentative systems, were vainly seeking;[a] but if a man would understand this, he must "become a fool that he may be wise;"[b] he must undergo a disciplinary and progressive training, if he would listen to the Apostles "speaking the wisdom of God in a mystery, even the hidden wisdom, which none of the princes of this world knew."[c] And then he goes on to tell the Corinthians, that he "could not speak unto them as unto spiritual, but as unto carnal, as unto babes in Christ. I have fed you," he says, "with milk"—that is, with elementary truth—"and not with meat"—that is, with a fuller measure of truth—"for hitherto ye were not able to bear it, neither yet now are ye able."[d] In the Epistle to the Hebrews we find the same distinction between the doctrines which are suitable for the weak and ignorant, and those which

[a] 1 Cor. ii. 6-10.
[b] *Ibid.* iii. 18.
[c] *Ibid.* ii. 7, 8.
[d] *Ibid.* iii. 1, 2.

a regenerate Christian might understand. When the inspired writer is about to speak of the great truths of our Lord and Saviour's Priesthood which were taught under the typical history of Melchizedek, he suddenly checks himself, remembering that some of his readers have not sufficiently advanced in Christian teaching to understand him. "We have many things to say," he observes, "and hard to be uttered, seeing ye are dull of hearing. For when for the time that has passed ye ought to be teachers, ye have need that one teach you again which be the first principles of the oracles of God; and are become such as have need of milk, and not of strong meat. For every one that useth milk is unskilful in the word of righteousness: for he is a babe. But strong meat belongeth to them that are of full age, even to those who by reason of use have their senses exercised to discern between good and evil."[b] Here, under the same figure of different kinds of food for the body, the difference of doctrine which the soul can receive at different stages of Christian instruction is very vividly taught us: and we see in this language the sanction for the discipline of the succeeding age, to which allusion has already been made. Nay rather, the system is to be referred, for its principle, to the example of the Teacher of teachers, our Lord Himself. What were His parables but an appeal to imagination? what was the explanation of the parables but a call for the first action of the reason? what were His longer discourses but a training of the aroused reason to move reverently and wisely among the things of faith? So again, first the Sermon on the Mount makes the conscience sensitive and true; then the sermon at Capernaum or the parables of the kingdom introduce the soul to many new and awful truths; and, lastly, the discourse in the Supper-Room

[a] Heb. v. 11-14.

teaches, among other things, union with the Father and the Son, through the Spirit; that great gift of an inward Presence, which is the consummation of the Christian life. Our Lord did not begin with the Last Discourse. He taught as men were able to bear His teaching.

Once more, are we not here reminded of the true method of educating children in religious truth? A careful mother or teacher will treat a child's mind with great tenderness and reverence. She will be careful to excite interest before gratifying it; and to gratify it in such degree as her child's capacities may admit. She will not think of the mind of her child as of a large bag, into which all the odds and ends of knowledge that are swept up from the table of common life may be thrown at random, but as a delicate and beautiful organism, to be handled with tenderness and respect, since one mistake in dealing with it may be fatal. A well-known writer has told us how she was taught by her mother the Nature and Attributes of God. "I asked her one day who God was, and was told to come again the next day, and at the same hour. I came, and repeated the question, 'Who is God?' and was again told to wait another day before I could be answered. And then, when my curiosity had been raised to the highest pitch, and my sense of the importance of the subject immensely enhanced by this repeated postponement of an answer, I came once more, and my mother explained, in words which I have never forgotten, how Great and Awful and Beautiful a Being God is; and what He has told us about His Attributes, and His relations to the world and to us, and all this in simple words, and so far as a child's mind could bear it."[a] Certainly such a lesson as that no child was likely to forget.

[a] Mrs. Schimmelpenninck; quoted from memory.

And lastly, this line of thought suggests the solemn interest of life. May not each of us have to learn something from the Great Teacher before the end comes, which we could not learn now? That which invests the life of a child with such pathos is the thought of all that it may have to go through before it dies. Our Lord bends over it in His tenderness, and bids it take its fill of joy, while yet it may. The day will perhaps come when He will say many things to it, under the discipline of sorrow and disappointment, which it could not bear now. There is a striking picture of Louis the Sixteenth and Marie Antoinette at their coronation. As yet all seems as bright as a great position and the smiles of friends, and splendid prospects, could make it; the young couple are scarcely more than children; it is the still unclouded morning of a summer's day. "I have many things to say unto thee" might well have been the motto of each of those young lives. As yet the years of deepening anxiety, the incapacity for dealing with stern times, the piteous indecision, the betrayal by trusted advisers, the hastened flight, the enforced return, the trial, the imprisonment in the Temple, the scaffold, are unsuspected. Each stage of suffering brought with it a lesson which might never otherwise have been learnt; but the lesson could not have been borne had it been given before its time. Many a man who dies quietly in his bed is in reality much more to be pitied than that King and Queen of France, as the sharp edge of the guillotine ushered them into the Presence beyond the veil.

Doubtless the future is veiled from us for other reasons; but especially as an accommodation to our real needs and capacities. Our "time is in His Hand,"[a] Who "knoweth

[a] Ps. xxxi. 17.

whereof we are made, and remembereth that we are but dust."[a] And few prayers will be more welcome to the soul that dwells constantly on this solemn truth than the Psalmist's: "Lead me forth in Thy truth, and learn me: for Thou art the God of my salvation: in Thee hath been my hope all the day long."[b]

[a] Ps. ciii. 14.  [b] Ps. xxv. 4.

www.ingramcontent.com/pod-product-compliance
Lightning Source LLC
Chambersburg PA
CBHW030807230426
43667CB00008B/1097